THE FOUR SEASONS

PAUL KOVI

THE
FOUR
SEASONS

WILLIAMS · SONOMA

THE FOUR SEASONS

by Tom Margittai and Paul Kovi

Recipes created by Chef Josef (Seppi) Renggli

Edited by Barbara Kafka

Foreword by James A. Beard

Simon and Schuster
New York

Published by Simon and Schuster
A Division of Gulf & Western Corporation
Simon & Schuster Building
Rockefeller Center
1230 Avenue of the Americas
New York, New York 10020
SIMON AND SCHUSTER and colophon
are trademarks of Simon & Schuster.

Designed by George Lois and Tom Courtos
Photographs by Gilles Larrain
Endpaper photograph by Tom Weihs
Manufactured in the United States of America
Printed by The Murray Printing Company
Bound by Economy Bindery

1 2 3 4 5 6 7 8 9 10

Library of Congress Cataloging in Publication Data

Margittai, Tom.
    The Four Seasons.

Includes index.
1. Cookery.   2. Four Seasons (Firm)
I. Kovi, Paul, joint author.   II. Renggli, Josef, date.
III. Four Seasons (Firm)   IV. Title.
TX715.M32   641.5   80-19710

ISBN 0-671-25022-1

THE FOUR SEASONS

is a trademark
registered in the U.S. Patent
and Trademark Office.

This book is lovingly dedicated to all those
who delight with us in the joys of food and wine
and to all who toiled with us over the years to make
The Four Seasons a restaurant loved by so many.

Acknowledgments

The editor would like to acknowledge the extraordinary contributions
of Susan Frank and Paula Wolfert without whom this book could not
have been prepared. She also wants to thank Chef Renggli and his staff,
as well as George Lois, for their creative participation.

Contents

Foreword

by James A. Beard

For more than twenty years I have shared the delights of a gastronomic legend. That legend is one of the most fascinating restaurants in the world, The Four Seasons. It began as a dream in several minds before it became a reality. It was a dream of the architect Philip Johnson. It was a dream of one of the owners of the Seagram Building, a lady of extraordinary taste, who happened to be a collector of fine paintings and artifacts. And it was a dream of Joe Baum, at that point the pivotal personality of an organization called Restaurant Associates.

This superb restaurant was planned so that it would provide the finest food and wine, so that its architecture would have an amazing grace, so that its appointments would be simply perfect. It was to be a backdrop for works of art by great creative masters like Picasso and Chagall. The dream, in short, was of a restaurant of peerless magnificence for New Yorkers, a restaurant whose food was splendid and whose very ambiance mirrored the seasons of the year. The recipes for The Four Seasons, the trees that grew indoors, the uniforms of the staff, the menu itself, all became emblems of the seasons. Thus, in the spring one rejoiced in the first primeurs, and one received the newly ripened fruits as they arrived by nature's clock, beginning with rhubarb, then strawberries, followed by other succulent ornaments of spring, like the first asparagus, which to me is always a certain affirmation of spring's arrival. There were fiddleheads and baby lamb and capretto, or kid, and all such wonderful things that defined the seasons. And I know so well what labor it was to create the menu for a restaurant of such awesome size every three months because for a long time I worked at creating menus for the changes in seasons, and I know so well the troubles of trying to keep those items that were ever in demand and combining them with others that were purely seasonal. It was an exciting time of my life.

This legend, I know, has been realized, and continues to flourish. First, the beauty of the restaurant is still breathtaking in its utter simplicity. Indeed, The Four Seasons is a perfect background for fine living. I have always reveled in its lovely environment as the ideal backdrop for beautifully dressed women and smartly tailored men. It is a setting that defies improvement. And I love the fact that outdoors is brought indoors in so many ways, that trees grow around the glittering pool and in the Bar Room, and that the subtle rippling of the curtains gives a feeling of a delicate breeze blowing ever so gently through the restaurant. And oh my, how it all enhances the feeling of gracious living! The appointments, the paintings, everything heightens this lovely setting for the finest food and drink. The napery and crystal, the uniforms of the pages and the waiters and the captains all express a totality of vision, a fullness of the imagination that is surely remarkable. Everything in The Four Seasons blends into a deeply fulfilling experience—the background and the colors and the flowers and the uniforms and, of course, the food. The effect is a triumphant, joyous whole.

Although Joe Baum is no longer associated with The Four Seasons, its legend was lovingly continued when Tom Margittai and Paul Kovi became its new owners in 1973. Tom and Paul had been there before and were intimately involved in creating the great traditions of this great restaurant.

The food, which started out under the aegis of Albert Stockli, was different in many ways from that of any other restaurant in the country at that time. In a word, The Four Seasons food was sensational. Over its twenty-year span, there were predictable variations—some interesting food and some less interesting—but this has now been transformed by the Margittai-Kovi stewardship, determined to keep the food always imaginative, pleasing to the palate, and rich with eye appeal. To be sure, it is still seasonal food, and the triumvirate which now directs the progress of the legend (Tom, Paul and, of course, the head chef, Seppi Renggli) takes great pains to bring in delicious seasonal foods at the peak of their greatness.

Great emphasis was placed on the wines from the beginning. When The Four Seasons opened in 1959, the restaurant was blessed with one of the greatest wine cards in the country. Considerable research and effort had gone into its inventory of great vintages and country wines. As the seasons changed, there was always a little card of summer wines or spring wines or winter wines, chosen from odd vineyards here and there, and seemingly everywhere. The Four Seasons was also one of the first great restaurants to recognize the importance of fine American wines, and since the beginning, people with a curiosity about American wines, including many Europeans, have flocked there to try them.

The Four Seasons has always operated without a sommelier. Paul Kovi, endowed with a noble palate, is an authority on fine wine. Along with his partner, Tom Margittai, Paul has kept the wine list timely and up to date, so there is always a grand variety to choose from. Once a year they feature something called a Barrel Tasting. Major vintners of California bring to The Four Seasons their new wines (as well as one wine which has been patiently aged) for a memorable tasting dinner that consists of appropriate fine dishes, each served in a tiny portion, for each particular wine. It is an event of no mean importance. The synchronized cooperation between the front of the house and the kitchen is an act of sheer choreography as it progresses through the evening. It is one of the most exciting and worthwhile wine events in New York.

It is fortunate that both Tom and Paul have the intensely professional interest in food and wine that they do, because it makes the restaurant so much more exciting and more important. Moreover, they are both outgoing and have warm personalities to which people readily respond. And this is just one of the reasons among so many that their diverse and large clientele remains so steady and loyal.

The food is created by a man whose taste and whose genius in cooking one must recognize. Seppi Renggli is as creative a man as I've ever known. He is an artist. He has amazing cooking hands that can make things look exquisite. He has a sense of color, a sense of composition and a sense of taste, all combined in one. And the result is food that is extraordinary, beautiful and entirely delicious. He is farseeing; he is not a part of one school of cookery or another; he is a great chef who has imagination, artistry and untiring love for his profession. He is surrounded by a staff of very loyal people, foremost among them Christian (Hitsch) Albin, a young Swiss chef who has worked with Seppi for the past ten years. Whether one dines or lunches in the Bar Room, where eminently simple broiled foods take the seat of honor, or in the Pool Room, where the menu is much more involved and its presentation much more spectacular, there is the comfort of knowing that all the food is supervised by this marvelously gifted man.

In compiling a book such as this one, there had to be the feeling, the background of the seasons, as well as a selection of recipes which have stood the battle of time, have remained popular and have been prepared with great relish and eaten with true appreciation by a large public.

It is not the run-of-the-mill cookbook. You will not find breakfast dishes and various simple bits of cookery. You will find dishes that have earned their place in this collection because they have been accepted, loved and greatly cared for by the discerning people who frequent The Four Seasons. I am sure that the variety, the chiaroscuro of tastes and textures will appeal to many, many people.

It is a cookbook that people will love to cook from. And it appeals to what I call the "bedside cook" who enjoys *reading* cookbooks for the gastronomic dreams they induce and thereby cause a much more peaceful sleep knowing the secrets of one's beloved delicacies.

It is a book to cherish and a book to use. It is not a coffee-table book, but rather a kitchen book that we expect will improve some people's cookery, increase the repertoire of other cooks and, overall, give people a mouth-watering picture of this great tradition-inspired restaurant as it enters its third decade.

Introduction

by Tom Margittai and Paul Kovi

If you turn to the endpapers of this book, you will see the two of us. We, of course, are separate people, with personal histories and lives of our own; but as owners and directors of The Four Seasons, we are a happy entity. While we worked together at times, we became partners in an official sense in 1973 when we bought The Four Seasons.

Many people felt that we were foolish. Nineteen seventy-three was a trying year for the economy and a difficult year for luxury restaurants. But we saw it as a challenge. We also knew that there were many positive things we felt about the restaurant and what we could do with it. We believe in New York City and in its life, present and future. We saw The Four Seasons as the quintessential restaurant of New York.

Indeed, we view food and restaurants as a part of general culture. They change and develop as other elements of the culture do. We felt that there was an enormous and growing interest in food and wine on the part of New Yorkers as well as the rest of the country; and from this group of seriously interested people—the same people who are interested in ballet, opera and literature—would come an audience that would *understand* what we wanted to do with the restaurant.

The Four Seasons has always served food of elegant simplicity. Its traditions have been recast in a newer, lighter mode. Coupled with a determined emphasis on the best and freshest seasonal foods, we felt this was the correct direction for our beloved restaurant. Our food would not slavishly imitate French, Italian or even Oriental recipes. Instead it would be food recreated in an American idiom. We were fortunate to have Chef Renggli join us to actually create these dishes.

We also realize that people come to The Four Seasons for different reasons. They come to the Bar Room at lunch as one would come to a club where they can eat simple, direct and good food. They come for dinner or lunch in the Pool Room to celebrate occasions, to feel indulged, pampered and even challenged by the food. Each kind of food requires the same care—a paillard as much expertise, technique, respect for ingredients and judgment in the balance of flavors as the most complex sauced dish.

Now, eight years later, we feel that we have indeed made The Four Seasons our own and have made it new. We believe our guests and friends agree with us; they frequently ask us for our recipes. It is true that ten years ago there was a Four Seasons cookbook, and it was very successful. However, we feel that our cooking has evolved, and with Chef Renggli we now have these new dishes to share with you. We hope they will give you pleasure in reading and in cooking.

This book takes for granted that you know how to cook and that you want from us at home what you want from us in the restaurant—memorable and exciting foods to make entertaining and perhaps even daily meals more rewarding. So we will not presume to teach you to cook, but we hope to share with you our feelings about the seasonal and unusual ingredients that are so important in our restaurant. We will share with you our feelings about the entity of a meal. A meal is not a recipe. It is a sequence of foods and wines, complementary and contrasting, that takes into account texture, color, taste and, in our case, the style we have developed.

The Four Seasons is not something we created by ourselves. We are indeed fortunate to have a deeply professional staff who enjoy our adventure as much as we do. And we have our cherished friends, those people who have shared their creative criticism with us, eaten our food and helped us to do our job. We wish to thank them.

There is Joseph Baum, who created the original Four Seasons. Both of us worked for Joe Baum at various times in our careers. From him we learned a great deal of the actual content that makes our restaurant great today. But perhaps more important, we received from him the motivation to grow, to develop and to insist always on the highest standards. There is James Beard, who has been associated with the restaurant since its earliest days. Originally he helped to develop its foods. Today he is a friend and one of our staunchest supporters. We never feel better than when he is sitting at one of our tables, eating our food. For us food is friendship and should be shared. There is H. Gregory Thomas, the supreme gastronome. Over the years his educated palate and clear, critical comments, combined with style and humor, made him one of our teachers. There is George Lois. Not only is he the designer of this book; he is also the designer of our graphics and the person who creates our advertising. There is Barbara Kafka, with whom we enjoy eating and drinking, and who has helped us to organize and create this book.

You may have noticed that we have not described the physical appearance of the restaurant. It is very hard to describe your own home. We hope, if you do not know the restaurant already, that you

SEPPI RENGGLI

will come and enjoy, as we do, the open spaces, the high ceilings and the brilliant design of Philip Johnson and the special accessories of Garth and Ada Louise Huxtable. If you can't come, we hope that the pictures in this book will give you an idea of what the restaurant is like, just as the recipes will give you an idea of what our food is like.

If it is difficult to describe one's home, it is even more difficult to describe one's family; and our staff, from Oreste Carnevali in the dining room to Seppi Renggli and his staff in the kitchen, are those superb professionals with whom we have worked for many years and who, indeed, have become our family.

Perhaps if we tell you a little about Chef Renggli and the way he cooks, you will know more about us. He is Swiss and has had a long training in many parts of the world. It is a pleasure to watch Chef Renggli work because he enjoys it. He goes so far as to say that you should not cook if you don't enjoy it; it will always show in the food. In the same way, he wants the public to come here to enjoy the food. He demands the best ingredients. That does not always mean caviar, but it does always mean the best butter, the best tomatoes. Best means the best for the purpose—which explains, for example, why we use sweet butter on the table and sweet butter to finish a sauce, while in the kitchen we generally use lightly salted butter. Chef Renggli feels that because of its lower butterfat content, the lightly salted butter gives lighter, less fatty-tasting sauces. In the same way he prefers to use peppers and fresh herbs rather than many dry spices in order to give fresh tastes. He is constantly experimenting and therefore our menus are constantly changing. Our recipes constantly change. He brings this enthusiasm and respect to every dish. He makes a dish from tripe which may cost as much as or more than a sirloin steak because of the time and attention required. Seppi Renggli is an innovative professional. We cannot imagine a better way to share his recipes with you than through this book.

TOM MARGITTAI

PAUL KOVI

The Entrance

The Four Seasons is located in the Seagram Building on Park Avenue in midtown Manhattan. There are two entrances. The Fifty-second Street entrance opens into a foyer with a generous stairway that leads directly to the maitre d's area. The lobby of this entrance area is adorned with pictures of treescapes.

The other entrance, from the Park Avenue side, leads through the stately Mies van der Rohe lobby of the Seagram Building and up six wide steps. Through the doors that open into The Four Seasons, the eye is initially overwhelmed by the world's largest Picasso, a stage curtain that measures 20 feet by 22 feet. It was created by Picasso in 1919 for the Diaghilev and Massine ballet *Le Tricorne*.

On either side of the Picasso are the two great dining rooms. The corridor that separates them is known as "Picasso Alley." The incomparable Picasso curtain is part of the collection of Joseph E. Seagram & Sons, Inc.

The Bar Room

New York has only one Mies van der Rohe building: the Seagram Building. Nestled securely in this masterpiece is The Four Seasons restaurant.

The first of its two resplendent rooms, The Bar Room (sometimes referred to as The Grill Room), has reinstated the classic American grill menu and has recaptured the ambience of New York's turn-of-the-century clubs.

The staircase leading up from the Fifty-second Street entrance (seen in the right of the First Overleaf) opens onto the maitre d' station. The room has been called New York's "Power Room," acknowledging its prestigious luncheon clientele from the worlds of media, finance, publishing, politics, advertising, theater.

Out of range of the camera's eye is the balcony of The Bar Room, where guests seated at a row of tables look down on this auspicious setting.

The Bar

The bar area in The Bar Room features a Richard Lippold sculpture, reflecting light from 3,000 suspended brass rods. Light flows through the Philip Johnson–designed looped chain window curtains as they subtly vibrate and shimmer from the gentlest flow of air.

The Pool Room

The Pool Room is one of the most perfectly proportioned rooms in the world.

Its dramatic central focus is a white Carrara marble pool. As in The Bar Room, its flowers, plants, and menus change four times a year to herald the arrival of each new season.

Mies-designed Brno chairs are in the main dining areas, Hans Wegner's classic chairs are used in a small dining room above The Bar Room, and the Barcelona chairs by Mies grace the street entrance lobby and "Picasso Alley."

The Day Cellar

The Day Cellar, in "Picasso Alley," contains 4,000 bottles of wine for the restaurant's daily supply. A collection of 30,000 bottles is stored in the Wine Cellar below the main floor.

To Paul and Tom
Who run the best restaurant I
over a perfect taste and manner
Seagram Building

Edgar M. Bronfman

Cold Appetizers

Cold appetizers are the party giver's delight, since most can be prepared ahead. They lend elegance to a meal even with the simplest of main courses. Leftovers can be saved and provide an instant fillip of hospitality to any guest stopping by for a drink.

When composing a gala buffet, these appetizers can supply much of the glamour. Add a hot stew that only improves in the keeping, and a green salad. Follow with an impressive dessert, cookies or some fruit and cheese, and your meal is complete.

While the usual place for the cold appetizer is at the beginning of the meal, before a main course or soup, some of our fish and game dishes are sufficiently unusual for you to serve them as a main course for lunch or a light dinner after a clear soup, such as a broth or consommé.

Red Snapper and Salmon Tartare

This tartare, not so dissimilar from a steak tartare, is beautiful on the plate, contrasting as it does the light-colored flesh of the snapper with the dark, rich color of salmon. This recipe was originally developed for a Barrel Tasting dinner (page 361), and you'll note that the dressing avoids the use of lemon juice or vinegar so as not to interfere with the wine. The dressing should be prepared a day ahead to allow its flavor to develop fully.

While the tartare will keep for some time in the refrigerator, the liquid from the fish will dilute the dressing and make the mixture mushy.

The slices of French bread can be toasted under the broiler and kept warm at the bottom of a turned-off oven.

9 ounces salmon fillet, skin removed
9 ounces red snapper fillet, skin removed
Kosher salt
Freshly ground white pepper
2 tablespoons Olive Oil Dressing (recipe follows)

Check the fillets to be sure all bones have been removed. Cut both fillets
into slices about ⅛ inch thick.
Stack the slices and cut them into ⅛-inch-wide strips.
Cut across the strips to make ⅛-inch cubes.
As you cut, discard any bones that may be remaining.
The pieces should be small but not mushy.
Place the fish in a serving bowl
and season lightly with salt and pepper.

Shake the dressing well and strain 2 tablespoons
through several layers of cheesecloth
into the fish in the bowl.
Mix gently but thoroughly.
Keep cold until ready to serve.

Anchovy Butter

2 anchovy fillets
Pinch Hungarian sweet paprika
4 tablespoons softened lightly salted butter
Freshly ground black pepper
1 tablespoon Olive Oil Dressing (recipe follows)

Place the anchovies in a bowl.
With a wooden spoon,
smash the anchovies against the side of the bowl
until they are a paste.
Whisk in the paprika, butter and pepper.

When the butter mixture is smooth,
shake the dressing well and strain 1 tablespoon
through several layers of cheesecloth into the bowl.
Whisk until smooth and thick.
Chill.

To serve, slice French bread into ¼-inch slices.
Toast both sides and keep warm.
Tell your guests to spread some of the anchovy butter
on the toast and top with some of the fish mixture.

Serves 6.

Olive Oil Dressing

½ cup French olive oil
¼ cup Armagnac
2 cloves garlic
12 whole cloves
1 tablespoon freshly crushed black pepper
1 sprig fresh tarragon
1 sprig fresh lemon thyme

Place all the ingredients in a jar.
Shake well and let rest overnight before using.

Serving Suggestions:
If serving a small group, place the Tartare and Anchovy Butter in bowls and the French bread toast in a basket; let your guests serve themselves. Leave any leftover Anchovy Butter on the table, since it is practically irresistible and will disappear before the end of the meal. At a formal occasion for more people, place slices of toast on individual plates, a spoonful of Tartar in the middle and a dab of Anchovy Butter on the side. Serve with butter knives.

The Freemark Abbey Chardonnay that we served with this dish at the Barrel Tasting is an ideal complement, but any full-bodied, non-sweet white wine would be shown at its best at this course.

*With admiration,
to America's most
beautiful restaurant.*

(And to the dill sauce.)

Charles Kuralt

CHARLES KURALT

'On the Road'

Marinated Salmon with Dill Sauce

The Four Seasons uses about 120 pounds of marinated salmon each week, and even more in the summer. It is a Bar Room favorite, served cold as a first course and lightly grilled as a main course. The salmon will keep in the refrigerator for two weeks, although the flavor intensifies after three days.

One 3-pound center-cut piece salmon
2 tablespoons plus ½ teaspoon sugar
4 teaspoons freshly crushed white peppercorns
2 tablespoons kosher salt
4 whole bunches plus 2 tablespoons snipped fresh dill
3 egg yolks
3 tablespoons imported Dijon mustard
Freshly ground black pepper
1 cup vegetable oil
Juice of ½ lemon
3 lemons, halved and hollowed
Boston lettuce leaves
Dill sprigs for garnish
6 scallions, trimmed

Fillet the salmon, leaving the skin on.
Be sure to remove any small bones with a tweezer.
Pat the fish dry. You will have two fillets.

Mix 2 tablespoons sugar with
the crushed peppercorns and salt.
Sprinkle a shallow dish large enough
to hold the fish with a third of the sugar mixture.
Place one of the salmon fillets,
skin side down, over the mixture.
Lightly pound the dill stalks of the dill bunches
with the side of a mallet
and spread them over the salmon in the dish.
Sprinkle with another third of the sugar mixture.
Cover with the remaining salmon fillet, skin side up.
Sprinkle with the remaining sugar mixture.

Set a plate on top of the salmon but do not weight it.
Cover with foil and refrigerate for 3 days,
turning the salmon each day.
Baste with the juices that accumulate around the salmon.

When ready to serve,
remove the salmon and wipe off most of the marinade.
Reserve 2 tablespoons strained marinade juices
and 3 dill sprigs from the marinade, chopped,
for the sauce.
Discard the remaining dill and marinade.
Slice the salmon on the diagonal into thin slices
as you would smoked salmon.

In a mixing bowl, beat the egg yolks with the mustard.
Season with pepper.
Gradually beat in the oil in a slow, steady stream,
whisking constantly, until smooth and thick.
Stir in the chopped reserved dill, marinade juices,
½ teaspoon sugar, lemon juice and snipped fresh dill.
Use the hollow lemon halves
as containers for the sauce.
Line a serving platter with lettuce leaves.
Arrange the salmon slices overlapping like a fan
on one side of the plate.
Garnish with sprigs of fresh dill,
the lemon cups filled with sauce, and the scallion shoots.
Sprinkle with freshly ground pepper.

Serves 6.

Note:
As a luncheon dish, serve with boiled potatoes and creamy
scrambled eggs. If you wish to serve the salmon grilled as a
main course, cut the fish on the diagonal into 1-inch-thick
slices and grill like a paillard.

Serving Suggestions:
The ideal bread for this is Swedish limpa rye, thinly sliced
and lightly buttered with sweet butter.

Marinated Salmon and Scallops

There could not be a prettier, lighter, or more simply prepared first course than this, but because the salmon and scallops are not cooked, they must be impeccably fresh and redolent of the sea.

Watercress leaves, stems removed
Arugula leaves, stems removed
Virgin olive oil
4 ounces salmon,
    cut crosswise on the diagonal into 16 slices
8 sea scallops
Grains of paradise or black peppercorns

Line four individual plates
with a mixed layer of watercress and arugula leaves.

Place some olive oil on a plate
and gently pass the salmon slices through the oil
so it *very* lightly coats them.
Arrange four slices on each plate.

Slice the scallops against the grain
into paper-thin rounds.
Lightly coat these with oil
and arrange on top of the salmon.

Grind fresh grains of paradise or black peppercorns
over the fish.

Serves 4.

Serving Suggestions:
In all probability, you will not need a salad course, what with the arugula and watercress in this dish. As it is so lightly seasoned, it makes a nice counterpoint to a curried main course.

Chicken Liver Mousse

This mousse transforms chopped chicken livers into a creamy, elegant purée. Kidney fat is used for its pure, clear taste. The mousse can be made in large quantities several days ahead and carefully wrapped in plastic; or pour a thin layer of cooled, melted butter onto the set mousse to seal. When serving, remove from the refrigerator, wrapped or sealed, and let rest for 20 minutes. Then remove the wrap or seal just before serving. Of course this can be made in one large dish rather than in individual ramekins.

¼ pound veal kidney fat
¼ pound chopped onions
1 pound chicken livers, trimmed
¼ teaspoon kosher salt
Freshly ground black pepper
1 cup heavy cream

Place six individual 6-ounce ramekins in the refrigerator to chill.

In a 10-inch skillet,
heat the fat in ⅓ cup cold water.
Cook until the fat dissolves and the water evaporates.
Pour into a small bowl,
then strain back into the pan.

Add the onions to the fat and cook over low heat,
stirring, until the onions are transparent and glossy,
but not brown, approximately 10 minutes.
Add the livers and sauté over medium heat, stirring,
for 3 minutes, or until the livers are seared on all sides.
Season with salt and pepper and add the cream.
Bring to a boil and continue to simmer over low heat
until the livers are completely cooked, about 5 minutes.
With a slotted spoon, remove the livers and onions
to the work bowl of a food processor.
Let cool.
Reserve the cooking juices.

Purée the livers and onions
in the food processor until smooth.
Beat in the cooking juices.
If you do not have a food processor,
push the livers and onions through the fine blade
of a food mill or purée in a blender
with the cooking juices.
Spoon the mixture into the chilled ramekins.
Tap them against the work surface to settle the mixture
and eliminate any air holes.
Chill for at least 2 hours.

Serve with toasted white bread.

Serves 6.

Serving Suggestions:

Liver is not the easiest meat to pair with wine. We
recommend a fruity, light red, such as a young Beaujolais;
or, recalling the fabulous fat livers of Europe, a sweet white
wine such as a Moselle or a California Riesling. Should you
happen to have any leftover brioche, toasted slices would
be even posher than white-bread toast.

HENNY YOUNGMAN

Ham Mousse with Peaches

This has been on the menu of The Four Seasons since its earliest days. The recipe has evolved, becoming lighter and more complex. The original, called Mousse of Ham in Whole Peaches, was a semi-liquid mixture of ham, port and mayonnaise, which was stuffed into a whole, peeled and pitted peach. Today, the evolved Ham Mousse with Peaches is a genuine, light, ham mousse custard, which is cooled, unmolded and served with thinly sliced peaches and toasted salted almonds. This new version gives more contrast in texture, is easier to eat, and easier for the cook to prepare ahead, since all the elements can be prepared and simply assembled at the last minute.

½ pound boiled ham, ground fine
2 egg yolks
2 tablespoons imported Dijon mustard
5 eggs
1 tablespoon tomato paste
Freshly ground black pepper
1 tablespoon port wine
½ cup heavy cream
2 cups milk
Kosher salt, if necessary
One 8-ounce jar watermelon rind,
    drained and finely chopped
8 medium, firm but ripe peaches,
    peeled, quartered and cut into thin wedges
½ cup toasted, salted almonds

Heat the oven to 350°F.

Blend the ham, egg yolks and mustard
in the work bowl of a food processor.
With the machine running,
add the whole eggs, one at a time, through the feed tube.
Add the tomato paste, pepper, port, cream and milk.
Blend completely.
Taste for salt and add if needed.

Divide the mixture among eight lightly buttered
1-cup custard cups.
Place in a roasting pan
lined with a double layer of newspaper.
This helps keep the heat even during cooking.
Set the pan on the lower shelf of the preheated oven.
Add enough hot water
to come halfway up the sides of the cups.
Cover the pan with foil and
bake for 35 to 40 minutes,
or until the custards are set.
Do not overbake.

Carefully remove the custard cups from the pan and
let them cool on a rack.

To serve, unmold onto individual serving plates.
Garnish each with a dollop of watermelon rind,
sliced peaches arranged in parallel lines on the plate and
the toasted, salted almonds.

Serves 8.

Serving Suggestions:

This is an appetizer, or indeed a luncheon dish, for a warm
summer day, perhaps in late August when ripe peaches are
available. For a light but spectacular main course to follow,
you might try Sweetbreads and Spinach Millefeuille
(page 127), then a salad of all the tenderest greens, and
Fresh Fruit Salad (page 454). It is a time for a young Italian
white or an Alsatian Riesling, crisp and bone-dry, one wine
for the entire meal—clear, copious and cold.

Bill Bernbach
to Tom & Paul with respect
and warm feelings

BILL BERNBACH

Smoked Salmon Mousse

While this recipe will be as gala as the salmon and caviar
that you use for it, a very small amount of each of these
luxuries will go a long way. With the pale pink of the
mousse, the pale, pale green of the sauce, the more robust
color of the salmon and the summery black accent of the
caviar, this is a beautiful dish.

12 ounces Nova Scotia smoked salmon,
    cut into ½-inch pieces
Kosher salt
Freshly ground white pepper
½ cup Aspic (see recipe, page 511), at room temperature
1¾ cups heavy cream
1 cup Mayonnaise (see recipe, page 517)
1 teaspoon wasabi mustard powder
1 tablespoon imported Dijon mustard
Six 1 x 4-inch thin slices smoked salmon, for garniture
1 tablespoon caviar

    Place the smoked salmon pieces
in the work bowl of a food processor
fitted with the metal blade or in a blender.
Season lightly with salt and pepper.
Process until smooth.
With the machine running,
slowly pour in the liquid aspic through the feed tube.
Stop the machine and scrape down the sides with a spatula.
Re-cover.
With the machine running,
slowly pour in 1¼ cups heavy cream.

    Spoon equal amounts of the salmon mixture
into six ¾-cup custard cups.
Smooth the top surfaces with the back of a spoon.
Chill the mousse in the refrigerator for 2 to 3 hours.

When ready to serve,
whip the remaining ½ cup cream until soft peaks form.
Mix the mayonnaise, whipped cream, mustard powder
and Dijon mustard together thoroughly for the sauce.

Spoon·equal amounts of the sauce
onto the centers of six individual serving plates.
Spread the sauce into a 4½-inch circle.

To unmold the mousses, place the bottoms
of the custard cups in very hot water for 4 or 5 seconds.
Dry the cups.
Quickly invert each mousse
over the center of the sauce on a serving plate.

Fold each thin slice of smoked salmon in half
and wrap it around your finger to make a small crown.
Top each mousse with the rolled salmon
and spoon ½ teaspoon caviar in the center of the roll.

Serves 6.

Serving Suggestions:

This mousse is delicious before a roast meat or even a cold
fish main course; or, at a summer lunch, before one of the
Salad Entrées. For visual reasons as well as those of taste,
this is a recipe that calls for a good rosé in its most gala
incarnation, a marvelous rosé Champagne or a comparable
California bubbly. A warm French loaf should be available
for those who want every last bit of sauce.

*Cu cele mai alese sentimente
Restaurantului „Faur Lemon"*

N. Năstase

ILIE NASTASE

3 Aug. 1976

Crabmeat Mousse

This is another of the elegant, extravagant Four Seasons mousses.

1 pound lump crabmeat, drained and picked over
2 cups heavy cream, whipped
⅓ cup Aspic (see recipe, page 511), at room temperature
1 to 2 tablespoons brandy
¼ cup caviar

Place the crabmeat in the work bowl
of a food processor and process until smooth.
Then push the mixture through a drum sieve
so it is silky smooth.
Stir in about ½ cup of the whipped cream.
Fold in another ½ cup.

Slowly stir the remaining whipped cream in its bowl
and, at the same time, pour in the aspic.
Fold the mixture into the crabmeat with the brandy.
When the mixture is smooth,
divide it among twelve ¾-cup ramekins.
Do not smooth the tops; let them peak.
Chill until set.

Just before serving,
top each portion with 1 teaspoon caviar.

Serves 12.

Serving Suggestions:
A cool Chablis or an informal sparkling wine such as
Mousseux and a bit of toast are all this dish requires. It
would be lovely as a first course before practically anything
except a seafood dish.

Avocado with Tomato and Basil Vinaigrette

This is a dish to make at some perfect point of the year when avocados are ripe and inexpensive, tomatoes ripe and full of flavor, and the basil so plentiful that you are looking for new ways to enjoy its peppery goodness.

1 cup finely chopped red onion
8 large fresh basil leaves, finely chopped
½ cup red wine vinegar
2 cups peeled, seeded and chopped ripe tomatoes
1 teaspoon freshly cracked black pepper
1 tablespoon kosher salt
1 teaspoon sugar
1 cup olive oil
6 ripe avocados, chilled

Blend the onion, basil and vinegar together in a wooden bowl.
Add the tomatoes, pepper, salt, sugar and olive oil.
Allow to stand 2 to 3 hours.

Halve the avocados lengthwise.
Remove the pits.
Using a melon ball cutter, scoop out two balls from each hollow.
Make crisscross lines in the remaining flesh.

Heat the dressing gently; then spoon it into the chilled avocado halves.
Top with the avocado balls and serve at once.

Serves 6 to 12.

Marinated Breast of Capon

Prepared for one of our Foursome Dinners, this dish—as beautiful as any Japanese dish of sashimi—requires advance planning not only because you need squash blossoms and tarragon sprigs for what is clearly a summer dish, but because the capon breast must be marinated and carefully sliced as well. This is a dish to prepare for friends who look at what they eat before they eat it.

Marination

2 whole boneless capon breasts, split
⅓ cup olive oil
6 shallots, sliced
1 leek, well washed and chopped
1 teaspoon kosher salt
1 teaspoon freshly ground black pepper
¼ cup fresh tarragon sprigs
1 cup Chicken Stock (see recipe, page 497),
    reduced to ½ cup
1 cup dry white wine, slowly reduced to ¼ cup

Remove and discard the skin and fat from the breasts.
Place the breasts in a glass or earthenware dish.

Heat the oil in a small pan.
Add the shallots and cook until soft.
Then, add the leek.
Cook until very soft, about 10 minutes.
Do not let the mixture brown.
Spread the mixture over the capon breasts.
Sprinkle with salt and pepper and the tarragon.
Turn the breasts to coat.
Pour the chicken stock and wine over the top.
It should just cover the capon breasts.
If not, add a little more stock and wine.

Cover the dish and refrigerate 2 to 3 days.

Assembly

Vegetable oil
1 red pepper, peeled, seeded, de-ribbed and cut into julienne
*   (see note)*
50 tarragon leaves (approximately)
12 squash blossoms, washed and dried
Kosher salt

Heat about 4 inches of vegetable oil in a 2-quart saucepan to 375°F.

Remove the capon breasts from the marinade.
Wipe off any marinade, but reserve.
Slice each piece on the diagonal into paper-thin slices.
You should get fifteen to eighteen slices per half breast.
Arrange about six slices
on one side of each of twelve dinner plates.
They should look like the petals of a flower.
Lightly brush each slice
with some of the oil from the marinade
and top with a tarragon leaf.
Arrange some julienned peppers
on each plate to look like the stem.

Place the remaining marinated vegetables and liquid
in a blender and blend until smooth.
Place in a small saucepan and heat through.

While the purée is heating, dip the squash blossoms
into the vegetable oil and fry for about 1 minute,
or until crisp.
Sprinkle with salt.

Garnish each plate
with a dollop of the puréed marinade and
a fried squash blossom.

Serves 12.

Cooked variation:

Wipe the marinade off the breasts
and purée the marinade as above.
Sear the meat on a hot grill
as for a paillard, 1 minute on a side.
Then, place in a preheated 375°F. oven for 8 minutes,
or until cooked through.

Slice on a diagonal into thin slices
(eight per piece).
Fan them on plates and serve with the puréed marinade.

Serves 4 as a main course.

Note:

To peel a bell pepper, begin with a vegetable peeler
and remove all the peel you can easily reach.
Then with a small knife,
cut the pepper into its natural sections,
discarding the core and seeds.
Use the small knife to cut around each section
and remove any remaining peel.

Serving Suggestions:

This dish suggests fine crystal, fine porcelain, fine wine such
as a great Montrachet or a wonderfully balanced light white
Bordeaux. We feel that it is a shame that the great wines
often come late in the meal when people's taste buds are
sated and their attention perhaps less keen. If looking to the
wines of California, try a dry Fumé Blanc from Napa.

INGRID BERGMAN

Seasonal Greens with Cracklings

At the Foursome dinner at which this salad was served, pork, duck and chicken skins were used to make the cracklings. You can be as creative as your larder or butcher provides. This is a rich, aromatic salad and a good first course to keep in mind when you have a heavy main course such as sausage, which is hard to precede with an appetizer.

Vegetable oil
Skin from roast or broiled chicken, duck or pork, cut into strips
½ cup Beef Bouillon (see recipe, page 503)
1 clove garlic
2 teaspoons imported green-herb Dijon mustard
   (see page 518)
1 tablespoon red wine vinegar
¼ cup walnut oil
2 tablespoons crème fraîche
Kosher salt
Freshly ground black pepper
3 cups seasonal greens, washed and crisped
   (see list of suggested seasonal greens, page 174;
   include fresh coriander and field cress)

Heat oil in a deep pot to 375°F.
Add the skin and cook until very crisp.
Drain and crumble.
(These are the cracklings.)

Place the bouillon in a saucepan
and cook until reduced to half.

Rub the garlic around the inside
of a wooden salad bowl;
discard the garlic.

Place the mustard in a mixing bowl.
Whisk in the vinegar.
Then slowly whisk in the walnut oil.
Then, whisk in the hot, reduced bouillon,
crème fraiche, salt and pepper.

Place the crisp, very dry
greens in the prepared salad bowl.
Toss with the dressing.

Top with the cracklings.

Serves 6.

GLORIA SWANSON

Fruit Salad with Curried Mayonnaise

We seldom serve fruit as a first course because it is hard to balance with wine. However, this is sufficiently interesting so that you might enjoy having the recipe.

Fruit
1 mango, peeled and pitted
1 kiwi, peeled
1 small tangerine, pith and peel removed
1 small pineapple, peeled, quartered and cored
1 apple, peeled, quartered and cored
½ cantaloupe, peeled and seeded
1 pear, peeled, quartered and cored
Juice of ½ lemon
1 pink grapefruit
1 navel orange
½ cup seedless green grapes

Cut the mango crosswise into ¾-inch slices.
Cut the kiwi, tangerine, pineapple, apple, cantaloupe and pear crosswise into ¼-inch slices.
Sprinkle the lemon juice over the apple to prevent discoloration.

Peel grapefruit and orange
with a knife to remove the white pith along with skin,
inserting the blade of the knife close to the membranes
to release the sections.
Discard the membranes.

Pat all the fruit slices dry.

26. 1. 77

Sauce

1 cup Chicken Stock (see recipe, page 497)
¼ cup curry powder
¾ cup Mayonnaise (see recipe, page 517)
½ cup sour cream

Place the stock in a small saucepan and bring to a boil.
Stir in the curry and cook until reduced to 6 tablespoons.
Let cool slightly.

Mix the curry with the mayonnaise and sour cream.

Assembly

Mix all the fruit, except the kiwi and tangerine,
with the sauce.
Toss to coat well.

Place the sauced fruits in a large glass bowl
or eight to ten tulip glasses.
Top with the kiwi and tangerine slices.

Serves 8 to 10.

Serving Suggestions:

This best precedes something simple and not too heavy,
such as chicken or grilled fish. In that case accompany it
with the same light white wine.

I love your food !
Thanks —

ARTHUR RUBINSTEIN

If
Rubinstein
says its
good — who
am I to argue!

Art Buchwald

ART BUCHWALD

Pâtés and Terrines

Pâtés, terrines, galantines and ballottines are all related. The word "pâté" is the same word, with different accents, as the French word for dough (*pâte*); they both come from the same root as the English word "paste." What is meant is a forcemeat or a farce, which is not only the substance of all these dishes but is the binding (paste) ingredient.

These dishes may be served hot or cold. Their major distinction has to do with cooking methods or serving methods. Traditionally the pâté was baked and served in a crust. The terrine was cooked in an earthenware dish (also called a terrine, from *terre,* the French for "earth"). Both the galantine and the ballottine were made by boning a bird and using the skin as a casing—the galantine poached, the ballottine baked. Today's lexicon of these dishes has increased and there are more fish and vegetable preparations than there were years ago.

All need to be prepared and cooked ahead. Some need to mature for several days in order to fully develop flavor. Be sure to allow enough time for all these procedures.

Sweetbread and Crayfish Pâté

This unusual combination of ingredients provides a balance between the creaminess of the sweetbreads and the resilient texture and unctuous flavor of the crayfish. If crayfish are unavailable, you can substitute an equal weight of medium shrimp and their shells.

6 to 8 paper-thin slices fatback
1 pair (about 1 pound) veal sweetbreads
1 cup dry white wine
1 small carrot
1 medium onion, quartered
1 small bunch parsley
1 celery rib
¼ teaspoon dried tarragon
Kosher salt
½ teaspoon freshly cracked black pepper
½ pound cooked, shelled crayfish;
   shells reserved
1¼ pounds lean veal
¼ pound chicken fat
¼ teaspoon freshly ground white pepper

   Line a 6- to 8-cup rectangular mold with the fatback, letting the excess hang over the edges.
Chill thoroughly.

   Place the sweetbreads in a bowl.
Add water to cover and refrigerate overnight.
Carefully cut away the connective tubes,
gristle and fatty parts.

Place the sweetbreads in a saucepan
with cold water to cover (about 3 cups),
the wine, carrot, onion, parsley, celery,
tarragon, 1½ teaspoons kosher salt
and the black pepper.
Slowly bring to a boil;
cover and lower the heat to a simmer.
Cook for 30 minutes.
With a slotted spoon,
remove the sweetbreads to a side dish.
Let cool.

Chop the crayfish shells
and add them to the sweetbread liquid.
Cook slowly, uncovered, for 45 minutes.
Strain the liquid into a small pan
and cook over high heat
until reduced to ¼ cup.
Let cool slightly.

While the liquid reduces,
put the veal and chicken fat
through the fine blade of a meat grinder.
Season with 1½ teaspoons kosher salt
and the white pepper.
Stir in the crayfish.
Set aside.

Heat the oven to 350°F.

Break the sweetbreads gently apart
into ½-inch pieces,
discarding any tough or fatty tissue that still remains.
Add to the veal and crayfish mixture.
Stir in the reduced liquid.

Spoon the mixture into the prepared mold
and tap against the work surface to settle.
Smooth the top
and bring the excess fatback up to cover the top,
adding extra fat if needed.
Cover the top of the mold with aluminum foil,
sealing tightly.

Place the mold in a larger pan
and fill that pan with hot water
to come halfway up the sides of the mold.
Place in the preheated oven
and bake for 1 hour.

Remove the mold from the water bath
and let cool to room temperature.
Refrigerate overnight.

Cut into ½-inch slices to serve.

Serves 18.

Serving Suggestions:

This dish merits a carefully chosen wine. If you like the fruitier wine taste of the Moselles, here is a pâté that makes a delightful background for them. Try a Johannisberg Riesling or, for a similar taste, the wines from Mendocino made with the same grapes. This dish may well precede a grilled bird or even a richly flavored meat stew. Depending on what you choose for a main course, you may wish to serve an herb mayonnaise or other sauce with the pâté.

This has li ke

the greatest restaurant in the world —

Anthony Quayle.

ANTHONY QUAYLE '76.

Pâté of Pike and Salmon, Sorrel Sauce

This extremely decorative fish pâté stays moister than most because of the unusual method of its poaching. The white background sets off the pink salmon and the black truffles, all framed with the green of the Sorrel Sauce. If fresh sorrel is not in season, you can use jarred sorrel (see Notes on Ingredients for more information).

1½ pounds pike fillets, skin removed
½ pound salmon fillet, skin removed
3 eggs
4 teaspoons kosher salt
Large pinch cayenne pepper
¼ teaspoon freshly ground black pepper
Pinch freshly grated nutmeg
1¾ cups heavy cream
2 black truffles, cut into ⅜-inch cubes
¼ cup green peppercorns packed in salt water, drained
Olive oil
5 tablespoons snipped fresh dill

Check over the pike and salmon and remove any small bones.
Push the pike through the finest blade of a meat grinder.
Place in a bowl, cover and chill.
Cut the salmon into ½-inch cubes.
Set aside.

I think so too,
Tony Randall

TONY RANDALL

Place the chilled pike
in the work bowl of a food processor
fitted with the metal blade.
With the machine running,
add the eggs, one by one, through the feed tube.
In the same way,
add the salt, cayenne, black pepper, nutmeg and cream.
Process 20 seconds after everything is added,
or until the mixture is smooth.

Transfer mixture into a large mixing bowl.
Fold in the truffles, 2 tablespoons green peppercorns and
the salmon.
Cover and chill 1 hour.

Place a 12 x 20-inch piece of plastic wrap
on your work surface.
Brush a center area of the wrap of
about 10 x 14 inches with olive oil.
Scatter 3 tablespoons snipped dill
and the remaining green peppercorns
over the oiled surface.
Spoon the fish mixture across the prepared area
so you have a cylinder
about 14 inches long and 4 inches wide.

Roll the plastic wrap around the cylinder,
tie the ends with string
and wrap again in plastic to make it watertight.

In a saucepan large enough to hold the roll flat,
bring enough water to a boil
to cover the pâté.
Lower the heat to a simmer and add the pâté.
Cook at the simmer for 45 minutes.

Remove from the water and let cool.
Unwrap, slice
and serve with the Sorrel Sauce (recipe follows).

Serves 12.

Sorrel Sauce

1¼ cups Mayonnaise (see recipe, page 517)
½ cup heavy cream, whipped
1 tablespoon sorrel purée (see note)
2 tablespoons imported green-herb Dijon mustard
  (see page 518)
½ cup fresh sorrel leaves, shredded
Freshly ground black pepper

Combine the mayonnaise, cream, sorrel purée and mustard, mixing well.
Fold in the fresh sorrel shreds
and season with black pepper to taste.

Note:

To make sorrel purée,
cook 1 bunch chiffonaded sorrel leaves in butter
until well wilted.
Push the cooked sorrel through a fine sieve.
If using canned sorrel purée,
use ¼ cup for a sufficiently strong flavor.

Serving Suggestions:

This pâté is so decorative that the serving plates should be simple. The acidity of the sorrel in the sauce calls for a somewhat more acid white wine than you might normally choose. Look to young, attractive whites such as the Pomino or the white wines of the Loire. This would be a wonderful first course before one of The Four Seasons' duck dishes (see pages 257 to 273).

Delicious! Thanks!
love Olivia Newton-John

OLIVIA NEWTON-JOHN

Galantine of Capon

A galantine is a bird which is boned and left whole or cut in only one place so the skin may be used as a kind of sausage casing. Galantines are poached and served cold, whereas the closely related ballottines are baked and served hot or warm.

The method for making this galantine has a modern-age twist—it is wrapped in plastic wrap. Use a good quality thick plastic wrap because thin wraps could melt in the cooking.

If you have never made a galantine before and have never boned out a bird this way, we recommend doing it when you have a calm and unhurried day ahead of you. Since the galantine will last at least three days, it gives you your choice of times.

One 3½- to 4-pound capon, cleaned, liver reserved
¾ pound boneless veal shoulder
¾ pound boneless pork shoulder
1½ tablespoons lightly salted butter
½ pound boneless chicken breasts, skin removed,
    cut into 1-inch chunks
¼ pound (about 5) chicken livers,
    trimmed and cut into 1-inch chunks
3 tablespoons brandy
⅓ cup shelled, blanched and peeled pistachio nuts
¼ pound fatback, cubed,
    blanched 1 minute in boiling salted water
    and drained
2 tablespoons plus ½ teaspoon kosher salt
½ teaspoon cracked black pepper
1 cup crushed ice
¼ teaspoon dried rosemary
¼ teaspoon dried thyme
¼ teaspoon dried sage
2 tablespoons chopped parsley
2 black truffles, cut into ¼-inch cubes
1 sprig rosemary
3 bay leaves

Bone the capon as follows,
making sure the skin remains in one piece
without tearing.
Cut off the wings and set aside.
Place the bird breast side down
on your work surface.
Just to one side of the backbone,
cut through the skin and meat
until your knife presses against the carcass.
Make sure the cut runs
the entire length of the bird
from the neck to the tail.

Holding the meat and skin flap
with one hand,
gently pull the meat away from the carcass.
As you pull the meat away,
release it from the carcass
by scraping against the bone with your knife.
The knife should follow
the natural curvature of the carcass.
When the thigh joint is exposed,
cut through it.
When all the meat has been released on one side
and is lying flat on the board,
repeat on the other side.

The breast meat will still be attached
to the white cartilage
which runs down the center of the breast.
With your knife pressed against the white cartilage,
cut down the sides of the cartilage
so the carcass can be removed.
Grasping the carcass securely in one hand,
lift up and pull it out.
As you lift,
use your knife to cut away
any ligaments or meat still attached.

Locate the thigh bone on one side of the bird.
Now, with the tip of a sharp knife,
starting at the exposed joint,
cut around the bone toward the drumstick,
scraping against the bone
and releasing the meat and ligaments as you work.
When you come to the joint
connecting the thigh bone to the leg bone,
cut through the joint with the knife point.
Lift out the bone,
scraping off any remaining meat or ligaments.

Pull the drumstick out from under the meat
and cut completely around the bone
and through the skin, meat and ligaments
about ½ inch from the end.
Holding the end of the leg bone
which was exposed inside the bird with two fingers,
cut completely around the bone just below the knob,
making certain to release not only the meat
but also the thin white ligaments
which hold the meat to the bone.
Using the edge of the knife,
scrape the meat down the bone.
Lift out the bone.
Repeat with the other thigh and leg.
Cut off the leg meat
and set aside for another purpose.
Use the bones and scrapings for stock.

Leaving the breast meat attached to the skin,
cut off slices on either side
which are half the thickness of the breast meat.
Slice these pieces in half again,
in the same way.
Set aside.

Cut the veal and pork into 1-inch cubes
and put them through the finest blade
of a meat grinder.
Cover and set in the refrigerator to chill.

Heat the butter in a skillet until hot.
Add the chicken breasts and sauté,
tossing, for 30 seconds.
Add the chicken livers and reserved capon liver
and cook 30 seconds longer,
turning them to sear lightly on all sides.
Pour in the brandy and flame.
Cook over moderate heat for 1 minute,
shaking the pan until the flames die down.
Place the cooked mixture in a bowl
with the pistachio nuts and fatback.
Season with 1½ teaspoons salt and pepper to taste.
Cover and let stand 15 minutes.

Place the ground pork and veal
in the work bowl of a food processor
fitted with the metal blade.
Add the crushed ice, rosemary, thyme,
sage, parsley, 1½ teaspoons salt and pepper to taste.
Process until smooth.
Add to the chicken breast and liver mixture,
mixing thoroughly.
Fold in the truffles.

Place a double layer of 24-inch-long sheets
of heavy plastic wrap on your work surface.
Butter the center of the sheet.
Lay the sprig of rosemary and the bay leaves
lengthwise down the center.
Place the boned capon, skin side down,
on top of the herbs.
Use the reserved breast slices to fill in
and make an even rectangle of meat over the skin.
Season with ½ teaspoon salt.
Spoon the prepared mixture over the capon meat.
Smooth the top evenly with a spatula,
then lift the plastic wrap at one end
and shape the capon lengthwise into a firm roll,
the edges of the capon skin meeting.
Roll up securely and twist the ends of the plastic
so that it will hold its shape during the cooking.
Wrap in one or two more layers of plastic.

Thank you — Liv Ullmann

LIV ULLMANN

In a pan large enough to hold the roll flat,
bring enough water to a boil to cover the roll.
Lower the heat so the water simmers.
Gently lower the capon roll into the simmering water
and cook, partially covered, for 2 hours.

Let rest in the water for 10 minutes.
Remove from the water and let cool.
Chill in the refrigerator overnight,
then unwrap, slice
and serve with Cranberry Relish (see recipe, page 421),
cornichons and Pickled Onions (see recipe, page 423).

Serves 10.

Serving Suggestions:

Follow the galantine with a rich, saucy meat course. Let the
wine of the main course determine your choice of wine for
the galantine. For a luncheon main course, serve with a
salad and a fresh, fruity, chilled Beaujolais or a Napa
Gamay.

January 8, 1980

To a very special

piece of New York

All the best,

Cy Coleman

CY COLEMAN

Terrine of Venison

This elegant late autumn dish is ideal for the homes of hunters where every saddle of deer yields many, many pounds of less choice, stew-type meat. However, this meat can also be purchased inexpensively, either fresh or frozen. If using frozen venison, defrost it thoroughly, save the juices, and put them through the meat grinder with the meat. If you have gone through the effort of getting the venison, consider making several extra terrines to give away as presents.

If you plan to keep the terrine for any length of time and it does not cover with fat as it cools, melt a little butter, let it cool, and pour it over the terrine until only the fat is visible. This will seal the terrine and will permit it to keep in the refrigerator for several weeks.

2 tablespoons lightly salted butter
6 large (about 6 ounces) mushrooms, sliced
1 McIntosh apple, peeled, cored and cut into eighths
One ½-pound celery root, peeled
   and cut into ¼-inch cubes
1 pound venison, 10 ounces cut into chunks,
   6 ounces cut into ¼-inch cubes
14 ounces pork fat, 12 ounces cut into chunks,
   2 ounces cut into ¼-inch cubes
½ pound pork butt (half lean, half fat),
   cut into chunks
1½ cups dry red wine
1 tablespoon green peppercorns packed in salt water,
   drained and crushed
4 bay leaves
2 cloves garlic, minced
6 shallots, minced
¼ teaspoon celery seed
½ cup calvados
2 eggs
⅓ cup shelled, blanched and peeled pistachio nuts
1 black truffle, cut into ¼-inch cubes
¼ pound boiled ham, cut into ¼-inch cubes
2 tablespoons kosher salt
½ teaspoon freshly ground black pepper
6 to 8 paper-thin fatback slices

In a 10-inch skillet, melt the butter.
Add the mushrooms, apple pieces
and the celery root.
Cook until softened but not brown.
Remove from the heat and let cool.
Stir in the 10 ounces venison,
12 ounces pork fat and the pork butt,
all cut into chunks.
Put through the fine blade of a meat grinder.

In a saucepan,
mix the red wine, the
green peppercorns, 1 bay leaf, garlic,
shallots and celery seed and heat through.
Heat the Calvados in a small pan.
Flame it and while it flames,
pour it over the wine mixture.
Shake the pan until the flames die down.
Cook the mixture over high heat
until only 2 tablespoons of liquid remain.
Remove and discard the bay leaf.
Let cool, then stir the contents of the saucepan
into the ground-meat mixture.
Stir in the remaining 6 ounces venison,
2 ounces pork fat, the eggs, pistachio nuts,
truffles and ham.
Season with salt and pepper.
Mix until well blended.

Heat the oven to 350°F.

Line a 2-quart terrine or pâté mold
with the fatback slices,
their edges slightly overlapping.
Spoon the mixture into the terrine.
Smooth out the top.
Bang the terrine against the counter a few times
to eliminate any air bubbles.
Lay 3 bay leaves across the top.
Cover with a double thickness of aluminum foil.
Place the terrine in a large pan.
Add hot water
to come halfway up the sides of the terrine.
Place in the preheated oven to bake 1 hour 15 minutes.

Remove the terrine from the pan.
Let stand until cool, then chill.
For full flavor to develop, wait 2 or 3 days before serving.
Serve sliced, directly from the terrine.

Serves 18.

Serving Suggestions:
If you are serving from a decorative terrine, you can do it at
the table. You may want to remove a single slice of the
terrine in the kitchen to facilitate removing the slices you
wish to serve. Have bowls on the table filled with cornichons
and/or cranberry sauce, pickled onions and mustard. If you
prefer a more formal service, put your chosen garnitures on
each plate with the slice of terrine. Here is a good place to
serve a rich, fine Piedmontese red or a full-bodied
California Pinot Noir. In an all-game dinner, this terrine
provides variation.

BETTY FRIEDAN

WILLIAM ROGERS

PHYLLIS DILLER

BELLA ABZUG

STEPHEN SONDHEIM

A Game Bird Terrine

This is a terrine of many days: day one and day two of preparation, as listed, but clearly a day three as well, since the finished terrine must be refrigerated a day before serving. There may well be a day four too, a day of shopping—and, in fact, a fifth day for making the chicken stock. The list of ingredients would seem to apply only to a restaurant or a great house where a shoot has just ended and the cook is trying to think of what to do with the extra partridge, quail and ducks. Today, however, quail as well as wild ducks can be found frozen in some stores. You may substitute any combination of wild birds as long as you end up with 1½ pounds of boned meat.

Day 1

Marinade
6 cups dry white vermouth
6 carrots, roughly chopped
12 garlic cloves, lightly smashed
3 small white onions, quartered
30 juniper berries,
    toasted in a dry skillet for 5 minutes
¾ cup white wine vinegar
¾ cup Genever (Dutch gin)
6 tablespoons olive oil

    Place all the ingredients in a saucepan
and bring to a boil.
Remove from the heat
and let cool to room temperature.

Meat

Two ¾-pound partridges, cleaned, giblets reserved
Four 3½-ounce quail, cleaned, giblets reserved
One 2-pound mallard duck, cleaned, giblets reserved
¾ pound pork butt, cut into chunks

The partridges, quail and mallard duck are
all prepared in the same way, as follows:
Cut a large circle around the thigh
and through the joint
to separate the leg from the body.
Scrape the meat from the thigh bone,
then from the skin, and set aside.
(The leg is too full of sinews to bother using the meat.)
Cut off the wings
and reserve for the glaze.
Remove the breast halves in one piece
and scrape off the skin.
Set the thigh and breast meat aside
with the livers.

Take the breasts
and remove the fillets in one piece.
Cut the remaining breast pieces into strips
½ to 1 inch wide.
Place all the breast pieces, including the fillets,
and the livers in a bowl.
Pour half the marinade over them,
cover and refrigerate overnight.

Place the thigh meat and pork in another bowl
and pour the remaining marinade over the meat.
Cover and refrigerate overnight.

Reserve the bones and trimmings
for the glaze.

Glaze

2 tablespoons lightly salted butter
30 juniper berries, toasted in a dry skillet
    for 5 minutes, crushed
6 cups Chicken Stock (see recipe, page 497) or water

Cut off and discard the feet; chop the carcasses.

Heat the butter in a 10-inch skillet.
Add the carcasses, giblets and other trimmings
and cook, stirring, for 10 minutes.
Do not let the bones really brown.
Add the juniper berries and stock.
Bring the mixture to a boil,
then lower the heat and simmer 1½ to 2 hours,
until well reduced.

Strain the reduced stock into a saucepan
and discard the solids.
Skim off any fat.
Continue cooking the stock
until you have a glaze,
about ¼ cup.
Scrape into a small bowl and chill.

Day 2

2 tablespoons lightly salted butter
½ apple, peeled, cored and sliced
3 mushrooms (about 3 ounces), sliced
1 garlic clove, sliced
3 shallots, sliced
2 tablespoons Genever (Dutch gin)
½ pound fatback, approximately, cut into paper-thin slices
1 egg
1 tablespoon kosher salt
¼ cup shelled, blanched and peeled pistachio nuts
1 bay leaf
2 sprigs fresh savory

Remove the thigh meat and pork from the marinade.
Pat dry and set aside.
Remove the breast meat and livers from the marinade.
Pat dry and set aside.

Pour all the marinade into a large skillet
and reduce to 3 cups.

With all good wishes,
Lorne Greene 10/23/79

LORNE GREENE

While the liquid reduces,
heat the butter in a second skillet.
Add the apples, mushrooms, garlic and shallots.
Sauté over medium-low heat,
without letting the vegetables brown, for about 2 minutes.
Add the thigh and pork meat.
Cook just to sear, about 2 minutes.
Add the gin; flame and toss.
When the flames die down,
remove the pan from the heat.
Let the mixture cool to room temperature,
then place in a bowl,
cover and refrigerate until cold.

Line a 4½ x 9½ x 2½-inch terrine
with the thin slices of fatback,
letting the excess hang over the edges; chill.

Strain the reduced marinade into a clean saucepan.
Continue to cook until reduced to ¼ cup.

Heat the oven to 350°F.

Push the pork mixture
through the fine blade of a meat grinder.
Process the pork mixture, the chilled glaze,
the reduced marinade and the egg
in a food processor until smooth.
It may be necessary to do this in two batches.
Season with about 1 tablespoon salt.

Place a quarter of the pork mixture (farce)
over the bottom of the prepared terrine.
Next, make a layer of
about a third of the marinated breasts and livers,
running the strips of breast lengthwise.
Sprinkle a third of the pistachio nuts over the meat.
Continue in this way,
alternating farce with marinated meat, and nuts,
ending with the farce.
Bring the excess pieces of fatback up
to cover the top of the terrine.
Place a bay leaf and the savory over the fatback.
Cover the terrine top with aluminum foil,
sealing tightly.

Place the terrine in a larger pan
and fill that pan with water
to come halfway up the sides of the terrine.
Bring the water to a boil,
then place the terrine and pan
in the preheated oven to bake for 1 hour 20 minutes.

Remove the terrine from the water bath
and let cool to room temperature.
Place a board and some weights (cans do well)
over the terrine and refrigerate overnight.

Serve in slices with cornichons
and Pickled Onions (see recipe, page 423).

Serves 12.

Serving Suggestions:

Instead of wine—although wine goes very well with this
terrine—you might want to serve ice-cold Dutch gin in tiny
glasses or a very good aquavit. Following Northern
European tradition, offer cold beer as well. It makes a
festive, but slightly bibulous, beginning to a meal. This is a
fragrant and nicely flavored terrine; choose a simple main
course.

Dear Tom —
Someday, I will come here
When I am not on a diet!

Erica Jong

ERICA JONG

Pheasant Terrine

Since this terrine demands at least three days of mellowing, after one day of preparation, you might prepare it on one weekend before serving it at a dinner on the following.

One 2½-pound young pheasant
¾ pound pork fat
¼ pound belly bacon, cut into ¼-inch cubes,
    or substitute fatback
2 large cloves garlic
5 large shallots
6 chicken livers, cleaned
¼ cup Cognac
1 cup dry red wine
1 cup orange juice
1 bay leaf
2 fresh sage leaves or ⅛ teaspoon dried sage
Pinch ground ginger
Pinch ground allspice
Pinch ground cloves
Pinch ground nutmeg
½ pound lean pork, cut into 1-inch pieces
¼ cup chopped blanched almonds
¼ cup julienned orange rind
1 large black truffle, cut into ¼-inch dice
1½ tablespoons kosher salt
¾ teaspoon freshly ground black pepper
½ pound fatback, approximately, cut into paper-thin slices
½ cup Aspic (see recipe, page 511), at room temperature

Remove the meat from the pheasant.
Reserve the liver.
(If desired, reserve the bones, skin and trimmings for stock.)
Cut the breast meat into chunks.
Cut up the leg and thigh meat.
Dice the pork fat.
Set aside.

In a large skillet,
sauté the belly bacon until it begins to render its fat.
Cook for 1 minute, stirring constantly.
Add the garlic, shallots, chicken livers
and the reserved pheasant liver.
Cook 1 minute longer, just to sear the livers.
Add the Cognac and flame.
Set aside four livers; let everything cool.

Place the wine, orange juice, bay leaf,
sage, ginger, allspice, cloves and nutmeg
in a saucepan.
Cook until reduced to ½ cup.
Remove and discard the bay leaf;
let the mixture cool.

Push the cooled chicken-liver mixture,
the pheasant meat, fatback and lean pork
through the fine blade of a meat grinder.
Mix well.
Stir in the reduced wine, almonds, orange rind,
truffles, salt and pepper.

Heat the oven to 350°F.

Line the bottom and sides of a 2-quart terrine
with the thin slices of fatback,
letting the slices hang over the edges.
Pack the terrine with half the mixture.
Top with the reserved livers in a layer.
Pack in the rest of the mixture,
tapping hard against the work surface
to settle the mixture and eliminate air bubbles.
Bring up the excess fatback
to cover the top.
Cover the terrine top with aluminum foil,
sealing tightly.
Place the terrine in a large pan.
Fill the pan with enough hot water
to come halfway up the sides of the terrine.

Bake in the preheated oven for 1 hour 45 minutes.

Allow to cool overnight.
Scrape off the fat and pour in the aspic.
Allow to ripen
at least 3 days in the refrigerator before serving.

Slice and serve at room temperature with Pickled Onions
(see recipe, page 423).

Serves 12.

Serving Suggestions:

Think of this as a first course at a game dinner before one of
the civets (pages 346 to 350) or the Scallops of Venison
with Purée of Chestnuts (page 243). Or follow it with
Barbecued Leg of Lamb (page 307). With such a meal,
serve a big Burgundy or Chianti,
both red wines of character.

Wish you were here
Glad I was here

Harold Rome
HAROLD ROME & FLORENCE ROME
& Florence Rome

Cold Appetizers / 65

Vegetable Terrine, Pepper Sauce

Every nouvelle cuisine restaurant has featured a vegetable terrine in recent years. The Four Seasons' version, while vegetable, is not vegetarian. It calls for an unusual group of vegetables which may be varied according to the season as long as you preserve a balance of taste, texture and color. This terrine, a pale pink color, slices better than most and lasts for about a week.

½ pound fatback, approximately, cut into paper-thin slices
Kosher salt
¼ cup celery root, peeled and cut into ½-inch cubes
¾ cup carrots, peeled and cut into ½-inch cubes
¾ cup kohlrabi, peeled and cut into 1-inch cubes
2 artichoke bottoms, trimmed and cut into about 10 wedges
½ cup asparagus, cut into 1-inch pieces
¼ cup turnips, peeled and cut into ½-inch cubes
1¼ pounds boiled ham
1¼ pounds lean veal
½ teaspoon fresh thyme or ¼ teaspoon dried thyme
10 tablespoons heavy cream
5 egg whites
½ teaspoon freshly ground black pepper
½ cup leeks, cut into ¾-inch pieces
¾ cup zucchini, cut into ¾-inch cubes
¾ cup yellow squash, cut into ¾-inch cubes
¼ cup green bell pepper, peeled and cut into 1-inch squares
    (see note, page 37)
3 or 4 black truffles, cut into ¼-inch cubes (optional)
½ cup dry white wine
2 bay leaves

Line an 8-cup rectangular terrine with fatback slices, letting them drape over the edges.
Chill until ready to use.

Bring a pot of salted water to the boil
and add the celery root, carrots, kohlrabi, artichoke bottoms,
asparagus and turnips.
Let the vegetables cook for about 5 minutes.
Rinse in cold water.
Drain well and wrap in a towel to dry.

Heat the oven to 350°F.

Working in batches, place the ham, veal and thyme
in the work bowl of a food processor to chop.
Return all the chopped meat to the work bowl.
With the machine running,
slowly pour in the cream and egg whites.
Season with the pepper.
Process until very smooth,
then push through a drum sieve.
Scrape into a bowl.

With a spatula, spread a layer of about 1 cup
of the ham-veal mixture (farce) on the bottom
and sides of the prepared terrine.
Add all the vegetables and truffles
to the remaining farce in the bowl.
Toss to mix well.
Spoon into the terrine and spread the top smooth.
Bring up the fatback from the sides to cover the top.
Pour in the white wine and top with the bay leaves.
Cover the top with a double layer of foil
and press to seal.

Place the terrine in a larger pan
and fill it with water to come halfway up the sides
of the terrine.
Bring to the boil, then place in the preheated oven
for 45 to 50 minutes.

Remove the terrine from the water bath
and let cool to room temperature.
Then refrigerate overnight, until firm.

To serve, remove the pâté from the terrine.
Cut into slices using a back-and-forth motion.
Serve with the Pepper Sauce (recipe follows).

Serves 12 to 18.

very much a pleasure to be here!

ALEX HALEY

Note:
Other vegetables, such as string beans or peeled broccoli stems, can be substituted for those used in the terrine. Blanch all hard vegetables.

Pepper Sauce
1 cup green bell pepper, peeled
  and cut into ⅛-inch squares (see note, page 37)
1 cup red bell pepper, peeled
  and cut into ⅛-inch squares (see note, page 37)
½ cup virgin olive oil, approximately
Kosher salt
Freshly ground black pepper
⅓ cup chopped chives
Juice of 1 lemon

Mix the green and red peppers in a bowl.
Add just enough oil to coat.
Season with salt, pepper, chives and lemon juice.
Let rest for at least 1 hour.

Serving Suggestions:
This vegetable terrine is light enough to go before a fish course and may also be more appealing before a rich meat main course than a sauced fish dish would be.

Spoon the sauce in a thin line around each slice. For more color, place a sprig of watercress on top of each slice of terrine. A warm, crusty bread would be good here.

This recipe, and particularly its sauce, which uses raw peppers and lemon juice, calls for a coarse wine, perhaps a dry Italian Pinot Grigio, good and cold, or a California Cabernet Rosé.

With Thanks and Kindest Regards.

Rachel Roberts

RACHEL ROBERTS

SEPT 9. 1975

Purée of Scallops

This delicate purée requires some advance thought, since it requires making an aspic. However, we think the result is well worth the effort.

½ cup dry vermouth
1 pound scallops (see note)
1 cup Aspic (see recipe, page 511), at room temperature
1 cup heavy cream
Kosher salt
Freshly ground white pepper
Red or black caviar

Heat the vermouth in a saucepan.
Add the scallops and simmer for 2 minutes,
or until just opaque.
With a slotted spoon,
remove the scallops to a side dish and reserve.
Cook the pan juices until they have reduced
to a syrupy glaze—about 2 tablespoons.

In a food processor fitted with the metal blade,
or using the fine blade of a food mill,
purée the scallops until they are a smooth paste.
With the machine running, pour in the aspic.
Scrape in the syrupy glaze and process until absorbed.

Whip the cream until stiff but not overwhipped.
Gently fold the scallop paste into the whipped cream.
Season to taste with salt and pepper.
Pack the mixture into a 1-quart terrine or soufflé mold.
Chill 1 hour before serving.

Garnish the purée with red or black caviar,
or a combination.

Serve with hot toasted bread cut in half diagonally, crusts removed after toasting.

Serves 6.

Note:
Bay scallops will give a finer result than sea scallops but they are also more expensive. Both types work well.

Serving Suggestions:
Place the dish in the center of the table with serving spoons so the guests can help themselves. The toast can be passed in a basket separately. A light and pretty white wine such as Chenin Blanc or a fresh Italian Pinot Grigio would be nice to serve here.

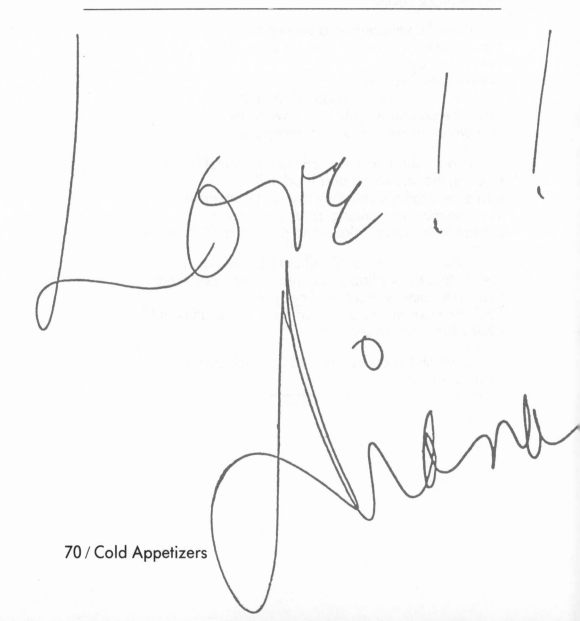

Hot Appetizers

DIANA ROSS

1976

There is nothing that increases the festivity of a meal so much as a hot first course. And while it is usually more work and more difficult to do than a cold first course, or no first course at all, it does permit a very simple main course such as a roast or a grill. Many of the recipes in this section are substantial enough to serve as a main course for lunch or for a light dinner. In either case, increase the size of the portions and add a light salad and a Fruit Tart (page 464) or a sorbet (pages 473 to 479) to complete the meal.

Oysters in Champagne Velouté

This is a fine, light version of a classic recipe. The rock salt serves the purpose of holding the oysters steady so that they will not spill their precious liquor, and it helps to retain their heat at the table. If you have a large fireproof platter or ravier and wish to cook several portions of oysters in the one dish, fill it with rock salt and heat thoroughly before putting the oysters in place. This is necessary because that quantity of salt will not heat through in the short time it takes the oysters to cook.

3 tablespoons lightly salted butter
3 tablespoons all-purpose flour
1 cup Fish Stock (see recipe, page 505)
½ cup Champagne
¼ cup heavy cream
¼ cup finely chopped mixed herbs
    (any combination of chives, sage, rosemary, parsley,
    savory, marjoram, thyme)
Freshly ground black pepper
24 oysters on the half shell
Rock salt

Melt the butter in a 2½-quart saucepan
and stir in the flour.
Cook for 2 minutes without letting the mixture brown.
Gradually beat in the fish stock.
When thickened and smooth,
let the sauce simmer gently for 20 minutes, whisking often.

Preheat the broiler.

Stir ¼ cup Champagne and the heavy cream
into the saucepan.
Simmer until the mixture is reduced to 1 cup.

Meanwhile in a separate pan,
heat the remaining ¼ cup Champagne with the herbs.
Cook until the liquid is almost evaporated.
Scrape the mixture into the sauce.
Season highly with pepper.

Fill six foil pie plates with rock salt
and press four oysters on the half shell into each bed of salt.
Spoon about 2 teaspoons of the sauce on top of each oyster.
Slide the pie plates under the broiler to glaze the tops
and heat the oysters through.
Place the pie plates on serving dishes and serve hot.

Serves 6.

Serving Suggestions:

Following the idea that the wine of the sauce should be the wine of service, a brut Champagne, possibly a Blanc de Blancs, would be a festive accompaniment. If your budget is less lavishly endowed, use a sparkling California wine such as Mirassou's Au Naturel.

A perfect way to start a late fall or early winter dinner, these oysters might be followed by Green Pepper Duck (page 269) or Braised Calf's Liver (page 291), ending with a light sorbet—and even Champagne to finish up if you have used Champagne throughout the meal.

with my regards

John Cheever

JOHN CHEEVER

August 30/1978

Lobster Ragout

We tend to think of lobster as white-wine food, and although the lobster is in fact prepared with white wine, this dish was designed to accompany a red wine, Joseph Phelps vineyard Syrah, 1977 and 1976 at the 1978 Barrel Tasting. This is a fruity wine, but one of great strength and one which certainly needs a dish that will not be dominated by it. Since lobster is so expensive, a dish that provides four servings out of one 2¼-pound lobster minimizes the cost.

1 cup dry white wine
1 tablespoon crushed black peppercorns
1 tablespoon crushed white peppercorns
Four 3-inch sticks dry fennel
2 tablespoons dill seed
¼ cup kosher salt
One 2¼-pound live lobster
2 cups Fish Stock (see recipe, page 505)
1 tablespoon lightly salted butter
½ cup carrots, peeled and cut into ¼-inch dice
½ cup leek greens, cut into ¼-inch squares
½ cup celery root, peeled and cut into ¼-inch dice
2 cups heavy cream, reduced to 1 cup
2 tablespoons Lobster Butter (see recipe, page 515)
2 tablespoons Armagnac
2 packed tablespoons fresh chervil leaves

Fill a 14½-inch-long fish poacher half full of water. Add the wine, peppercorns, fennel, dill seed and salt. Bring to a boil; lower the heat and let simmer 30 minutes. Add the lobster and let cook, covered, for 12 minutes.

Place the fish stock in a saucepan and cook to reduce to a glaze.

Melt the butter in a small saucepan. Add the carrots, leeks and celery root. Cook until soft.

When the lobster is done cooking,
remove it from the liquid and let it cool until you can handle it.
With a heavy knife,
cut the lobster in half lengthwise from head to tail.
Spoon out the green tomalley and red roe
and set aside in a small bowl.

Pull out the tail meat in two pieces (one from each side).
Slice them crosswise into ½-inch pieces.
Remove and discard the bands from the claws.
Break off the three joints
and remove the meat in pieces as large as possible.
If wider than ½ inch, slice them.
Break off the small pieces of claw and
add their meat to the rest.
Crack the large pieces of claw with a hammer
and try to remove the meat in one piece.
Slice crosswise into ¼-inch pieces.

Pour the cream into the fish glaze; whisk until smooth.

In a 10-inch skillet, melt the lobster butter.
Do not let it get too hot.
Add the lobster pieces, roe and tomalley.
Sauté the pieces until heated through.
Add the Armagnac and flame.
Shake the pan until the flames die down.
Add the cooked vegetables and the cream mixture.
Toss to mix and blend everything.
Season to taste with salt and pepper.

Divide the mixture among four heated plates
and sprinkle the fresh chervil on top.

Serves 4.

Note:
If lobster is unavailable, substitute shrimp.

Serving Suggestions:
If using a wine like the Syrah, you might want to continue it
with a lamb dish such as the Saddle of Lamb Baked in Salt
(page 304). There is something appealing about a meal in
which the food is sophisticated and the wine simple and
direct.

Wild Mushrooms with Herbs

There is an increasing interest in this country in wild mushrooms. If it is true that the world is divided into mushroom and non-mushroom people, we are firmly with the mushroom people. One wild mushroom that is beginning to appear in markets in the larger cities is the chanterelle, a fragrant, delicious variety, also called egg mushroom and crater mushroom in this country. Its season runs from June through October, depending on geography and climate. These mushrooms are available dried as well. Canned chanterelles also exist, and while somewhat mushy and lacking in the flavor of the fresh, they are adequate if well rinsed and patted dry before use. You may wish to cut the canned chanterelles into smaller pieces.

Six ¼-inch slices French bread
1 glove garlic, halved
4 tablespoons olive oil, approximately
½ cup thinly sliced shallots
1½ pounds (about 4 cups) fresh chanterelles (see note),
*   pulled apart lengthwise into 3 or 4 pieces*
½ cup finely chopped mixed herbs
*   (summer savory, chives, tarragon, thyme, chervil, etc.)*
1 cup finely chopped fresh parsley
Kosher salt
Freshly ground black pepper
1 cup heavy cream, reduced to ⅓ cup,
*   or ⅓ cup crème fraîche*

    Rub the crusts of the bread with the garlic halves.

In a 12-inch skillet, heat 2 tablespoons olive oil.
When the oil is smoking, add the bread slices in a layer.
When the bottoms are light brown,
turn the bread over and brown the other sides.
If necessary, add more oil to the skillet.
The bread should be crisp, not soggy.
Keep warm.

In the same skillet,
heat the 2 remaining tablespoons olive oil until smoking.
Add the shallots and cook until soft.
Add the mushrooms.
Cook until coated with oil and warm, 1 to 2 minutes.

Add the mixed herbs and parsley; toss to blend well.
When everything is soft (not before),
season lightly with salt and pepper.
Add the cream and stir to blend.

Place 1 slice of toast on each of six warm salad plates.
Top with some of the mushroom mixture.
Serve hot.

Serves 6.

Note:

Any wild mushrooms, alone or in combination, can be used.
If using dried mushrooms, first soak until soft; drain well.

Serving Suggestions:

Since this is a first course which uses neither fish nor fowl nor
beef, it will go well with any meal. Its other advantage is that
should you find—in wood or field or market—wild
mushrooms, here they star on their own and not used simply
as accompaniments to other food. Tournedos of Veal with
Oyster Purée (page 281) would be a lively contrast in color
and taste. You might think of starting this meal with a red
wine rather than a white because of the intense meaty taste
of wild mushrooms.

Savory Flans

Flan is one of those confusing culinary words. In Spanish-speaking countries it signifies the standard dessert—the inevitable caramel custard which always seems to end each meal. By extension, all such egg-and-cream custards, whether sweet or not, have come to be called "flans." (The metal ring that is placed on a baking sheet and draped with pastry to create a pie shell is also called a flan.)

Here is an unusual group of savory flans, rich in flavor, unctuous in taste and delicate in texture, to act as starters for memorable meals.

Calf's Brain Flan with Fried Capers

Mustard and capers, the classic accompaniments of calf's brains, are used to garnish this pale, creamy white custard.

1 pound calf's brains
5 egg yolks
6 eggs
2 cups milk
2 scant cups heavy cream
2¾ teaspoons kosher salt
Freshly ground black pepper
Pinch freshly grated nutmeg
4 tablespoons lightly salted butter,
   heated to nut-brown and cooled

Sauce

2 cups heavy cream
2 tablespoons Glace de Viande (meat glaze)
   (see recipe, page 502)
3 tablespoons imported green-herb Dijon mustard (see page
   518), or any strong imported Dijon mustard
Freshly ground black pepper

    Soak the brains in cold water to cover for 2 hours.
This helps with the removal of the membrane.
Slip your fingers under the membrane
and carefully peel off the filaments.
Clean the brains of all traces of blood.
Rinse and pat dry.

    Heat the oven to 350°F.

I love it here !

Push the brains through a drum sieve
or purée in a blender or food processor
and then push through a drum sieve.
Whip the egg yolks and whole eggs together
in a mixing bowl.
Whisk in the brains.
Stir in the milk, cream, salt, a generous amount of pepper
and a pinch of nutmeg.
Slowly whisk in the melted brown butter.
Strain the mixture through a fine strainer
and spoon into eight buttered 1-cup custard cups.
Place the cups in a deep roasting pan
lined with a double layer of newspaper.
This helps keep the heat even during cooking.
Set the pan on the lower shelf of the preheated oven.
Add enough hot water
to come halfway up the sides of the custard cups.
Cover the pan with aluminum foil.

Place in the preheated oven and
immediately lower the temperature to 250°F.
Bake for 50 to 60 minutes,
or until the flans are firm to the touch.
Do not test by piercing with a needle
because you risk breaking this delicate flan.
Remove from the oven and
leave in the water bath for 10 to 15 minutes.

While the flan cooks, make the sauce.
In a deep saucepan, reduce the cream by boiling
to 1½ cups.
Whisk in the glace de viande, mustard and pepper to taste.

Unmold the warm flans onto serving plates.
Spoon the sauce over the flans
and scatter Fried Capers (recipe follows) on top.

Serves 8 as an appetizer.

ESTELLE PARSONS

Fried Capers

Vegetable oil
½ cup very large capers

Heat the oil in a saucepan to 375°F.

Dry the capers well and add them to the hot oil.
Cook for a few seconds until the buds open.
Drain.
Serve immediately.

Makes ½ cup.

Serving Suggestions:

Although this is a first course containing meat, it is so light and creamy that it could even be served before a fish main course, reversing the usual order. It would be particularly nice, however, before Partridge with Champagne Cabbage (page 330) or a Civet of Venison (page 346), both winter party dishes.

You've brought the "5ᵗʰ season" to the world of cuisine — always a delight.

Frank Gifford

FRANK GIFFORD

Duck Liver Flan

Here the clearly defined taste of duck livers permeates the flan, and marrow provides a tasty added fat. One can reduce the cost of this festive first course by serving the flan with the lighter Shallot Butter (page 201).

Three 1-inch marrow bones
¾ pound (about 6) duck livers
2 egg yolks
1 small clove garlic
Freshly ground black pepper
Pinch freshly grated nutmeg
2 teaspoons kosher salt
½ cup heavy cream
3 eggs
2 cups milk

Crabmeat Sauce
1¼ cups Fish Velouté (see recipe, page 507)
½ cup heavy cream
1 teaspoon kosher salt
Freshly ground white pepper
2 tablespoons lightly salted butter
1 pound lump crabmeat, picked over
2 tablespoons snipped fresh chives
2 tablespoons Cognac
½ teaspoon lemon juice

Dip the marrow bones in warm water to loosen the marrow. Scoop the marrow out of the bones and soak in cold water for 2 hours. Pat dry and chop coarsely.

Heat the oven to 350°F.

Place the marrow in a food processor. Add the livers, egg yolks, garlic, pepper, nutmeg and salt. Process until smooth. With the machine running, add the cream, the whole eggs, one by one and the milk. Strain the mixture through a fine sieve into a bowl.

Pour the mixture into six 8-ounce buttered custard cups.
Place in a roasting pan lined with newspaper.
This helps keep the heat even during cooking.
Set the pan on the lower shelf of the preheated oven.
Add enough hot water to the pan
to come halfway up the sides of the cups.
Cover the pan with foil and place in the preheated oven.
Immediately lower the oven temperature to 250°F.
Bake 50 to 60 minutes, or until firm.

Remove the pan
and let the cups stand in the water bath for 10 to 15 minutes.
Run a knife around the edges of the flans
and turn them out onto individual serving plates.

While the flans cook, prepare the sauce.
Heat the velouté in a 2-quart saucepan.
Stir in the cream and season with salt and white pepper.
Set aside.

In a well-seasoned skillet, melt the butter.
Add the crabmeat and sauté for 30 seconds.
Add the chives and Cognac.
Do not stir, but shake the pan gently to combine the flavors.
Pour the crabmeat and juices over the velouté
and reheat while shaking and tossing to combine.
Add lemon juice and
adjust seasonings to taste with salt and pepper.
Spoon over individual flans and serve at once.

Serves 6.

Serving Suggestions:

If you use the Crabmeat Sauce, you will want a very simple main course to follow this complex first one. Beef Paillard (page 320) or Veal Scallops, Lemon Butter (page 283) would be light and appropriate. If you use the Shallot Butter, then the dish becomes lighter and simpler and could be followed by Baked Striped Bass on Sea Salt with Black Pepper (page 220) or Crisp Duck (page 259) served with Stuffed Apples with Red Cabbage (page 271), which would be nice because you would have the duck livers from the ducks you are preparing. With the Duck Liver Flan, you might serve a fruity, light Riesling. Try a new Riesling from Washington state or Oregon; California Rieslings have more alcohol.

Crabmeat Flan with Crayfish Sauce

This is the savory flan to follow caviar in a meal where only the most luxurious will do. However, in the interest of practicality, if not economy, we have suggested shrimp as a substitute for the hard-to-find crayfish.

If you are fortunate enough to live in Louisiana or the Pacific Northwest, you might consider taking up "crawfishing." Not all crayfish are edible, however, so we advise you to consult your local conservation agency. In general, the time to catch crayfish is from April through October.

Take a look at our Notes on Ingredients for information on buying, rather than catching, crayfish.

Flan
7 eggs
4 egg yolks
2 cups heavy cream
3 cups milk
1 tablespoon kosher salt
Freshly ground white pepper
Freshly grated nutmeg
1 pound crabmeat, picked over
    and pushed through the fine blade of a meat grinder
    or chopped well in a food processor

Garnish
1 large black truffle, cut into very thin julienne

Sauce

2 cups heavy cream
½ teaspoon Glace de Poisson (fish glaze)
   (see recipe, page 506), optional
Kosher salt
Freshly ground black pepper
4 tablespoons Crayfish Butter (see recipe, page 515)
¼ cup julienned celery root
¼ cup julienned carrot
¼ cup julienned leek (both white and green parts)
2 shallots, finely chopped
½ pound cleaned and shelled crayfish tails (see note)
3 tablespoons Cognac
1½ tablespoons snipped fresh chervil
Juice of 1 lemon

Heat the oven to 350°F.
Butter eight 8-ounce custard cups.

In a large mixing bowl,
whisk together the eggs, egg yolks, cream and milk.
Season with salt, pepper (a generous amount) and nutmeg.
Stir in the ground crabmeat.
Pour the mixture into the prepared cups.
Place in a deep roasting pan lined
with a double layer of newspaper.
This helps keep the heat even during cooking.
Add enough hot water to the pan
to come halfway up the sides of the custard cups.
Place in the preheated oven and
immediately lower the temperature to 250°F.
Bake for 50 to 60 minutes.

While the flans bake, prepare the sauce.
In a large deep saucepan,
cook the cream until it reduces to half.
Stir in the glace de poisson.
Add salt and pepper to taste. Set aside.

In a second saucepan, heat 2 tablespoons crayfish butter.
Add the prepared julienne of vegetables and the shallots.
Sauté, stirring, over low heat for 2 minutes,
until everything is tender but still crisp.
With a slotted spoon,
remove the cooked vegetables to a side dish.

Add the remaining 2 tablespoons crayfish butter
to the same pan.
Add the crayfish tails and quickly sauté.
Stir in the Cognac and cook, stirring, for 1 minute longer.

Fold the vegetables, crayfish and pan juices
in the reserved cream.

Stir in the chervil, then the lemon juice.
Taste the sauce for salt and pepper
and readjust seasoning if required.
Keep hot over boiling water.
If necessary, thin the sauce with a little cream.

Remove pan from the oven
and let the custard cups rest in the hot water bath
for 10 to 15 minutes.
Run a knife around the edge of the custard cups
and turn them out onto individual plates.
Carefully spoon the crayfish sauce over
and around each flan.
Top with a sprinkling of truffle julienne.

Serves 8.

Note:

If crayfish are not available, you may substitute ½ pound
shrimp. Use small shrimp (40 to 50 per pound). Peel them
and halve them lengthwise, removing the vein. Sauté them in
a little walnut oil until barely done. In that case, substitute
Shrimp Butter for Crayfish Butter (see recipe, page 515).

Serving Suggestions:

Since crayfish are a spring food par excellence, we suggest,
in tune with the spring season, Fillet of Veal with Fiddlehead
Ferns (page 278) as a main course and fresh fraises de bois
with crème fraîche for dessert—and Champagne throughout
the meal. If you have made the flan with shrimp sauce, a
Roast Rack of Lamb with Leeks and Spinach (page 309)
would be a good follow-up. The wine: Chenin Blanc or
Pouilly Fumé to start and a fine Bordeaux after. End this
meal with the Hazelnut Cake with Chocolate Chunks
(page 447).

Puréed White Beans with Confit d'Oie

Confit d'oie, goose cooked and then preserved in its fat, is native to Southwest France. Like other confits, it is often served with beans to provide a hearty meal during the long, sometimes cold, winters. In our kitchens we take this robust dish, lighten it by puréeing the beans and pare down the portion size to make a refined first course. You can, of course, serve larger portions for a main course. In that case, add garlic and tomato coulis to make the tastes more aggressive.

While the confit may seem like a time-consuming preparation, the results are worth the effort and it will keep for a year. In fact, the flavors need a month to develop sufficiently. It is a wonderful treat to have on hand when unexpected company arrives. In that case, not having had time to cook the beans from scratch, you might drain canned cannellini beans, toss them with a little olive oil, garlic and parsley and heat with the confit for a quick, impressive supper.

Confit d'Oie

One 10- to 15-pound fatty goose
2 tablespoons sea salt
¾ pound lard, approximate

With a knife, make large circles around the thighs and through the leg joint of the goose to remove from the body.
Cut out the breast with the wings in two pieces (one per side).
Remove all the loose fat and reserve it with the carcass.

Place the goose pieces in a bowl.
Sprinkle them with the sea salt to coat evenly.
Cover and refrigerate 24 hours.

Meanwhile, chop up the carcass with its fat.
Place in a 6- to 8-quart casserole
with the reserved fat and ¼ cup water.
Heat slowly.
When the fat has melted,
add cold water just to cover the bones.
Bring liquid to a boil,
lower the heat and simmer for 2½ hours.

Place a colander over a wide, shallow bowl.
Pour the contents of the pot into the colander.
When the liquid has drained through, discard the bones.
Let the stock cool, uncovered, then refrigerate.

When the stock is cold,
lift off the fat that has risen to the top.
Place the fat in a large casserole and heat.
You should have about 2 pounds of goose fat.
Rinse the goose pieces in cold water and dry well.
Place them in the fat
and add enough lard to cover the goose—about ½ pound.
Cover and cook over low heat for 3 hours.

Meanwhile, place the goose stock over high heat
and reduce by boiling to 4 cups.
Cool, uncovered, at room temperature.
Freeze until ready to prepare the purée.

When the goose pieces are done cooking,
place them in a large earthenware crock.
Pour the fat over the goose pieces,
lightly cover the crock
and let rest at room temperature for 6 hours.
Refrigerate the crock for 2 days.

Melt the remaining ¼ pound lard just until liquid.
Don't let it get too hot.
Pour the lard over the top of the goose and fat in the crock.
Lard will harden and seal the crock.
Goose fat will not get firm enough to seal.
Leave in the refrigerator for 1 month.
(It will keep, sealed, for 1 year.)

Puréed White Beans

1 pound dried navy beans
½ cup goose fat
1 cup coarsely chopped onions
4 cloves garlic
1 cup kosher salt
½ cup all-purpose flour

Place the beans in a bowl.
Add cold water to cover by 1½ inches.
Leave overnight in the refrigerator.

Heat the oven to 325°F.

In a heavy casserole with a tight-fitting lid,
melt the goose fat.
Add the onions and garlic.
Cook over high heat until the onions are transparent.

Drain the beans
and add to the pot with the 4 cups reserved goose stock.
Bring to a boil.
Cover the pot.
Combine the salt, flour and ⅓ cup water.
The mixture should be a thick paste.
Spread it along the crack between the pot and lid to seal.

Bake in the preheated oven for 3 hours.
Remove from oven, lift off salt sealer and lid.
Let beans cool for 15 minutes.

Purée the bean mixture in a food processor or blender,
a little at a time, or force through a food mill or fine sieve.

If the mixture is too thick, thin it with a little chicken stock.
Consistency should be thick and smooth.

Assembly

2 tablespoons dry bread crumbs

Heat the oven to 375°F.

Prepare the confit for serving.
Remove the meat from the fat.
Pull the thigh and leg meat from the bones and slice.
Place the slices in individual 1-cup ramekins,
removing the fat as you work.

Spread the puréed white beans over the goose slices,
completely covering the meat.
Sprinkle with the bread crumbs.

Bake in the preheated oven until browned, 20 to 30 minutes.

Serves 30 to 40.

Note:

The breast can be eaten cold. Slice it thinly against the grain. Serve with French bread, sliced into ¼-inch-thick rounds, spread thinly with goose fat and toasted. Serve cornichons and Pickled Onions (see recipe, page 423) on the side.

Serving Suggestions:

Even in its lightened version, this is not a first course for timid eaters. As a surprise, serve it with a strong red wine of the Languedoc or perhaps a tiny glass of Armagnac. Follow it with a light fish dish such as Escalope of Salmon with Caviar (page 203). The ramekins are an advantage when you plan a party, since they can be prepared early in the day to be put in the oven as your guests arrive. For dessert, try the Pine Nut Galette (page 440).

APRIL 19.76

Rudolf Nureyev

RUDOLF NUREYEV

Fettuccine with Smoked Salmon and Cream Sauce

A New York dish that cheerfully combines Italian pasta and that New York favorite, smoked salmon, has actually popped up in Italy. We think you will find the colors and flavors delicious together. By Italian and restaurant standards this is a first course, but done in somewhat larger portions it should make you happy for lunch.

Kosher salt
2 cups heavy cream
1 pound fresh fettuccine in ¼-inch-wide strips (recipe follows),
  or substitute dried imported fettuccine
½ pound Nova Scotia smoked salmon,
  cut into 1½ x ⅓-inch strips
¼ cup freshly grated Parmesan cheese
Freshly ground black pepper

In a large pot, bring 3½ quarts of water with 3 tablespoons salt to a boil.

In a large, heavy skillet, bring the cream to a boil. Cook, stirring constantly with a wire whisk (so the cream doesn't boil over), until the cream is very thick, about 8 minutes.

Add the fettuccine to the boiling water. Cook until it is just done but still firm to the bite. If using fresh pasta, this will take less than a minute after the water returns to the boil. Dried pasta will take longer. Drain well.

While the fettuccine is cooking,
stir the salmon and cheese into the cream.
Cook over high heat for 2 to 3 minutes.
Add the drained fettuccine to the skillet.
Toss gently.

Place the fettuccine and sauce in a serving dish.
Grind fresh pepper over the top.

Serves 4.

Fettuccine

1 ½ cups all-purpose flour
2 eggs, lightly beaten
1 tablespoon olive oil

Place the flour in a bowl.
Make a well in the center and pour in the eggs and oil.
Using your hand and working in a circular motion,
slowly combine the flour with the liquid.
If the mixture is very moist and sticky,
add a little more flour.

Turn the mixture out onto a lightly floured board
and knead the mass,
folding it over and pressing it out,
until you have a smooth ball of dough.

Either with a rolling pin or in a pasta machine,
roll out the dough until it is 1/16 inch thick.

If using a pasta machine,
set the rollers to cut 1/4-inch-wide strips
and cut the pasta.
Otherwise, use a sharp knife.

Let dry for 20 minutes before cooking.

Makes about 1 pound pasta.

Serving Suggestions:

Follow your fettuccine with either Veal Scallops, Lemon
Parmesan (page 284) or Veal Chop with Tomato, Basil and
Mushrooms (page 286), salad, cheese and fruit. Italian
wines make this a light version of an Italian evening. We
recommend a Corvo di Salaparuta from Sicily.

Spaghetti with Peppers and Prosciutto

This is a pasta dish that can be composed at the last minute. On your way home, pick up two ounces of prosciutto and a few red and green bell peppers. This, of course, presumes that onions, olive oil, garlic and parsley are on hand, and basil plants are growing on your windowsill, a part of your ongoing kitchen. Colorful, immediate and flavorful, it respects all the basic rules of Italian cooking.

Kosher salt
1 pound spaghetti (imported variety No. 3)
¼ cup Italian olive oil
1 cup finely chopped onion
2 cloves garlic
1 cup prosciutto, cut into ⅛-inch cubes
1 cup peeled green bell peppers, cut into ⅛-inch cubes
  (see note, page 37)
1 cup peeled red bell peppers, cut into ⅛-inch cubes
  (see note, page 37)
⅓ cup finely chopped parsley
½ teaspoon dried oregano
6 fresh basil leaves, finely chopped
2 tablespoons lightly salted butter
2 ounces Parmesan cheese, grated
Freshly ground black pepper

   Bring 4 quarts of salted water to a boil.
Add the spaghetti and cook until tender, about 12 minutes.

Meanwhile, heat the olive oil in a wide skillet.
Add the onions and garlic and sauté slowly, stirring,
until the onions are soft.
Add the prosciutto and sauté 1 minute, stirring.
Then add the peppers and cook 1 minute more
before adding the parsley, oregano and basil.
Discard the garlic.

Drain the spaghetti and
add to the skillet with the butter and 1 tablespoon cheese.
Toss well.
Season with pepper and salt to taste.
Serve at once with the remaining cheese sprinkled on top.

Serves 6.

Serving Suggestions:
A Valpolicella or a young, light Zinfandel from Napa echo
the ampleness of this course. You can then go on to a simple
and easy roast chicken, a grilled steak or, more elaborately,
to Shrimp and Scallops Sautéed with Tarragon (page 224).
Follow with the red or white wine you started with.

JOHN W. MITCHELL

Gnocchi

Gnocchi are little poached pillows of flour or potatoes or
semolina. They occupy the same place in the meal as a
pasta dish. Here is a light and easy version with a touch of
Seppi's Swiss heritage, evident in the Swiss cheese, and a
touch of our Hungarian heritage in the paprika.

2 cups milk
¼ pound lightly salted butter
1 teaspoon kosher salt
⅛ teaspoon freshly grated nutmeg
1¼ cups all-purpose flour, sifted
7 eggs
½ cup freshly grated Parmesan cheese
1 cup Béchamel Sauce (see recipe, page 516)
½ cup grated Swiss cheese
⅓ cup dry bread crumbs
Hungarian sweet paprika

Place the milk, butter, salt and nutmeg
in a saucepan.
Bring to a boil.
Add the flour all at once
and stir over high heat until the mixture comes together
and away from the sides of the pan.
Remove the pan from the heat
and beat in the eggs one at a time.
Stir in the Parmesan cheese.
Set aside to cool.

In a 10-inch skillet,
bring 3 inches of salted water to a simmer.
Divide the mixture into about twenty equal rounds
and drop them into the simmering water.
Cook about 3 minutes,
or until the balls are firm and rise to the top.
They will still be raw inside.
Remove them with a slotted spoon
to a flat pan lined with a kitchen towel
and let drain.

Heat the oven to 325°F.

August 22, 1975

Butter a 12-inch au gratin dish
and spoon in a thin layer of béchamel sauce.
Place the dumplings over the sauce.
They should fit tightly.
Pour the remaining béchamel sauce over the dumplings.
Sprinkle the Swiss cheese over the top,
then sprinkle on the bread crumbs.
Dust with paprika.

Bake in the preheated oven for 30 minutes,
or until the dumplings are puffed and soft
and browned on the top.

Serves 8.

Serving Suggestions:
The various cultural influences on this dish indicate a wide
latitude in the choice of wines. Everything from a Swiss Dôle
through a Hungarian red or an Italian white, depending on
the contents of your wine cellar or local store, will work. You
could follow the gnocchi with a nice Crisp Duck with Black
Pepper Sauce (page 259 and 268) or, more simply, a
Barbecued Leg of Lamb (page 307).

As long as New York has the Four Seasons I'll never leave again...

Leonard Garment

LEONARD GARMENT

Risotto Primavera

A risotto is an especially creamy rice dish cooked by adding
liquid to rice that has been sautéed in butter or oil. This
version, for spring, is made when the first vegetables are
beginning to ripen. Fresh and fragrant, it can be used as a
side dish with simple veal dishes.

¼ cup olive oil
½ cup finely chopped onion
1 clove garlic
1 pound Arborio rice (see Notes on Ingredients)
½ cup dry white wine
6 cups Chicken Stock, approximately,
    (see recipe, page 497), heated
1 cup (6 ounces) thinly sliced mushrooms
6 ounces green beans, cut into 1-inch pieces
1 large red bell pepper, peeled, seeded
    and cut into 1-inch squares (see note, page 37)
1 large green bell pepper, peeled, seeded
    and cut into 1-inch squares (see note, page 37)
¼ pound fresh snow peas, stringed, ends trimmed,
    cut in half on the diagonal
8 asparagus, woody ends broken off, cut into 1-inch pieces
1 medium zucchini, cut in half lengthwise,
    then crosswise into ¼-inch slices
½ cup peeled, seeded and cubed tomatoes
¼ cup finely chopped parsley
Pinch grated nutmeg
Kosher salt
Freshly ground black pepper
¼ pound lightly salted butter
½ cup freshly grated Parmesan cheese

    Heat the olive oil in a 12-inch skillet.
Add the onion and garlic; cook over moderate heat,
stirring, until the onion is soft and golden.
Add the rice and stir to coat,
using a flat-bottomed wooden spoon.
Add the wine and stir until absorbed.

Begin adding the chicken stock, ⅓ cup at a time.
Keep stirring until each addition is absorbed
before adding the next.
Continue adding stock until 4 cups have been absorbed.
This takes about 15 minutes.
Discard the garlic.

Begin adding the vegetables in the following order
(don't add too much at a time
since many of the ingredients will give off their own liquid
as they cook and that liquid must be absorbed):
mushrooms, beans, peppers, snow peas, asparagus,
zucchini and tomatoes.
Add more stock as needed.
When all the liquid has been absorbed,
add the parsley, nutmeg, salt, pepper
and remaining stock, if needed.
Cook, stirring,
until the rice is very creamy and tender but not mushy.
Remove from the heat
and stir in the butter and cheese.
The whole process should take 20 to 25 minutes.
Serve at once.

Serves 6.

Serving Suggestions:
If using this risotto as a first course, you might follow it with
duck or with a lighter dish such as a Lime Broiled Breast of
Chicken (page 238).

GINA LOLLOBRIGIDA

fantastica!
energia!
dlove
give

A Seafood Risotto

We have told you about our very special seasonal Foursome Dinners. This seafood risotto, the third course at the dinner on October 3, 1979, honoring Peter Sichel, has been inspired by many stays in Venice, a favorite city of ours, whose way with seafood we much admire. Delicious in taste, creamy and rich in texture, this risotto would make an ideal dinner or supper dish. The method of gradual addition and absorption of liquid to and by the rice is critical and is the single fact that defines the risotto. Risottos may have any number of ingredients and seasonings, but they are always prepared in the same way. This risotto, with its vivid colors, is particularly festive.

3 tablespoons olive oil
½ cup onion, cut into ¼-inch pieces
1 pound Arborio rice (see Notes on Ingredients)
½ cup dry white wine
6 cups, approximately, mixed Fish Stock and Chicken Stock
    (see recipes, pages 497 and 505), heated
1 cup shrimp, peeled and halved lengthwise
6 ounces bay scallops
12 oysters, shucked
12 littleneck clams, shelled
¼ pound shelled and cooked crayfish tails (optional)
¼ pound squid, cleaned, blanched in boiling water
    until soft, and cut into ¼-inch rings
1 cup shelled and cooked mussels with their cooking liquid
    (see note)
1 red bell pepper, peeled, seeded and
    cut into ¾-inch squares (see note, page 37)
1 green bell pepper, peeled, seeded
    and cut into ¾-inch squares (see note, page 37)
¼ pound fresh snow peas, stringed, ends trimmed,
    cut in half on the diagonal
¼ pound thin string beans, ends trimmed,
    cut into 1½-inch pieces
3 asparagus, woody ends broken off, cut into 1-inch pieces
    (if thick, cut in half lengthwise)
¼ pound zucchini, seeded, cut lengthwise into thirds,
    then crosswise into ¼-inch slices

1 large tomato, peeled, seeded and cut into 1-inch pieces
¼ cup dried Italian mushrooms, soaked, liquid reserved,
   or 4 fresh shiitake mushrooms
¾ cup freshly grated Parmesan cheese
6 ounces lightly salted butter
1 tablespoon Madeira wine

Heat the olive oil in a 12-inch skillet.
Add the onion and sauté until transparent.
Add the rice and stir to coat,
using a flat-bottomed wooden spoon.
Add the wine and stir until absorbed.
Begin adding the stock, ⅓ cup at a time.
Keep stirring until each addition is absorbed
before adding the next.

Continue adding stock until
about 4 cups have been absorbed.
This takes about 15 minutes.

Begin adding the fish and vegetables
in the following order (don't add too much at a time
since many of the ingredients will give off their own liquid
as they cook and that liquid must be absorbed):
shrimp, scallops, oysters, clams, crayfish, squid, mussels,
then the vegetables and mushrooms.
Add more stock as needed.
When all the liquid is absorbed (rice should not be soggy),
stir in the Parmesan cheese.
Remove from the heat and stir in the butter and Madeira.
The entire process should take 20 to 25 minutes.

Serves 6 as a first course.

Note:
To cook the mussels, follow the procedure in the recipe for
A Feuilleté of Mussels in Saffron Sauce (page 116), omitting
the saffron.

Serving Suggestions:
A main course to follow this risotto might be Tournedos of
Beef with Herb and Mustard Butter (page 316). Follow with
a Fruit Sorbet (pages 475 to 477) for a light dessert.
Excellent wines are a Pinot Grigio from the Veneto region or
a light Chardonnay from Mendocino.

Calf's Brains in Mustard Crumbs

Brains are an underused delicacy and therefore
underpriced. Be sure of your audience before preparing this.
However, if you do make it, you will be rewarded with a
crisply crusted, creamy dish balanced between bland and
spicy.

Three 12-ounce pairs calf's brains
Kosher salt
Freshly ground black pepper
All-purpose flour
Fresh bread crumbs
3 egg yolks
6 tablespoons imported green-herb Dijon mustard (see page
   518), or any strong imported Dijon mustard
12 tablespoons lightly salted butter

Soak the brains in cold water to cover for 2 hours.
This helps the removal of the membrane.
Slip your fingers under the membrane
and carefully peel off the filaments.
Clean the brains of all traces of blood, rinse and pat dry.
It is not necessary to poach them.

Season the brains with salt and pepper.
Spread some flour on one plate and
soft bread crumbs on another.
Mix the egg yolks and mustard in a small bowl.
Roll the brains in the flour,
then brush to coat with the egg yolk-mustard mixture.
Roll to coat in the bread crumbs.
Pat each into a nice oval shape if possible.
They are very fragile and tend to break up.
If they do, pat them together as best you can.

Heat the oven to 350°F.

Heat 6 tablespoons butter
in a well-seasoned, ovenproof skillet.
Add the brains
and sauté quickly on one side until golden brown.
Add the remaining 6 tablespoons butter to the skillet.
Turn the brains and sauté on the other side.
Place the skillet in the preheated oven
to continue cooking for about 8 minutes.

Serve piping hot,
with a spoonful of the browned butter over each serving.
Sprinkle ½ cup Fried Capers (see recipe, page 82) on top.

Serves 6.

Serving Suggestions:
This dish could be the prelude to a meal that goes happily
with lots of good beer or ale. You might, for instance, serve
Boiled Beef (page 321) as the main course; and two
supposedly prosaic preparations will become a feast.
If you wish to serve a wine, choose a light Burgundy or
a Pinot Noir from California.

*Always pleased
to refine and reconsider*

Robert Morley

ROBERT MORLEY

Ramekin of Oysters and Periwinkles

This recipe, created for the Fall Four Seasons Foursome Dinner in 1979, is flavored by greens delicate though rich in taste. It was accompanied by a 1977 Chardonnay of Robert Mondavi. The dish is well worth doing and is one of the few hot first courses of this kind light enough to precede even a fish main course.

Following the major recipe, we give instructions for cooking periwinkles. These small sea snails make a delicious and very pretty component of the dish. Should periwinkles be unavailable, small canned land snails could be used instead. Rinse the canned snails in clear water. Then, combine 1½ cups water, 2 tablespoons white wine, ⅓ cup red wine, 1½ tablespoons diced onion, 1½ tablespoons diced celery, a splash of lemon juice, a bit of salt, a grind of fresh pepper, and cook over medium heat until the vegetables are soft. Reduce the heat, add your washed and drained snails and simmer for a few minutes until the snails are plump, hot and tasty.

---

2 cups Fish Stock (see recipe, page 505)
16 oysters, shucked (liquor reserved)
1 tablespoon lightly salted butter
½ cup leek greens, cut into ¼-inch squares
½ cup carrot, peeled and cut into ¼-inch dice
½ cup celery root, peeled and cut into ¼-inch dice
1 cup cream, reduced to ½ cup
1 cup cooked, shelled periwinkles (see cooking instructions)
Kosher salt
Freshly ground black pepper
Fresh snipped chervil

Place the fish stock in a saucepan.
When boiling, add the oyster liquor.
Cook down to a glaze.

Heat the butter in a small saucepan.
Add the vegetables and cook until soft.
Heat the cream and add the cooked vegetables to it.

Over high heat, add the oysters to the fish glaze.
Cook for a few seconds.
Remove them with a slotted spoon and add the periwinkles.
When they are hot, return the oysters to the pan.
Pour in the cream sauce with the vegetables
and cook until the oysters curl.

Season to taste with salt and pepper.
Spoon into four ¾-cup ramekins and top with chervil.
Serve hot.

Serves 4.

To Cook Periwinkles:

1 cup dry white wine
1 cup dry red wine
¼ cup diced onion
¼ cup diced celery
Juice of ½ lemon
2 teaspoons kosher salt
5 peppercorns
2 pounds periwinkles, well washed

Place 3 cups water, the wines, onion, celery,
lemon juice, salt and peppercorns in a saucepan.
Bring to a boil, then simmer for 15 minutes.
Strain into a clean saucepan and discard vegetables.
Bring the liquid back to a boil and add the periwinkles.
Lower the heat and simmer for about 12 minutes.
The little rounded tops will rise to the edge.
Drain and let cool.

When the periwinkles are cool,
pull them out of their shells with toothpicks.

Makes about 1 cup shelled, cooked periwinkles.

Serving Suggestions:

Look at the Foursome dinner menu on page 360 for
suggestions as to what to serve with this first course. It is a
dish that merits a good Chablis or a fine, dry Alsatian
Riesling.

Quail Eggs with Chopped Sirloin

Quail eggs are clearly not an everyday event. Should you find some in their fragile, beautiful, varicolored speckled shells, then this recipe, developed for the Barrel Tasting of March 1978, is a beautiful way to present them. Their tiny, quivering whites and yellow yolks are set off with a ring of chopped sirloin tartare.

1 finely chopped anchovy fillet
1 teaspoon finely chopped capers
2 tablespoons finely chopped shallots
1 egg yolk
1½ tablespoons olive oil
½ teaspoon imported Dijon mustard
½ teaspoon kosher salt
Freshly ground black pepper
1 tablespoon snipped chives
6 ounces chopped sirloin
6 slices white bread
12 very thin 1-inch squares mildly smoked bacon
12 quail eggs

In a bowl, combine the anchovy, capers and shallots. Add the egg yolk, olive oil, mustard, salt, pepper, chives and meat. Using a fork, work the mixture until well blended and smooth.

Cut two 1¾-inch rounds out of each slice of bread.
Spread a ¼-inch layer of the meat mixture on one round.
Punch out ½-inch circles from the center of the rounds.
Scrape the meat from the small round
to use on the next large round.
Continue in this way
until you have twelve rings of bread covered with meat.

Place one ring on top of each bacon square
and arrange them side by side
in a heavy skillet over low heat.
Drop a shelled quail egg in the center of each ring
and cook slowly until the whites are barely set.
The meat should not change color.

Makes 12.

Serving Suggestions:
If you have access to quail eggs, you may even have quail.
In that case, follow this first course with Roast Quail with
Sage and Fried Grapes (page 333) or Broiled Quail with
Bacon and Mustard (page 335). Look at the Barrel Tasting
menu for wine suggestions.

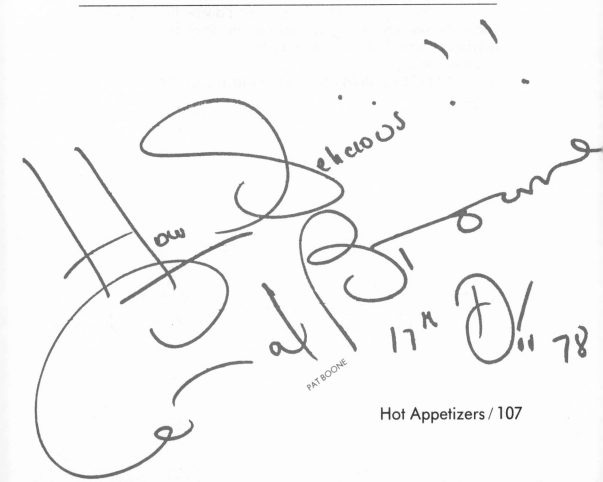

PAT BOONE

Breast of Quail on Crouton

If quail is one of the most elegant of birds, then surely its breast isolated on a crouton that has been sautéed in goose fat must be the epitome of style. This dish acquires a full and unctuous taste from the use of the livers.

8 quail
3 tablespoons lightly salted butter
1 shallot, chopped
8 quail livers
3 chicken livers
1 tablespoon dry sherry
Kosher salt
Freshly ground black pepper
One 2-inch-thick piece white bread (unsliced)
½ cup goose fat or clarified butter

Bone the quail, skin the breasts and divide them in two. Leave the skin on the legs but remove the thigh bone, leaving only the bone in the drumstick.
Reserve the legs
for the Quail Legs in Mustard and Pistachio Crumbs
(page 110).

Thank you for a splendid meal.

In a small saucepan, heat 1 tablespoon butter.
Add the shallot and simmer until transparent.
Add the livers and simmer until almost cooked through.
Deglaze with sherry,
scraping the bottom of the pan with a wooden spoon.
Season with salt and pepper.
Press the mixture through a fine sieve
and mix well.

Trim the crusts from the bread.
Cut it diagonally in half.
Trim the halves to a teardrop shape
and slice the pieces into sixteen ¼-inch slices.

In a skillet, heat the goose fat or clarified butter
and brown the croutons on both sides.
Lift them out to drain on absorbent paper.

Divide the liver mixture and spread on the croutons.
Arrange them in a circle on a warmed round platter.

Heat the remaining 2 tablespoons butter in a skillet
until it starts to brown.
Sprinkle the quail breasts with salt and pepper.
Sauté them quickly for a few seconds on each side
until pink.
Do not overcook.
Place one breast piece on top of each crouton
and serve at once.

Makes 16.

Serving Suggestions:
A fall savory on the Four Seasons Fall Foursome dinner in
1979, this tiny breast was part of a duo of extraordinary
tidbits. The other was Quail Legs in Mustard and Pistachio
Crumbs (recipe follows). At the Foursome dinner a Dom
Ruinart, Blanc de Blancs 1973, was served.

SEAN CONNERY

Quail Legs in Mustard and Pistachio Crumbs

5 slices white bread, or the equivalent in bread trimmings
4 sprigs fresh coriander
½ cup shelled, blanched and peeled pistachio nuts
3 tablespoons imported green-herb Dijon mustard (see page 518)
2 egg yolks
16 quail legs (reserved from the quail for the Breast of Quail on Crouton)
All-purpose flour
Kosher salt
Freshly ground black pepper
3 tablespoons lightly salted butter

Place the bread, coriander and pistachio nuts
in the work bowl of a food processor
fitted with the metal blade.
Process until you have fine crumbs.

Beat the mustard and the egg yolks until well blended.

Dust the legs with flour,
then season with salt and pepper.
Drop them into the mustard mixture and coat well.
Remove the legs and coat them in the bread crumbs.

In a skillet, heat the butter
until it gets foamy and brown.
Add the legs
and fry them to a nice, crisp light brown, 5 to 7 minutes.
Arrange in a circle on a preheated platter.
Serve at once.

Makes 16.

MARGOT FONTEYN

21ˢᵗ Sept 1976

Sweetbreads with Saffron and Melon

Another Barrel Tasting creation, a pairing of the delicate, creamy taste of the sweetbreads with a gentle saffron sauce set off by the pale orange of the melon.

Sweetbreads

1 pair sweetbreads
½ cup dry white wine
1 small leek, washed, trimmed and halved
1 celery rib
½ medium onion

Soak the sweetbreads in cold water
to cover for 3 hours.
Drain and place in a 2-quart saucepan
with the wine, leek, celery, onion and water to cover.
Bring the liquid to a boil;
lower the heat and simmer for 20 minutes.
With a slotted spoon,
remove the sweetbreads to a bowl.
Cut into 1-inch pieces.
Keep warm.

Thanks from
Bibi Andersson

BIBI ANDERSSON

Sauce

1 tablespoon lightly salted butter
2 large shallots, finely chopped
1 teaspoon green peppercorns packed in salt water, drained
¼ cup Madeira wine
1 cup Brown Veal Stock (see recipe, page 498)
1 cup heavy cream
1 teaspoon dried saffron dissolved in white wine just to cover

Heat the butter in a small heavy saucepan.
Add the shallots and green peppercorns
and sauté for 3 minutes.
Add the Madeira and boil until reduced to a glaze.
Add brown stock and bring to a boil;
reduce heat and simmer until reduced to a thick glaze.

Whisk in 1 cup heavy cream in a slow steady stream.
Stir in the saffron-and-wine mixture.
Cook, stirring, over high heat for 5 minutes,
or until thick and shiny.
Strain into a clean bowl and keep warm.

Melon

½ cantaloupe, peeled and seeded
3 tablespoons lightly salted butter

With a ¾-inch melon baller, cut the melon into balls.

Heat the butter in an 8-inch skillet.
When hot and foamy, add the melon
and sauté until lightly browned and heated through.

Assembly

Divide the sweetbreads and melon balls
among six ¾-cup ramekins.
Spoon the sauce evenly over all.
Stir gently to mix.

Serves 6.

Serving Suggestions:

Chef Renggli created this dish to go with a fine California
Fumé Blanc; its character can be a guideline for your own
choice. This first course combines well with almost any main
course.

Puff Pastry

There is a special mystery and elegance to any dish using puff pastry—a special dough with a long and complex history. As it is made today, puff pastry is an intricately formed combination of butter and dough repeatedly rolled and folded to make it light and flaky.

Historically, a similar effect was created in many parts of the world without the rolling and folding but by separating paper-thin layers of dough with layers of butter or oil. Recipes exist from nations as diverse as China, Greece and Hungary.

The Arabs form their very thin dough on a flat pan called a tobsil del warka. The Sicilians, who had frequent contact with the Arabs, developed a rich, multilayered, shell-shaped pastry called sfogliatelli, which has become the name of Italian puff pastry in general.

Puff pastry is also related to the phyllo dough of Greece, which many cooks use interchangeably with the Austro-Hungarian strudel dough. Because of the high natural gluten content of Hungarian wheat, cooks in Hungary were able to make their strudel dough especially thin. In France, when the famous La Varenne wrote his cookbooks, puff pastry still meant individual sheets of dough separated by butter layers and baked. By the time of Carême, in the early nineteenth century, puff pastry, known in France as feuilletage, had already become what it is today. Most of our modern techniques were well known to him.

From the nineteenth century until recently, puff pastry was presented ornately as vol-au-vents, bouchées or fleurons. Following the modern trend toward lighter food, less ornate feuilletés and millefeuilles have become popular.

Feuilletés are small squares or rectangles cut out and baked. When they puff up, the top is cut off, a sauced preparation is spooned over the bottom, and the top replaced. For millefeuilles, the dough is pricked all over to allow air to escape during baking, resulting in a flatter pastry which is layered, flaky and buttery, but not light and puffy. Millefeuille dough can be used as a base for a tart; but for a true millefeuille, the pastry is stacked like a layer cake with filling between the layers, such as for a Napoleon.

Feuilletés and millefeuilles can be served with either sweet or savory fillings. The method for preparing the puff pastry dough is in the Basic Preparations chapter (page 523).

A Feuilleté of Mussels in Saffron Sauce

The mussels in their pale saffron sauce create a fragrant counterpoint to the crisp feuilleté. The mussels and sauce can be prepared ahead. Pour the sauce over the mussels and reheat just before serving. The feuilletés themselves will be at their best if baked at the last moment rather than reheated.

2½ quarts (about 4½ pounds) mussels
1 cup dry white wine
1 ounce sliced shallots
½ teaspoon black peppercorns
½ bunch parsley
1 clove garlic
1 cup heavy cream
1½ teaspoons saffron threads
   soaked in 1 tablespoon white wine
6 feuilleté boats, heated
   (see Puff Pastry recipe, page 523)
Softened butter

    Discard any mussels which do not close when tapped.
Also discard any mussels which are relatively heavy— they are probably full of sand.
Wash the mussels one by one under cold running water.
Scrub each until its shell is smooth.
Pull off the "beard."
Soak the mussels in fresh cold water until ready to use, then drain.

15 February 1977

In a deep pot, combine white wine with
the shallots, peppercorns, parsley and garlic.
Bring to a boil;
lower the heat and simmer for 10 minutes.
Add the mussels; cover and cook over high heat,
shaking the pan frequently, for 6 to 8 minutes,
or until the shells are open.
If some shells do not open,
cover the pan and cook for another minute.
If they still do not open, discard.

Remove all the open mussels.
Shell them.
Place the mussels in the top of a double boiler.
Strain the mussel cooking liquid
through a dampened kitchen towel
or several layers of dampened cheesecloth
into a clean saucepan.
Boil down to 1 cup.
Beat in the cream.

Allow to simmer gently, stirring often,
until reduced to 1 cup.
Stir in the saffron and its liquid.
Adjust the seasoning to taste.
Pour the sauce over the mussels
and keep hot over simmering water.

Slice the tops off the feuilletés
and place the bottoms on individual serving plates.
If the pastry isn't cooked through,
pull out and discard the uncooked middle.
Top each with about 2½ tablespoons mussels and sauce.
Cover with pastry top and
brush softened butter over each.
Serve at once.

Serves 6 as a first course.

GREGORY PECK

A Feuilleté of Bay Scallops

This fresh, lightly herbed scallop dish will melt in your mouth.
The muscle, the white stripe on one side of the scallop, tends to toughen as the scallop cooks, but can be picked off like the string on a bean. If you have feuilletés and fish stock on hand, the actual preparation takes only a few minutes.

1 cup Fish Stock (see recipe, page 505)
½ cup dry vermouth
½ cup heavy cream
1½ tablespoons lightly salted butter
1 pound bay scallops, muscles removed
3 tablespoons fresh chervil leaves
Kosher salt
Freshly ground black pepper
6 feuilleté boats, heated
   (see Puff Pastry recipe, page 523)
Softened butter

Place the fish stock and vermouth in a 1-quart saucepan.
Bring to a boil and reduce to a glaze.
Add the cream.
Stir and cook until the sauce is fairly thick, about 10 minutes.

Over medium-high heat, melt the 1½ tablespoons butter
in a skillet.
When the butter is foamy,
add the scallops and cook just until opaque,
about 2 minutes.
With a slotted spoon,
remove the scallops to a dish and keep warm.
Pour the liquid from the skillet
into the saucepan with the cream sauce.
Cook until reduced to original thickness.
Add 2 tablespoons chervil, the scallops
and salt and pepper to taste.

Slice the tops off the feuilletés
and place the bottoms on individual serving plates.
If the pastry isn't cooked through,
pull out and discard the uncooked middle.
Divide the mixture among the feuilletés.
Top with the remaining chervil and freshly ground pepper.
Brush the browned pastry tops with the softened butter
and place over the filled bottoms.

Serves 6.

I'll make it an annual event to attend my birthday with you!!!

Beverly Sills

BEVERLY SILLS

Hot Appetizers / 119

A Feuilleté of Crayfish and Asparagus

A combination of crayfish and asparagus is the quintessence of spring. If you feel less quintessential, substitute shrimp for the crayfish and Shrimp Butter made with shrimp shells for the Crayfish Butter (recipes for both, page 515). In any case, the pinkish orange of the shellfish and the crisp green of the asparagus make a lovely picture with the cream and the light-brown crust.

1 cup Fish Stock (see recipe, page 505)
½ cup dry vermouth
½ cup heavy cream
1 ½ tablespoons Crayfish Butter (see recipe, page 515)
¾ pound cooked and shelled crayfish tails
Kosher salt
Freshly ground black pepper
24 thin, cooked Asparagus tips (see recipe, page 390)
6 feuilleté boats, heated
   (see Puff Pastry recipe, page 523)

Follow the same procedure as for the Feuilleté of Bay Scallops (see preceding recipe), substituting crayfish butter for regular butter and crayfish tails for bay scallops.

Spoon the mixture into the feuilleté boats and top with asparagus tips, then the feuilleté tops.

Serves 6.

A Feuilleté of Vesiga with Chervil

This is one of our most extraordinary feuilletés. The vesiga—the marrow of the spinal column of the great sturgeon—becomes almost transparent and gives the cream sauce a mysterious texture.

1 pound vesiga
2 cups heavy cream
2 teaspoons Glace de Poisson (fish glaze)
   (see recipe, page 506)
2½ tablespoons snipped fresh chervil
Kosher salt
Freshly ground black pepper
6 feuilleté boats, heated (see Puff Pastry recipe, page 523)
Softened butter

Prepare the vesiga as explained in the recipe for Essence of Red Snapper with Vesiga (see page 162).

Heat the cream in a saucepan.
Bring to a boil and reduce to 1 cup.
Beat in the glace de poisson.
When smooth, fold in the vesiga and the chervil.
Season with salt and pepper.
Keep hot.

Slice the tops off the feuilletés
and place the bottoms on individual serving plates.
If the pastry isn't cooked through,
pull out and discard the uncooked middle.
Divide the mixture among the feuilletés.
Brush the browned pastry tops with softened butter
and place over the filled bottoms.
Serve hot.

Serves 6.

Millefeuille of Puréed Vegetables

This millefeuille is a delicate extravaganza in which the pastry leaves are layered with various puréed vegetables rather than with a heavy cream filling as in a Napoleon. All the purées, the sauce and the millefeuille pastry can be prepared ahead and quickly assembled shortly before dinner.

Kosher salt
Juice of ½ lemon
1 pound parsnips, scraped and cut into large chunks
Freshly ground black pepper
10 tablespoons lightly salted butter
½ cup heavy cream
1 pound broccoli, stems and flowers,
  cut into chunks
Freshly grated nutmeg
1 pound carrots, cut into chunks
1½ teaspoons olive oil
½ cup coarsely chopped shallots
1 clove garlic
½ cup dry red wine
1½ cups (4 to 5 ounces) mushrooms, finely chopped,
  sprinkled with the juice of ½ lemon
½ cup chopped parsley
1½ cups Chicken Stock (see recipe, page 497)
3 tablespoons Glace de Viande (meat glaze)
  (see recipe, page 502)
12-inch square Puff Pastry (see recipe, page 523),
  baked for millefeuilles

　　　Bring a saucepan of salted water to a boil.
Add the lemon juice and parsnips.
Cook until the parsnips are tender.
Drain well and purée in a blender
or food processor until absolutely smooth.
Season to taste with salt and pepper.

Melt 3 tablespoons butter in a saucepan.
When it begins to foam, add the parsnip purée
and cook over medium heat, stirring,
until heated through.
Beat in the cream.
The purée should be creamy but not too thick.
Keep warm.

Bring a second pot of water to a boil.
Add the broccoli and cook until very tender.
Drain, rinse under cold running water; drain again.
Process in a food processor until smooth.
Season with salt, pepper and nutmeg to taste.

In a second saucepan,
melt another 3 tablespoons butter.
When the butter begins to foam, add the broccoli purée.
Cook, stirring, until heated through.
Keep warm.

Place the carrots in a small saucepan
and cover with cold water.
Add salt and bring to a boil.
Cook until very soft.
Push through a sieve or process in a food processor
until very smooth.

Melt 3 tablespoons butter in the saucepan.
When butter is foamy, add the carrot purée.
Cook, stirring, until heated through.
Keep warm.

Heat the olive oil in a heavy saucepan
and add the shallots.
Sauté until transparent but not brown.
Add garlic and wine and simmer slowly
until completely reduced and dry.
Add the mushrooms and parsley and stir well.
Stir in the chicken stock and glace de viande.
Bring to a boil and reduce by half to about 1½ cups.
Remove from heat.
Discard the garlic and
whisk in the remaining tablespoon butter.
Check for seasoning and add pepper and salt if needed.

Cut the puff pastry
into twenty-four 2 x 4-inch rectangles.
Spread six with parsnip purée,
six with broccoli purée and six with carrot purée.
Stack them with the carrot on the bottom,
then the parsnip and the broccoli.
Top each stack with a remaining rectangle.
Press down lightly.
Brush the top of the pastry with melted butter.
Place some sauce on each plate
and a millefeuille on top.

Serves 6.

*I trust that this
will be the first
of many such lunches*

Chaim Herzog

CHAIM HERZOG

21 August 1985

Mussels and Spinach Millefeuille

For this delight, build up layers of puff pastry, mussels and spinach into a fragile tower for each person. As a first course rather than as a luncheon main course, make each portion one-half as large. At lunch, a crisp Alsatian Riesling would be perfect.

7 ounces leaf spinach, stems removed
5 tablespoons lightly salted butter
1 clove garlic, lightly crushed
Kosher salt
Freshly ground black pepper
12 x 9-inch rectangle Puff Pastry
    (see recipe, page 523), baked for millefeuilles
2 recipes Mussels in Saffron Sauce
    (without feuilleté boats) (see recipe, page 116)
Softened butter

Wash the spinach leaves well.
Place them in a pot of boiling water and cook until wilted.
Drain and rinse in cold water; press dry.

Heat 5 tablespoons butter in a large skillet
until nut brown.
Add the garlic and stir for 30 seconds.
Add the spinach and stir to coat with the butter.
Season to taste with salt and pepper; discard the garlic.

Cut the puff pastry into eighteen
1½ x 4-inch rectangles.
Place a rectangle on each of six individual plates.
Spread some spinach on each, then some mussels and sauce.
Repeat with another layer of pastry, spinach,
mussels and sauce.
Top with a pastry rectangle.
Press down gently to set
and brush some softened butter on top; serve hot.

Serves 6 as a luncheon main course.

A Gorgonzola Millefeuille

This millefeuille is a pungent bite to munch along with drinks before dinner or at a cocktail party.

6 ounces Gorgonzola cheese, broken into pieces
½ cup crème fraîche
10 x 15-inch rectangle Puff Pastry
  (see recipe, page 523), baked for millefeuilles

Place the cheese and 1 tablespoon crème fraîche
in the work bowl of a food processor
fitted with the metal blade.
Process until smooth.
With the machine running,
gradually pour in the remaining crème fraîche
through the feed tube.
Process until well blended.
Chill until firm but spreadable.

Using a serrated knife,
cut the baked pastry into three equal parts.
Spread the prepared cheese over
two of the sheets and stack them.
Cover with the third sheet and press lightly to set.
With the serrated knife,
trim off about ¼ inch of pastry all around.
Cut the remainder into 1 x 2-inch pieces.
Serve with cocktails.
Do not refrigerate.

Makes about 20 pieces.

NANCY M. KISSINGER

18 Aug 1977

Sweetbreads and Spinach Millefeuille

Of all the millefeuilles in this book, this rich and creamy version is perhaps the most suitable for a main course. It could follow a Smoked Salmon Mousse (page 31) and, in turn, be followed by poached fruit. You might choose a clear, lightly sweet Rhine wine to drink with it.

2 pairs sweetbreads,
    soaked in cold water to cover for 3 hours
1 cup dry white wine
1 leek, washed, trimmed and halved
2 celery ribs
1 medium onion, halved
8 tablespoons lightly salted butter
3 tablespoons all-purpose flour
1⅓ cups heavy cream
1 large or 2 small egg yolks
Kosher salt
Freshly ground white pepper
7 ounces leaf spinach, washed, stems removed,
    leaves cooked until soft
1 clove garlic, slightly crushed
13½ x 8-inch sheet Puff Pastry (see recipe, page 523),
    baked for millefeuille, warm
Softened butter

Drain the sweetbreads and
place them in a 3-quart saucepan
with the wine, 1 quart water, leek, celery and onion.
Bring the liquid to a boil;
lower the heat and simmer 30 minutes.
With a slotted spoon, remove the sweetbreads to a bowl.
By boiling, reduce the cooking liquid to 2 cups.

While the liquid reduces,
pull off the outer membranes of the sweetbreads.
Separate sweetbreads into 1-inch pieces;
remove and discard any hard fatty parts.

Melt 3 tablespoons of the salted butter in a saucepan.
Add the flour and whisk until smooth.
Let cook for a few minutes without browning.
Gradually whisk in the hot cooking liquid.
Simmer 5 to 8 minutes over gentle heat,
stirring with a spoon, until sauce is thick and smooth.

Stir in 1 cup cream and continue to cook, stirring,
until the sauce is again thickened, about 10 minutes.
Strain through a cone sieve into a clean saucepan.
Blend the remaining ⅓ cup cream and the egg yolks
in a small bowl.
Add some of the strained cream sauce to the egg yolks
to raise their temperature and prevent curdling.
Pour the warm mixture into the sauce, stirring constantly.

Fold in the sweetbreads.
Season with salt and pepper to taste and reheat gently.
Do not allow to boil; keep hot.

Press the spinach leaves dry.
Heat the remaining 5 tablespoons butter
in a large skillet until nut-brown.
Add the garlic clove, then the spinach.
Season with salt and pepper and
toss well over high heat for 1 minute.
Discard the garlic clove and remove the spinach from heat.

With a small sharp knife,
cut out eighteen 1½ x 4-inch rectangles of puff pastry.
Place a rectangle
on each of six individual serving dishes.
Spread some spinach on each rectangle;
cover with some of the sauced sweetbreads.
Cover with another pastry rectangle, more spinach,
more sauced sweetbreads and another pastry rectangle.
Press down gently to hold and
coat the top of each pastry rectangle
with a little softened butter.

Serves 6.

Savory Soufflés

Hot and savory soufflés are a dramatic way to begin a meal. They are perhaps the easiest soufflés of all to time, since you can seat your guests shortly before the soufflés are ready. The soufflé that we make at The Four Seasons is somewhat more stable than the classic soufflé and has been extremely dependable for us.

There are few wines that are particularly appropriate for a soufflé. Eggs are not the happiest background for wine. Therefore, the wine you choose to serve will be dependent on the other ingredients in the soufflé. A solution as airy as the soufflé itself is Champagne or the California bubbly wines of good quality.

Basic Soufflé

This is a recipe that you will need again when looking at the dessert soufflés. You can use it as the base for many variations.

4 tablespoons unsalted butter
4 tablespoons all-purpose flour
1 ½ cups milk, scalded
6 egg yolks
6 egg whites, at room temperature

Heat the oven to 400°F.

Butter and flour the appropriate soufflé mold.
Make a collar as follows:
Take a sheet of aluminum foil long enough
to go around the circumference of the mold plus 1 inch.
Fold the foil over twice lengthwise to make a sturdy strip.
Butter the foil, then wrap it around the mold
so three-quarters of the strip extends over the top of the mold.
Secure the overlapping ends with a straight pin.
Then tie it in place with string and set aside.

Melt the butter in a saucepan and stir in the flour.
Cook, stirring constantly,
for 2 minutes without letting the mixture brown.
Stir in the milk
and whisk until smooth and thickened.

Remove the pan from the heat
and stir in the egg yolks, two at a time,
beating well after each addition.

Season the mixture according to the specific recipe
and set the base mixture aside.

Place the egg whites in a clean bowl
and beat until stiff peaks form.
Stir about one-fourth of the whites into the base mixture. Fold
in the remaining whites.

Spoon into the prepared mold
and bake according to the recipe directions.

Ramp Soufflé

Ramps are wild leeks especially abundant in the mountains of West Virginia. Available from April to June, their appearance each spring harbingers the annual Feast of the Ramson, sponsored by the National Ramp Association. If you cannot find ramps, substitute ordinary leeks for a different, though equally delicious, soufflé.

1 recipe Basic Soufflé (see page 130)
1 tablespoon olive oil
6 heaping tablespoons finely chopped ramps
   (if unavailable, substitute leeks)
Kosher salt

Prepare a 6-cup soufflé mold as described in the basic recipe.

Heat the olive oil in a small skillet.
Add the ramps and sauté until soft, about 10 minutes.

Stir the cooked ramps, with salt to taste, into the base mixture before adding the egg whites.
Spoon into the prepared mold.
Bake in the preheated 400°F. oven for 35 minutes.
Serve immediately.

Serves 6.

Good luck and thanks for many pleasant occasions

DAVID SUSSKIND

Mushroom and Knob Celery Soufflé

The interesting combination of flavors in this soufflé is reminiscent of northern Italy.

1 recipe Basic Soufflé (see page 130)
1 tablespoon olive oil
⅓ cup finely chopped, peeled celery root (knob celery)
⅓ cup dried Italian mushrooms,
    soaked in cold water to cover for 3 to 4 hours
Kosher salt
Freshly ground black pepper

    Prepare a 6-cup soufflé mold
as described in the basic recipe.

    Heat the olive oil in a small skillet.
Add the celery root
and sauté over medium heat until cooked through.

    Squeeze the mushrooms until very dry.
(Save the liquid to flavor soup, if you wish.)
Chop them fine.

    Stir the celery root, mushrooms and seasonings
into the base mixture before adding the egg whites.

    Spoon into the prepared mold.

    Bake in the preheated 400°F. oven for 35 minutes.
Serve immediately.

    Serves 6.

A great pleasure to be here!

Spinach and Bacon Soufflé

The combination of the unctuous spinach purée and the crisp crumbled bacon works well. At The Four Seasons we serve this as a vegetable side dish for two rather than a first course on its own.

1 recipe Basic Soufflé (see page 130)
10 ounces (8 packed cups) fresh spinach leaves,
    well washed
¼ pound (4 or 5 slices) bacon
1 ½ teaspoons kosher salt
Freshly ground black pepper
Pinch freshly grated nutmeg

Prepare a 6-cup soufflé mold
as described in the basic recipe.

Bring a large pot of salted water to a boil.
Add the spinach and cook for 2 minutes.
Drain well and refresh under cold running water.
When the spinach is cool enough to handle,
squeeze out as much water as possible.
Wrap it in a towel and squeeze again.

Place the dry spinach in a food processor
and process until finely chopped.

Cook the bacon until crisp, then drain well and crumble.

Fold the spinach, bacon and seasonings
into the base mixture before adding the egg whites.

Spoon into the prepared mold.

Bake in the preheated 400°F. oven
for 35 to 40 minutes.
Serve immediately as a side dish.

Serves 8.

EUDORA WELTY

Gruyère and Prosciutto Soufflé

A small amount of prosciutto adds a touch of color and an edge of flavor to this cheese soufflé. Buy your prosciutto in one piece, not presliced.

1 recipe Basic Soufflé (see page 130)
1 cup shredded, loosely packed Gruyère cheese
    plus 1 thin 3½-inch square
⅓ cup (1½ ounces) minced prosciutto
¾ teaspoon kosher salt
Freshly ground black pepper
Pinch freshly grated nutmeg

Prepare a 6-cup soufflé mold as described in the basic recipe.

Stir the Gruyère, prosciutto, salt, pepper and nutmeg into the base mixture before adding the egg whites.

Spoon into the prepared mold and top it with the slice of cheese.

Bake in the preheated 400°F. oven for 30 to 35 minutes. Serve immediately.

Serves 4.

To the people who make dining out a creative experience —

Bill Moyers   March 12

BILL MOYERS

Soups

If "music be the food of love" and "bread the staff of life," then soup and a simmering stockpot are the warmth of hearth and home. With Chef Renggli we think we have developed a special selection of soups, both hot and cold. Many of them are dependent on stocks. Since these freeze well, and therefore may easily be made in quantity, you can make life easier for yourself, as well as providing variety for your menus, by having frozen stocks on hand.

We have few serving suggestions for soups. By and large, wines are inappropriate. Elsewhere in these pages, we have suggested some of the soups as first courses. In sufficient quantity, a good soup can almost be a meal if accompanied by a good crusty bread and followed by salad, fruit and cheese or a baked dessert.

Cold Soups

On a warm spring day or a sizzling day in summer, an interesting cold soup will often pique your guests' appetites.

Sorrel Vichyssoise

Years ago, in the kitchens of the New York Ritz, Louis Diat, a great chef, invented an ideal summer soup, cold but full of flavor. He based it on his mother's hot potato-and-leek soup. Since that time, vichyssoise has traveled around the world and back to France to become a summer menu staple. Chef Renggli, our brilliant chef, has played some interesting variations on this theme.

The first of these vichyssoise versions adds the tartness of sorrel.

6 tablespoons lightly salted butter
1 medium onion, chopped
2 garlic cloves, chopped
2 leeks, trimmed, washed well and chopped
6 cups Chicken Stock (see recipe, page 497)
2 large boiling potatoes, peeled and roughly cut up
5 bunches sorrel, well washed, stems removed
1¼ cups heavy cream
Kosher salt
Freshly ground black pepper
6 scoops Sorrel Sorbet (see recipe, page 166)

In a deep pot, heat the butter.
Add the onion and garlic
and gently cook for 2 to 3 minutes without browning.
Add the leeks and cook until soft but not brown.
Add the stock, potatoes and 4 bunches sorrel.
Bring to a boil, lower the heat and simmer 45 minutes.

Purée the soup in a blender
or food processor in batches, then stir in the cream.
Strain the purée through a fine strainer into a clean bowl.
Season with salt and pepper to taste and chill thoroughly.

Roll the remaining sorrel leaves, four at a time,
from stem to tip and cut crosswise into fine shreds.

Serve the soup cold in chilled bowls
garnished with the sorrel shreds and sorrel sorbet.

Serves 6.

Apple Vichyssoise

When Chef Renggli came to The Four Seasons, there was already an apple vichyssoise on the menu which replaced the potatoes with apples. Since that time, he changed the recipe and heightened its taste by the addition of ginger and applejack, among other ingredients. The presentation has also been embellished by a scoop of clear cider sorbet placed in the center of the cold soup.

4½ tart apples, such as Granny Smith
    or Rhode Island Greening
Juice of 1 lemon
1 cup dry white wine
2 cinnamon sticks
3 thin slices fresh ginger
5 tablespoons sugar
1 tablespoon applejack
¼ cup sour cream
1 cup Beef Bouillon (see recipe, page 503)
1 cup heavy cream
½ teaspoon kosher salt
6 scoops Cider Sorbet (see recipe, page 165)

Peel, core and quarter the apples.
Cut the half apple into fine julienne;
sprinkle with half the lemon juice and set aside.

Place the remaining 4 apples, the wine, cinnamon, ginger and sugar
in a heavy saucepan.
Bring to a boil, cover the pan,
lower the heat to medium and let cook for 10 minutes,
or until the apples are thoroughly cooked.
Let cool,
then remove and discard the cinnamon sticks and ginger.

Place the apples and their cooking liquid
in a food processor or blender
with the applejack and sour cream.
Process until smooth.

With the machine running,
pour in the bouillon in a slow steady stream.
Then pour in the cream in the same way.
Blend in the remaining lemon juice and salt.

Place in the refrigerator to chill thoroughly.
Serve in chilled bowls,
each garnished with a scoop of cider sorbet
and some raw julienned apple.

Serves 6.

Spring + poached snapper
at the Four Seasons!
Now I am in New York!

17 May '79   Jan Morris

JAN MORRIS

Red Snapper Madrilene

A madrilene is a clear, well-seasoned broth with enough natural gelatin so that when it is chilled it sets into a clear jelly and can be broken up with a fork into glistening jewels. Most madrilenes are based on tomatoes and beef stock. Our unusual madrilene is based on red snapper heads, bones and trimmings. If you cannot beg, borrow or steal these from your fish man, you might make this soup the day after preparing the snapper.

Stock

1 medium onion, peel on
4½ pounds red snapper heads, bones and tails
3 quarts water
½ bottle (about 1½ cups) Riesling wine
1 leek, halved and well washed
1 small bunch parsley stems
1 celery rib
1 small carrot
¼ head garlic, unpeeled
1 bay leaf
1½ teaspoons freshly crushed black peppercorns

Clarification

¾ pound red snapper skin and trimmings
½ cup chopped leek greens
½ cup chopped parsley leaves and stems
3 egg whites
½ cup chopped celery
½ cup chopped carrot
4 fennel sticks, broken into 1-inch pieces
1 very ripe beefsteak tomato, chopped
1 cup crushed ice
2 tablespoons unflavored gelatin
1 tablespoon kosher salt
¼ whole nutmeg, broken

2 tablespoons dry sherry

Garnish
18 cooked crayfish tails, shelled

Halve the onion and place it, cut sides down,
in a dry skillet over high heat to brown.
Put all the ingredients for the stock,
including the browned onion,
in a deep, non-aluminum stock pot.
Bring the liquids to a boil.
Skim carefully; reduce the heat and simmer for 1 hour.

Prepare the clarification
by grinding the skin and trimmings of the fish
through the largest blade of a meat grinder.
Mix with the remaining ingredients, except the sherry.
Pack into a deep container and chill.

Add the chilled mixture to the stock.
Slowly bring to a boil.
Lower the heat and simmer, uncovered and undisturbed,
for 1 hour.

Line a colander
with a damp kitchen towel and place over a metal bowl.
With a ladle, carefully transfer
the mixture to the colander.
Do not stir the mixture.
Allow the liquid to seep through the colander
without disturbing it.
Discard the solids.

Taste the soup and readjust the seasoning.
Stir in the sherry.
Chill.
When jelled, stir up with a fork.
Spoon into six chilled individual serving cups
and garnish each serving with three shelled crayfish tails.

Serves 6.

With gratitude for a splendid meal —

Wm Manchester

WILLIAM MANCHESTER

Chilled Gazpacho

Gazpacho, that paradigm of cold summer soups, is as varied as the regions of Spain from which it comes—and the ways of the cook. We think ours is especially good.

2 pounds ripe tomatoes, roughly cut up
3 cucumbers, peeled, seeded and roughly cut up
2 celery ribs, roughly cut up
5 red bell peppers, seeded, deribbed and roughly cut up
1 medium onion, roughly cut up
1 large clove garlic, blanched in boiling water
  in its skin 5 minutes, then peeled
4 fresh basil leaves
1 quart tomato juice
6 drops Tabasco
¼ cup fruity olive oil
2 tablespoons red wine vinegar
1 teaspoon sugar
2 teaspoons kosher salt
1 cup Beef Bouillon (see recipe, page 503)
Freshly ground black pepper

Garnish
Cubed bread, toasted in olive oil
Peeled, seeded and cubed cucumber
Peeled, seeded and cubed tomato
Peeled red bell pepper, cut into squares (see note, page 37)
Peeled green bell pepper, cut into squares (see note, page 37)
Diced onion

In the work bowl of a food processor fitted with the metal blade, place the tomatoes, cucumbers, celery, red peppers and onion. Process until fairly smooth. Add the garlic and basil and purée until smooth. Push through the fine blade of a food mill or sieve.

Stir in the remaining ingredients and chill well. Serve in chilled bowls accompanied by garnishes.

Serves 8 to 10.

Avocado Soup with Avocado Sorbet

This soup is seasoned with coriander and lemon and amplified by avocado sorbet. It would go best with a grilled main course.

2 medium-sized ripe avocados
¼ cup crème fraîche
¼ cup sour cream
Pinch ground thyme
6 drops Tabasco
1 teaspoon kosher salt
Pinch ground coriander
Juice of ½ lemon
1 cup heavy cream
2 cups Beef Bouillon (see recipe, page 503)
8 scoops Avocado Sorbet (see recipe, page 166)
2 tablespoons sliced almonds, toasted

Peel the avocados, pit them
and purée in a food processor.
Add the crème fraîche, sour cream, seasonings and
lemon juice and process until smooth.
With the machine running, pour in the heavy cream,
and then the bouillon, in a steady stream.
(If you do not have a food processor, purée the avocado
through the finest blade of a food mill
and continue with the recipe using an electric mixer.)
Strain the soup through a fine strainer and chill.

Serve the soup in small chilled bowls,
garnishing each with a scoop of avocado sorbet.
Top with toasted almonds.

Serves 8.

Tomato Bisque with Basil Sorbet

This is one of those seasonal dishes that can only be made in full summer or early fall when the tomatoes are fresh and fabulous, the basil precious and pungent.

2 tablespoons olive oil
½ pound chopped onion
1 celery rib, roughly cut up
2 garlic cloves
2½ pounds ripe beefsteak tomatoes,
    cored, seeded and cut into ¼-inch slices
24 fresh basil leaves
2 cups Chicken Stock (see recipe, page 497)
Kosher salt
Freshly ground white pepper
1 cup heavy cream
6 scoops Basil Sorbet (see recipe, page 166)

Heat the olive oil in a 10-inch skillet. Add the onion, celery and garlic and cook over low heat for about 10 minutes, or until the vegetables are soft but not brown.

Add the tomatoes and half the basil and stir to blend. Cook slowly for about 10 minutes.

Stir in the chicken stock and salt to taste. Bring to a boil, lower the heat; simmer about 1 hour, or until everything is very soft.

Purée the mixture in a blender or food processor, then push it through a fine sieve to give a smooth purée. Place in the refrigerator for an hour, or until cold.

Stir in the cream, adjust the seasoning and chill.

Serve in chilled bowls garnished with scoops of basil sorbet and the remaining basil leaves.

Serves 6.

Cold Peach Soup

In much of this country, we tend to be suspicious of fruit soups. In Europe they are popular in countries from Germany north. This summer soup is a spectacular way to overcome any prejudices your guests may have.

6 peaches, peeled and pitted
1 small orange, halved and pitted
½ lemon, pitted
1 bay leaf (preferably fresh)
One 1½-inch cinnamon stick
4 whole cloves
2 cups dry white wine
2 cups water
⅓ cup sugar
1 teaspoon cornstarch
3 tablespoons peach brandy
7 ounces ginger ale

Place peaches, orange, lemon, bay leaf,
cinnamon, cloves, wine, water and sugar in a saucepan.
Bring to a boil, lower the heat slightly
and cook for about 1 hour, or until everything is very soft.

Blend the cornstarch into the brandy.
Stir into the peach mixture; bring to a boil.
Remove from the heat and let cool.

Remove the orange and lemon rinds,
leaving the pulp in the mixture.
Discard the rinds with the bay, cinnamon and cloves.

Purée the mixture in a blender or food processor.
Then, push through a fine sieve into a metal bowl.

Divide 1 cup of the mixture among
four small containers and freeze.
Chill the rest of the soup.
Just before serving, stir in cold ginger ale.

Serve in chilled bowls, top with frozen soup.

Serves 4.

Hot Soups

Hot soup is indeed "Soup of the evening, beautiful Soup!" and its warming presence, even at its most refined, will start your guests off to a glowing evening.

Purée of Vegetables

This is a soup for fall. You can make potage for other seasons by choosing other vegetables, but respect the proportion of leafy to solid and the variety of tastes and colors.

This soup makes a fine main dish. Follow the soup with a light salad and cheese.

¼ pound lightly salted butter
4 cloves garlic
1 onion, roughly cut up
3 celery ribs, roughly cut up
1 leek, green and white parts, well washed and roughly cut up
2 tomatoes, peeled and roughly cut up
2 medium boiling potatoes, peeled and roughly cut up
1 large stalk broccoli, roughly cut up
6 large mushrooms, roughly cut up
½ rutabaga, peeled and roughly cut up
¼ cabbage, roughly cut up
1 summer squash, roughly cut up
3 carrots, peeled and roughly cut up
1 veal knuckle
2 cups heavy cream
2 cups milk
2 tablespoons kosher salt
Freshly ground black pepper

Melt the butter in a 5-quart saucepan.
Turn the heat to medium-low
and add the garlic, onion, celery and leek.
Sauté slowly until everything is soft but not brown.

Add the remaining vegetables
and the veal knuckle to the pot.
Add water to barely cover and bring to a boil.
Turn heat down; simmer 2 hours; discard veal knuckle.

Purée the soup in a blender or a food mill.
Return to the pot and reheat.
Add the cream and milk and bring to a boil.
Season with salt and pepper to taste.

Serves 12.

Onion Soup

This unusual onion soup with cream and potato and its eccentric touch of Camembert cheese is a soup for the most sophisticated of dinners.

¼ pound lightly salted butter
2 pounds onions, roughly cut up
4 cloves garlic
1 leek, washed, halved and thinly sliced
1 boiling potato, peeled and sliced
1 quart Beef Bouillon (see recipe, page 503)
½ cup dry white wine
1 cup heavy cream
Kosher salt
Freshly ground black pepper
1 completely ripe Camembert cheese, rind removed

Heat the butter in a heavy saucepan.
When it foams, add the onions, garlic and leek.
Cook, stirring, until the onions
just begin to brown around the edges.
Reduce heat to very low; continue to brown onions
in their own juices for about 20 minutes.

Mix in the potato slices and continue to cook
very slowly another 30 minutes, stirring occasionally.
Pour in the beef bouillon and the wine, bring to a boil.
Cover and cook at a simmer for 30 minutes.

Heat the oven to 375°F.

Remove the pan from the heat, uncover and allow to cool.
Purée in a food processor or blender.
With the machine running, slowly pour in the cream.
Adjust the seasoning with salt and pepper.

Ladle the creamy soup into individual cups.
Cover each cup with a dribbling of the cheese.
Set the cups on a baking sheet
and brown in the preheated oven; serve hot.

Serves 12.

Ramp Soup

Related to the Onion Soup is this briefly-in-season specialty.

1 pound ramps
¼ pound lightly salted butter
1½ pounds boiling potatoes,
    peeled and cut into 1-inch pieces
6 cups Chicken Stock (see recipe, page 497)
2 cups heavy cream
Kosher salt

Wash the ramps thoroughly in cold water.
Trim off the roots.
Set a few ramps aside to garnish the soup.

Melt the butter in a large saucepan.
Add the washed ramps and stir.
Cook over low heat until wilted, about 10 minutes.

Add the potatoes and stir to coat with the butter.
Pour in the chicken stock.
Bring to a boil slowly,
then reduce heat and simmer for 30 minutes.
Purée the soup a few cupfuls at a time
in a blender or food processor.
Bring purée to a boil, stirring with a wire whisk.
Stir in the cream and bring back to the boil.
Taste for seasoning, adding salt if necessary.

Push the mixture through a fine sieve
and whisk until smooth.
Skim off any froth that rises.

Serve hot in bowls garnished with raw ramps.

Serves 10.

Note:
Leftover soup is good cold.

Pumpkin Bisque

This soup makes an interesting first course, contrasting the texture and flavor of the puréed pumpkin with that of the baked acorn squash.

4 tablespoons lightly salted butter
2 cloves garlic
1 celery rib
¼ pound chopped onion
1 leek, white part only, chopped
One 2½-pound Spanish pumpkin (calabaza),
    peeled, seeded and cut into 2-inch chunks
1 quart Chicken Stock (see recipe, page 497), heated
6 small acorn squash
1 cup heavy cream
Kosher salt
Freshly ground white pepper
6 tablespoons crème fraîche
2 tablespoons toasted pepitas

In a deep saucepan, heat the butter.
Add the garlic, celery, onion and leek.
Gently sauté for 5 minutes, or until golden.
Add the pumpkin and cover with hot chicken stock.
Bring to the boil, cover the pan tightly,
lower the heat and simmer 30 minutes.

While the soup simmers, prepare the acorn squash.
Cut off the tops about ¾ inch down.
Scoop out and discard the seeds.
Trim the bottoms so they sit flat,
cutting away as little of the squash as possible.
Set aside.

Heat the oven to 350°F.

Con mucho gusto!

JOHN D. EHRLICHMAN

Strain the vegetables from the soup into a clean bowl,
reserving both vegetables and liquid.
In a food processor or blender, purée the vegetables.
Add enough of the cooking liquid to make 5 cups purée.
Return the purée to the saucepan, add the cream
and stir over medium heat until almost boiling.
Season well with salt and pepper.

Spoon about 1 cup of purée
into each prepared squash shell.
Spoon 1 tablespoon crème fraîche
over each portion of soup.
Do not stir in.
Place the squash on a baking sheet
and bake in the preheated oven for 45 minutes,
or until the squash is soft and the top brown.
Garnish with the pepitas.

Serves 6.

Note:

Leftovers can be served cold, seasoned with additional salt
and pepper.

WILLIAM STYRON

William Styron
Dec. 10, 1979
thank you!

Cream of Artichokes

There are more uses for artichokes in heaven and earth, Horatio, than boiling and plopping them on a plate with a vinaigrette or a Hollandaise sauce. When artichokes are relatively inexpensive and you can afford to discard the leaves, this is a lovely soup that uses the bottoms and stems. Should you be wildly ambitious, you can, of course, cook the leaves and scrape the base of each leaf to extract a small amount of the pulp. This can either be added to the soup or used as the base of small flans or soufflés. Do watch out for flavoring combinations and wines after any artichoke dish, because after you have eaten artichokes, other foods tend to taste sweeter.

½ pound lightly salted butter
1½ medium onions, finely chopped
3 celery ribs, roughly chopped
1 leek, white and green parts, washed and roughly chopped
½ cup all-purpose flour
3 quarts Chicken Stock (see recipe, page 497)
8 large artichokes, bottoms and peeled stems only,
   cut into small pieces
1 large boiling potato, peeled and halved
1 cup broccoli flowerettes
1¼ cups heavy cream
Kosher salt
Freshly ground black pepper

In a large deep pan, melt the butter.
Add the onions and sauté until soft but not brown.
Add the celery and leek
and stew over medium heat for 10 minutes,
stirring often, until the vegetables are soft
but not brown.

Blend in the flour,
stirring with a wooden spoon, to make a smooth roux.
Let cook for 2 minutes.
Gradually stir in the stock,
being careful not to form lumps.
Still stirring, bring soup to the boil.
Add the artichokes, potato and broccoli flowerettes.
Lower the heat
and let the soup simmer gently, uncovered, for 2 hours.
Do not cut down on the time.
The long simmering brings out the full artichoke flavor.

Push the soup through the fine disk of a food mill
or through a coarse sieve.
Do not put the soup
in a food processor or blender.
Return the soup to a saucepan; reheat gently.
Stir in the cream
and season with salt and pepper to taste.
Serve hot.

Makes 2½ quarts, serving 10 to 12.

PHILIPPE de ROTHSCHILD

in a house of all seasons
at their best

Oyster Broth

Although we call this recipe simply Oyster Broth, we are perhaps guilty of understatement. It is actually a rich and creamy soup that helps to puff up the pastry topping it for a spectacular presentation.

2 cups Fish Stock (see recipe, page 505)
9 shucked oysters (liquor reserved)
2 dry fennel stalks
1 cup heavy cream reduced to ½ cup
Kosher salt
Freshly ground black pepper
2 tablespoons chopped chives
½ lemon
Six 4-inch rounds Puff Pastry (see recipe, page 523),
    ¼ inch thick
1 egg

Place the fish stock,
oyster liquor and fennel in a saucepan.
Cook down until reduced to half.
Remove the fennel and add the reduced cream.
Season with salt and pepper to taste.
Chill thoroughly.

Chop the oysters into ¼-inch pieces.
Divide them among six ½-cup ovenproof cups.
(Deep espresso cups work better than ramekins.)
Sprinkle the chives over the oysters in the cups,
then place a drop of lemon juice in each.
Chill thoroughly.

Divide the cream mixture among the six cups.
They should be about two-thirds full.
Brush the puff pastry rounds with egg.
Place them, egg side down, over the tops of the cups.
Press to seal the sides; brush the tops with egg.
Refrigerate for 3 hours before baking.

Heat the oven to 400°F.
Place the cups on a baking sheet and bake for 25 minutes,
or until the pastry is puffed and golden brown. Serve.

Serves 6.

The Four Seasons is the Place to cell Season in the City New York! our faith Salisbury Harrison Salisbury October 21st 1975

Clear Soups

Clear soups—the consommé, the double consommé, the bouillon, the essence—have always been the particular province of restaurants and traditionally are included in any self-respecting dinner. To prepare them properly takes time; the flavoring elements must be allowed to cook relatively slowly so that the essences are extracted and come to join intimately with each other. Then the soups must be skimmed and clarified, since one of the hallmarks of such soups is that they be crystal-clear. We list in this section several outstanding soups of this kind.

Duckling Consommé

Here, as in the Essence of Pheasant (page 160), the basic ingredients are the by-product of a main dish. Most frozen ducks in supermarkets do not have heads and feet attached; ducks in Chinese markets, however, do, and are worth looking for.

Stock

Necks, heads, feet and wing tips from 2 ducklings
  or all the bones from 1 boned-out duckling
1 small leek, roughly cut up
1 small carrot, roughly cup up
½ medium onion, unpeeled, burnt on a hot griddle
1 parsnip, roughly cut up
4 garlic cloves
1 celery rib, roughly cut up
1 bunch parsley

Place all the ingredients in a stock pot
and add 2 quarts cold water.
Bring to a boil, skim the scum that rises to the top,
then lower the heat and simmer for 2 hours,
skimming occasionally, until you have 6 cups stock.

Strain the stock through a fine strainer into a clean bowl.
Chill thoroughly.
Remove and discard the fat.

A restaurant for all seasons

Clive Barnes

CLIVE BARNES

November 3, 1975

Clarification

1 small leek, roughly cut up
1 small carrot, roughly cut up
½ medium onion, unpeeled, burnt on a hot griddle,
    roughly cut up
1 parsnip, roughly cut up
1 celery rib, roughly cut up
1 bunch parsley
1 tomato, roughly cut up
1 pound lean beef, roughly cut up
4 whole cloves
⅓ whole nutmeg, cut into pieces
1 tablespoon freshly crushed black pepper
1½ tablespoons sea salt
4 egg whites
2 cups crushed ice

Put the leek, carrot, onion, parsnip, celery, parsley,
tomato and beef through a meat grinder
fitted with a medium blade.
Place the mixture in a bowl
and add the remaining ingredients; mix well.

Stir this mixture into the chilled stock.
Pour into a stockpot
and place the mixture over medium heat.
Place a wooden spoon in the pot and leave it there
so you can gently stir occasionally
to keep the mixture from sticking to the bottom and burning.
Leave the stock to cook gently for 1 hour.
The clarification mixture should rise to the top
and form a crust.

Line a colander with a dampened kitchen towel
or several layers of dampened cheesecloth.
Place the colander over a bowl
and slowly ladle the liquid in.
Do not stir.
Let the stock drain slowly.
The liquid should be clear.

Reheat and adjust seasonings to taste.

Serves 6 to 8.

Essence
of Pheasant

There are many special, and indeed some extravagant,
recipes in The Four Seasons repertoire. This does not mean
that we and Chef Renggli are not as concerned with
economy as other good cooks who know that thrift may
provide not only inspiration but also good taste. Therefore,
this soup uses pheasant bones and could well be made after
a party at which you have used the meat. The bones can be
placed in plastic bags and kept in the freezer for a long
period of time. The most compact way to keep them is to
crack them with a hammer first. The veal knuckle is added to
give a more gelatinous texture to the soup.
   We serve this soup as an intermezzo in a long dinner
and, therefore, keep the portions very small. For a simpler
meal, you may prefer more generous servings.

6 pounds pheasant bones, trimmings and skin
   (not the gizzards or liver)
One 2-pound veal knuckle
1 leek, halved and well washed
2 cabbage leaves
1 small white turnip, quartered
1 small sprig fresh rosemary
3 to 4 leaves fresh sage
1 whole head garlic, separated but not peeled
1 whole nutmeg, cracked
1 teaspoon black peppercorns, crushed

   Put the pheasant bones, skin and trimmings
in a large stockpot, together with the veal knuckle.
Pour in 6 quarts of cold water
and bring slowly to the boil.
Lower and heat and simmer, partially covered, for 1½ hours,
skimming as necessary.

Add the leek, cabbage, turnip, rosemary,
sage, garlic, nutmeg and peppercorns.
Simmer, uncovered,
until the liquid has reduced to 1 quart.

Line a colander with a dampened kitchen towel
or several layers of cheesecloth.
Place over a clean pot.
Pour the stock through; discard the solids.
Allow the stock to cool
and skim off most of the fat.

Clarify the stock as explained
in the Duckling Consommé recipe (page 158),
using the same ingredients.

To serve, reheat the soup
and pour into twelve demitasse cups.

Serves 12.

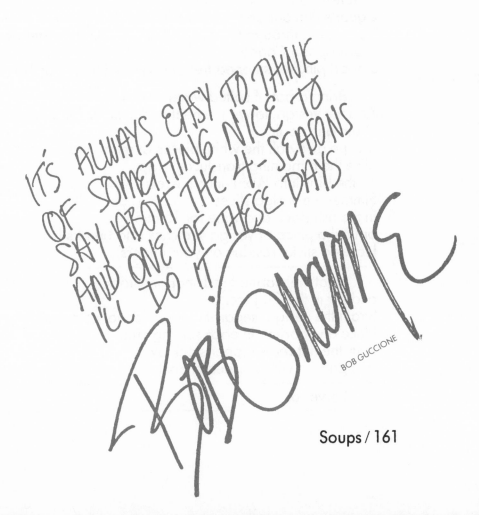

IT'S ALWAYS EASY TO THINK
OF SOMETHING NICE TO
SAY ABOUT THE 4-SEASONS
AND ONE OF THESE DAYS
I'LL DO IT!

BOB GUCCIONE

Essence of Red Snapper with Vesiga

People tend to think of fish soups as thick and zesty. Here, we have a special soup in the consommé tradition. While fresh vesiga (see Notes on Ingredients) is hard to come by, if you find it, we urge you to try this soup.

While chervil has a special flavor and aroma, dried chervil retains very little of this. If you cannot get fresh chervil, substitute fresh Italian parsley.

½ pound vesiga
1 cup Fish Stock (see recipe, page 505)
2 tablespoons dry white wine
2 quarts Red Snapper Madrilene (see recipe, page 141), prepared through the clarification, omitting the gelatin
1 tablespoon Cognac
6 good pinches snipped fresh chervil or Italian parsley

Bring a pot of salted water to a boil.
Add the vesiga, lower the heat and simmer for 3 hours.
Drain and cool.
Scrape away all the white pieces of meat and discard.
Slice the remaining translucent strip
on the bias into ¼ x 1-inch pieces.
Simmer the vesiga slices
in the fish stock and wine for 15 minutes,
or until a piece of vesiga stretches and breaks in half, or
leaves a sticky residue on your fingers.

Heat the clarified red snapper stock
and stir in the Cognac.
Strain the vesiga; separate into six equal portions.
Place one portion in each serving cup.
Pour the hot red snapper stock over
and garnish with snipped chervil.

Serves 6.

Intermezzo Sorbets

A long, classic French dinner often includes the Trou Normand, a sorbet made with Calvados. It is used as a palate cleanser in the middle of the meal between courses. In the same mode, there are Champagne and Armagnac sorbets. There are also spicier sorbets that we use in the middle of a long meal that we call intermezzo sorbets. These are a little different from the classic versions, but we think equally special. Ideally, these sorbets should be made just before serving and not allowed to freeze too hard. What you should have in your mouth is not really a firm ice, but the ice just as it is turning into a very cold liquid.

Clove Sorbet

⅓ cup whole cloves
1 cup water
1 recipe Simple Syrup (see page 474)
1 cup dry white wine
Juice of 1 lemon

Place the cloves and water in a pot.
Bring to a boil and cook for 2 minutes.
Let cool overnight, then strain; discard the cloves.

Combine the clove water with the remaining ingredients.

Pour mixture into an ice cream freezer
and freeze according to the manufacturer's directions.

Makes about 4 cups.

Cider Sorbet

1 cup hard cider
1 cup sweet cider
¾ cup sugar
1 apple, peeled, cored and thinly sliced
1 tablespoon applejack

Place the ciders and sugar in a heavy saucepan.
Cook over moderate heat, stirring, until the sugar dissolves.

Add the apples and cook for 3 minutes, or until tender.
Transfer the mixture to a blender and blend until smooth.
Stir in the applejack.

Place in an ice cream freezer
and freeze according to the manufacturer's directions.

Makes about 2 cups.

Avocado Sorbet

1 ripe avocado
Juice of ½ lemon
Pinch kosher salt
¼ cup sugar
1¼ cups cold water

Peel and pit the avocado.
Purée the pulp with the lemon juice in a food processor.

In a separate bowl,
whisk the salt, sugar and water together
until the sugar dissolves.
With the machine running,
pour the sugar mixture through the feed tube.
Process until smooth.

Place in an ice cream freezer
and freeze according to the manufacturer's directions.

Makes about 1½ cups.

Variation:
For either Basil Sorbet or Sorrel Sorbet, add ¼ cup very
finely chopped fresh leaves to the mixture before freezing.

*thank you,
i'm flattered and full*

Shelley Duvall

SHELLEY DUVALL

The Main Course

Vegetarian and Chinese cooking aside, it is generally agreed that there is a focal point to every meal. Even though the exclamation points of drama may come, as we indicated before, at any point in the meal, be it a spectacular dessert or first course, soup or salad, the center of the meal is still what we precisely call the main course. All the dishes described in the next six sections are proper, indeed dramatic, main courses. In smaller portions, some of the fish dishes might well be used as a fish course before a meat course. Certainly, the kidney and sweetbread dishes could be used as subsidiary rather than main courses. If you look at the composition of the Foursome dinners and Barrel Tasting dinners, you will see that, in fact, for special events at The Four Seasons we use small portions of various main courses in a sequence to provide a special kind of meal. Nevertheless, in looking at the recipes ahead, choosing those of interest and deciding how to organize your dinner, lunch or supper, it is as a rhythmic balance that the meal should be composed. You should not have all highlights, all big guns, all heavy dishes, all fruit, all wine or all green. Some of the main-course dishes have a simplicity that is very attractive when preceded by a complex appetizer.

Cold entrées, even though they may
be dramatic and interesting, can rarely take
the weight of an elaborate introductory course.
Should you wish to establish an unusual order,
you might proceed from a hot soup to the cold
entrée. Since most of these cold entrées are
dramatic in their presentation, follow with
a dessert that is visually simple, though
rich in taste.

Salad Entrées

It is not only in France that carefully arranged
and extravagant salads have risen to prominence.
In fact we may say that they are a significantly
American phenomenon. However, we must add
that at The Four Seasons these salads have risen
to new heights. These unusual and attractive light
main courses take pride of place on
summer menus.

Roast Breast of Capon

The capon is a bird with plump breasts that are even more delicious cold than hot. The presence of sunchokes, a new name for the old-time Jerusalem artichoke, indicates a recent recipe. The accompanying Carrot and Raisin Salad is equally delicious with a slice of cold, leftover roast lamb or pork, or even the breast of chicken left over from last night.

Two 2½- to 3-pound whole capon breasts, boned,
  skin left on
Kosher salt
Freshly ground black pepper
Sprigs fresh tarragon
1 tablespoon vegetable oil
2 tablespoons lightly salted butter
1 bunch watercress
3 or 4 sunchokes, peeled
  and cut into julienne strips

Heat the oven to 375°F.

Season the breasts well with salt and pepper. Place sprigs of tarragon underneath the skin.

Heat the oil and butter in a 10-inch skillet. Add the capon, skin side down, and place in the oven to brown for 6 minutes. Turn and brown another 6 minutes.

Let the capon rest 10 minutes before slicing. Slice the halves on the diagonal into four pieces each.

Serve garnished with the watercress and sunchoke with the Carrot and Raisin Salad (recipe follows) in a bowl on the side.

Serves 4.

Carrot and Raisin Salad

½ cup sour cream
Juice of 1 lemon
1 tablespoon honey
2 tablespoons red wine vinegar
Kosher salt
Freshly ground black pepper
½ cup black raisins,
   soaked in warm water to cover for 30 minutes
1 pound finely shredded carrots
¼ cup coarsely chopped walnuts

Place the sour cream, lemon juice, honey
and vinegar in a bowl.
Mix well with a whisk.
Season to taste with salt and pepper.
Drain the raisins well
and add to the bowl with the carrots.
Mix well.
Add the walnuts and mix to blend.

Serves 4.

Serving Suggestions:

On the hottest days a Gazpacho (page 143) might precede
your capon and a Fruit Tart (page 464) follow it. To make it
a more festive meal, you could begin instead with a Gruyère
and Prosciutto Soufflé (page 134). Then a dessert sorbet
(pages 473 to 479) is all that would be needed. A lightly
chilled Beaujolais would have both the fruitiness of taste and
the summery freshness to complete the meal.

JEAN-PIERRE AUMONT

Duckling with Oranges and Red Onions

While this recipe calls for three ducklings, you can make this salad from the legs and thighs of ducks you have prepared earlier, the breasts of which you have used at another meal. In that case, you will have the duck sauce ready and waiting. The accompanying Orange and Red Onion Salad creates a version of the classic Moroccan salad. It does for cold duck what orange sauce has long done for hot duck.

Since the salad itself has a fruit-tinged dressing, avoid a fruit dessert. Either the Cappuccino Soufflé (page 491) or the Caramel Ice Cream (page 483) is a good finish. The Seafood Risotto (page 100) or the Wild Mushrooms with Herbs (page 77) are hot appetizers that set the salad off well. If you prefer a cold appetizer, you might look to the Smoked Salmon Mousse (page 31), which has the advantage of being relatively easy.

Orange and Red Onion Salad

¼ cup olive oil
¼ cup walnut oil
Juice of ½ lemon
2 cups finely sliced red onion (sliced crosswise into rounds)
4 oranges
2 teaspoons sugar
½ cup water
1 teaspoon finely grated fresh ginger
2 tablespoons red wine vinegar
½ teaspoon coriander seeds, toasted in a dry skillet
    for 5 minutes and finely ground
½ teaspoon kosher salt
Freshly ground black pepper

Blend the olive and walnut oils
with lemon juice in a wooden bowl.
Toss with the onion slices and let stand until slices are limp.

Meanwhile, use a stripper
to make julienne strips of orange rind
from one of the oranges.
Cook the strips in boiling water for 1 minute to blanch.
Drain.
Place the strips in a small saucepan
with the sugar, water and ginger.
Cook until the mixture becomes syrupy.
Add the vinegar and allow to heat through;
then pour the mixture over the onions.
Add the coriander seeds, salt and pepper.
Let stand 3 hours.

Peel and thinly slice the oranges into rounds.

Just before serving, drain the onions,
reserving the sauce.
In a deep glass serving dish,
make layers of oranges alternating with layers of onions,
ending with a small pile of onions on top.
Pour the sauce over the oranges and onions.
Mix at the table.

Duckling

½ cup heavy cream, whipped
½ cup Orange Sauce (see recipe, page 263)
3 cooked ducklings (see Duck section beginning on page 259)
Orange slices, halved

Mix the cream and sauce until blended.
Set aside.

When the duck has been out of the oven for 1 hour
(do not refrigerate), cut off the legs and thighs.
Slice the breast meat into thin slices (scallops).

Border six serving plates with halved orange slices.
Spoon sauce on each plate.
Place a leg and thigh over the sauce
and cover with slices of breast meat.

Serve with the Orange and Red Onion Salad.

Serves 6.

Seasonal Greens with Duck Livers

If you prepare the duck feast that this book's recipe for roast duck merits (see page 259), you will not only have duck left for the preceding salad, but will also have a plethora of livers for this salad. If you wish to keep the livers for a few days before using, you can cover them with milk and freeze them. Bring back to room temperature and pat dry before use. Then you can proceed with the salad. The list of greens suggested below not only provides a palette of possibilities for use here, but may also inspire your other salad-making as it does that of The Four Seasons.

Suggested Seasonal Greens

Bibb lettuce	Boston lettuce (yellow leaves only)
Romaine	Ramp (in April)
Chicory	Field lettuce
Escarole	Dandelion
Arugula	Belgian endive
Watercress	Fresh coriander
Spinach	Chervil
Red-tipped leaf lettuce	Chives
Green leaf lettuce	Alfalfa sprouts

Salad

1 tablespoon imported Dijon mustard
2 teaspoons red wine vinegar
5 tablespoons olive oil
Kosher salt
Freshly ground black pepper
2 cups seasonal salad greens
   (see preceding suggestion list)

Prepare the mustard dressing
by combining the mustard and vinegar
with a wire whisk in a small bowl.
Add the oil, a few drops at a time,
constantly beating until mixture is thickened.
Season well with salt and pepper.

Pour the dressing over the mixed greens and toss.
Divide salad equally between two salad bowls.

Livers
1 tablespoon olive oil
¼ pound duck livers,
 cut on a bias into ¼-inch-thick slices
Kosher salt
Freshly ground black pepper
2 tablespoons red wine vinegar
Eight ¼-inch slices French bread,
 toasted in the oven until crisp
1 clove garlic, halved

Heat the olive oil in a small skillet until very hot.
When the oil begins to smoke, add the liver slices
and cook, stirring gently, for 15 seconds.
Season with salt and pepper.
Push the livers to one end of the pan
and add the red wine vinegar.
Cook for 15 seconds longer, then shake the pan,
moving the livers back over the bottom of the skillet.
The liver slices should be pink inside.

Divide the liver slices over the salads.

Rub the bread rounds with garlic halves.
Garnish each salad with 4 bread rounds (medallions).
Serve immediately so the liver is still warm.

Serves 2.

Serving Suggestions:
Since this salad makes a festive meal for two, serve a
California méthode champenoise such as Schramsberg
Blanc de Noir. If you have been provident enough to freeze
a few feuilleté boats (see Puff Pastry recipe, page 523), you
can bake them for a first course and fill them with either A
Feuilleté of Mussels in Saffron Sauce (page 116) or one of
the other saucy mixtures in that section (pages 118 to 121).
Finish with either a Frozen Chocolate Soufflé (page 432) or
a Grapefruit and Tequila Sorbet (page 475).

Lobster Salad

The lobster salad is, of course, not an everyday delight, and therefore merits both the variety of ingredients and the careful attention required. We think you will find it festive enough for the most elaborate luncheon.

Lobster

6 fennel sticks, broken into 1-inch pieces
¼ cup sea salt
1 bottle (about 3 cups) Riesling wine
¼ cup black peppercorns
Two 2-pound live lobsters

Bring 3 quarts of water to a boil
in a pot large enough to hold the lobsters.
Add the fennel, salt, wine and peppercorns.
Bring back to the boil and add the lobsters.
Lower the heat and simmer, covered, for 15 minutes.
Turn off the heat and allow the lobsters to cool
in the cooking liquid for 20 minutes.
Remove.

Working over a bowl, break off the claws of the lobster
and halve the body lengthwise.
Scrape the coral and the green tomalley into a bowl.
Collect the white fat and the lobster juices
as you shell the lobster.
Add these to the coral and tomalley.
Remove the lobster meat in large chunks and set aside.

ALEXANDER CALDER

Dressing

1 clove garlic, crushed
2 egg yolks
¼ cup imported green-herb Dijon mustard (see page 518)
2 teaspoons aged red wine vinegar
2 tablespoons olive oil
Sea salt
Dried green peppercorns (optional)
Freshly ground black pepper

Rub a wooden bowl with the garlic; discard.
Add the egg yolks and mustard to the bowl; whisk to blend.
Set a drum sieve or fine strainer over the bowl
and rub the coral-tomalley mixture through it.
Stir in the vinegar and the oil, whisking to blend completely.
Season with salt, dried green peppercorns, and black pepper.

Assembly

½ cup romaine lettuce leaves
½ cup watercress leaves, stems removed
½ cup arugula leaves, stems removed
½ cup Boston lettuce leaves
½ cup spinach leaves, stems removed
½ cup sorrel leaves, stems removed
6 thin slices black truffle
1 tablespoon chopped fresh coriander leaves
3 tablespoons chopped parsley

Toss the salad greens with half the prepared dressing.
Cut the lobster into 1-inch chunks
and coat with the remaining sauce.
Arrange the greens in a glass serving bowl
and set the pieces of lobster on top.
Scatter the truffle slices and herbs over all.
Serve at room temperature.

Serves 6.

Serving Suggestions:

Balance this festive cold main-course salad with an Italian
dish such as Spaghetti with Peppers and Prosciutto
(page 94). Accompany the salad with a good Riesling. Then
finish with the Poached Pears in Red Wine (page 461), or,
for a true Riesling celebration, the Cream Cheese and
Riesling Soufflé (page 489).

A Salad of Brains with Fried Capers

This salad contrasts the warm, creamy richness of calf's brains with the crisp, chilled freshness of the salad greens. It is a salad to satisfy the sophisticated palate.

Assorted fresh greens (choose among romaine, chicory, red leaf lettuce, escarole, spinach, arugula, watercress, bibb lettuce), stemmed where necessary and torn into bite-size pieces
1 tablespoon chopped fresh coriander leaves
1 tablespoon chopped fresh dill
2 tablespoons chopped fresh chervil
2 endives, leaves separated and cut in half crosswise
Three 6-ounce pairs calf's brains
2 egg yolks
½ cup imported green-herb Dijon mustard (see page 518)
Freshly ground black pepper
Fresh white bread crumbs
Oil for deep-fat frying

Salad dressing
¼ cup imported green-herb Dijon mustard (see page 518)
1 ½ tablespoons sherry wine vinegar
2 tablespoons red wine vinegar
1 cup virgin olive oil
1 teaspoon kosher salt
Freshly ground black pepper
¼ cup Beef Bouillon (see recipe, page 503) (see note)
2 very large or 4 medium shallots, finely sliced

Soak the brains in cold water to cover for 2 hours. This helps with the removal of the membrane.

While the brains are soaking, wash, drain and dry the salad greens and herbs. Set aside.

Remove the brains from the water and slip your fingers
under the membrane to carefully peel off the filaments.
Clean the brains of all traces of blood.
Rinse and pat dry, then cut them into 1¼-inch dice.

Beat the egg yolks, mustard
and freshly ground pepper (a generous amount) in a bowl.
Spread the bread crumbs on a tray.
Coat the pieces of brain with the egg mixture,
then lay them on the bread crumbs.
Sprinkle more crumbs over to cover
and shake to coat evenly.

Heat oil in a deep-fat fryer or deep pot to 375°F.
Line a rack or plate with several layers of paper towels.
Fry the brain cubes in batches until golden on all sides.
Do not cook too many pieces at a time
as they won't cook evenly.
Remove the golden cubes with a slotted spoon
to the paper towels to drain.
Roll in a kitchen towel to keep warm.

In a wooden salad bowl, make the salad dressing.
Whisk the mustard with the vinegars until well combined.
Add the oil in a slow, steady stream, whisking constantly.
Season with salt and pepper, then stir in the beef bouillon.

Toss the greens and shallots with the prepared dressing.
Arrange them on serving plates
and scatter the warm fried brains on top.
Serve with Fried Capers (see recipe, page 82)
and a fine julienne of leek and carrots crisped in ice water.

Serves 6.

Note:
Do not use canned bouillon in this recipe.

Serving Suggestions:
This rich main-dish salad might be preceded by Oysters in
Champagne Velouté (page 73) or A Feuilleté of Mussels in
Saffron Sauce (page 116). Pineapple Compote (page 456)
or Fruit Flan (page 466) complete the meal. This is that
special salad which calls not only for wine but for a red
wine at that, a light Bordeaux or a Côtes du Rhône.

The Four Seasons Pheasant Salad

This salad, calling as it does for two roast pheasants, is ideally suited to a great house the day after a banquet celebrating a pheasant shoot. Then one would have a larder of leftover roast pheasants crying out for adequate use. Today, restaurants are the great houses of yore, and their larders provide roast pheasants. This recipe is so good it would seem to justify cooking too many pheasants so you'll have a few left over. The bite of the turnip, the beauty of the nasturtium leaves, the various tastes and colors make this a feast indeed.

Two 2-pound young, plump pheasants
1½ teaspoons sea salt
½ teaspoon black peppercorns
4 juniper berries, toasted in a dry skillet for 5 minutes
1 bay leaf
5 tablespoons lightly salted butter, softened
5 tablespoons Cognac
Two 6-inch-square paper-thin slices fatback
3 tablespoons vegetable oil
2 cups very finely shredded green cabbage
¼ celery root, peeled and
   cut into 2-inch-long julienne strips
1 small leek, cut into 2-inch-long julienne strips
1 small carrot, peeled and
   cut into 2-inch-long julienne strips
1 white turnip, peeled and
   cut into 2-inch-long julienne strips
12 nasturtium leaves, stems removed
4 ounces belly bacon, cut into 1 x ¼-inch lardons
5 tablespoons imported green-herb Dijon mustard
   (see page 518)
10 tablespoons olive oil
2½ tablespoons red wine vinegar
5 tablespoons walnut oil
Kosher salt
Freshly ground black pepper

2 bunches watercress, stems removed
1 bunch arugula, stems removed
6 or 7 sprigs fresh coriander leaves, stems removed
6 large (about 6 ounces) fresh mushrooms,
  peeled and thinly sliced
Juice of ½ lemon
2 apples, peeled
1 head Boston lettuce

Heat the oven to 400°F.

Examine the pheasants
and remove any feathers that remain.
Wipe the insides carefully with paper towels.
Reserve the livers.
Carefully work your fingers between the flesh
and the skin around the breast to loosen the skin.
Be careful not to make any holes in the skin.

Grind the salt, peppercorns, juniper berries
and bay leaf to a powder in a spice mill or coffee grinder.
Whip the butter, then blend in the spices.
Slowly beat in 2 tablespoons Cognac.
Slip the prepared butter between the skin and flesh
to coat the entire breast of each bird.

Cover each pheasant with fatback,
tying the fatback in place with string.
Heat 2 tablespoons vegetable oil
in a wide, heavy ovenproof pan or skillet until hot.
Place the pheasants on their sides in the pan;
set it in the preheated oven to roast for 15 minutes.
Turn and roast 15 minutes on the other side,
then 15 minutes breast side up.
Baste two or three times during the cooking time
with the pan juices.

Remove the pheasants and let them cool on a platter.
Pour off the fat from the pan;
add the remaining 3 tablespoons Cognac to the pan.
Set the pan over high heat
and deglaze by scraping the bottom with a wooden spoon.
Add the livers and cook over moderate heat, tossing gently,
for 1 minute.
Scrape the livers and pan juices into a dish
and allow to cool.

Soak the cabbage, celery root, leek, carrot, turnip
and nasturtium leaves in cold water to cover
for at least 10 minutes,
or until ready to prepare the salad.
If necessary, they may soak for up to 2 hours.

Sauté the bacon lardons
in the remaining tablespoon of vegetable oil
until brown and crisp.
Remove with a slotted spoon, drain on absorbent paper
and reserve.
Discard the fat.

Rub the pheasant livers and pan juices
through a fine sieve into a mixing bowl.
Add any juices that the pheasants have given off
while cooling.
Add the mustard, olive oil, vinegar, walnut oil, salt
and pepper; mix well to combine.

Toss the watercress, arugula and coriander leaves
with half the dressing until well coated.
Sprinkle the mushrooms with lemon juice;
mix with the greens.
Arrange mixture on a large, long platter.

Drain the soaking julienne strips of vegetables.
Roll them in a kitchen towel
to press out as much moisture as possible.
Reserve the nasturtium leaves for the garnish.
Peel the apples
and cut them into very fine julienne strips.
Scatter the apples over the vegetables.

Quarter the pheasants.
Skin and bone the breasts and cut them
into thin even slices.
Reserve the legs for another dish (see note).
Arrange the breast slices randomly over the vegetables
with nasturtium leaves in between.
Dribble the remaining dressing over the breast slices.
Scatter the lardons on top.

Separate the lettuce leaves from the head
and pile them around the pheasant slices and vegetables.

To eat, fill a lettuce leaf
with some of the tossed greens, julienne vegetables,
pheasant and bacon.
Roll up and eat with your hands, like a taco.

Serves 6.

Note:

Seppi uses the pheasant leg meat to make a galette of
pheasant. Skin and bone the legs; grind the meat finely and
use it to replace the Champagne cabbage in the Potato
Galettes (see recipe, page 414).

Serving Suggestions:

Carry this beautiful platter forth with pride. At most, you may
want a cream soup and a light dessert to surround this
extravaganza. For the wine, we would suggest the German
way with game dishes—a lovely, lightly sweet Moselle of a
good year and a good grower.

thank you for your wonderful restaurant!!!

RUTH GORDON

Bar Room Chef's Salad

This is a famous dish in the Bar Room, the summer bread-and-butter of the advertising and editorial world as well as of the other movers and shakers who meet there and wish to eat lightly. The dressing, which has been a secret until now, is a gentle treasure that could be used on any finely grated or julienned vegetable served as a special first course or as an accompaniment to most cold main courses.

Tuna Sauce

4 egg yolks
1½ tablespoons imported Dijon mustard
¾ tablespoon tarragon vinegar
1½ teaspoons kosher salt
Freshly ground black pepper
1 cup olive oil
4 ounces tuna packed in olive oil (oil reserved)
½ cup sour cream
Juice of ½ lemon

In a salad bowl, combine the egg yolks with the mustard, vinegar, salt and pepper; beat until thick and creamy.
Add the olive oil in a slow stream, beating the mixture until it is well blended.
Stir in the oil from the tuna, the sour cream and the lemon juice.
Chop the tuna and gently fold in.

Salad

2 carrots, peeled and cut into julienne
1 zucchini, seeds discarded, cut into julienne
3 celery ribs, cut into julienne
1 red bell pepper, peeled, seeded, deribbed
  and cut into julienne (see note, page 37)
1 green bell pepper, peeled, seeded, deribbed
  and cut into julienne (see note, page 37)
1 small cabbage, cut into julienne

from the regular at table # 63 —

1 daikon, peeled and cut into julienne
12 ounces boiled ham, cut into julienne
12 romaine lettuce leaves
Small bunches watercress, sorrel, dandelion,
   arugula, etc.
12 ounces mortadella, cut into julienne
Grated Parmesan cheese
12 thin slices Genoa salami
3 pimientos, quartered
18 Niçoise olives

   Mix together the carrots, zucchini, celery,
red and green peppers, cabbage, daikon and boiled ham.
Add the sauce and toss lightly.

   Arrange the lettuce leaves on a large serving dish.
Place the mixed vegetables down the center of the dish
and decorate each side with small bunches of greens.
Scatter the mortadella over the vegetables
and top with a sprinkling of Parmesan cheese.

   Fold the thin slices of Genoa salami in half
and then in quarters.
Open them up
so three layers are on the bottom and one on top.
Use them to garnish the platter
with the pimiento quarters and the olives.

   Serves 6.

Serving Suggestions:

If you have the energy to make bread, this is the salad to
reward a thick and chewy crust. We persist in thinking of this
as a luncheon dish and think that people will eat enough so
that they will not want many courses with it. Follow the berry
season through the summer, serving your favorite with,
perhaps, heavy crème fraîche or sour cream, as well as an
assortment of sugars—for instance, finely granulated white,
natural brown, dark brown, and even demerara sugar. A
few sprigs of mint would not be amiss. Serve a California
Chenin Blanc in ample quantity.

Lenore Hershey
LENORE HERSHEY

Salade Niçoise

The whole world seems to love salade Niçoise. And there are enough "authentic" recipes to rival those for bouillabaisse. This version, while based on the classic potatoes, green beans, tuna, tomatoes and onions, improvises imaginatively. It has proved very successful in the restaurant.

2 beefsteak tomatoes, cored, halved and seeded,
    cut into 1-inch chunks
Olive oil
Kosher salt
Freshly ground black pepper
½ teaspoon sugar
3 large boiling potatoes,
    boiled in their jackets just before using
3 to 4 ounces mildly smoked bacon,
    thinly sliced and cut into ¼-inch squares
½ cup red wine vinegar
2 tablespoons imported Dijon mustard
4 scallions, finely chopped,
    including half the green tops
1 cup Chicken Stock or Beef Bouillon
    (see recipes, pages 497 and 503)
¼ cup finely chopped parsley
¼ cup finely chopped, peeled red bell pepper
    (see note, page 37)
¼ cup finely chopped, peeled green bell pepper
    (see note, page 37)
¼ cup finely chopped onion
1 small clove garlic, chopped
⅓ cup finely chopped mixed fresh herbs
    (chives, parsley, tarragon and basil)
One 1¾-ounce can anchovies, chopped
    (reserve 6 for the garnish)
Three 4½-ounce cans imported tuna packed in olive oil
1 head romaine lettuce
1 bunch watercress
1 pound string beans, frenched,
    blanched 2 minutes in boiling salted water
    and rinsed in cold water

1 head Boston lettuce
3 hard-boiled eggs, peeled and cut into wedges
¼ pound Niçoise olives
Fresh sorrel, dandelion and arugula,
 stems removed, coarsely chopped
½ red bell pepper, peeled, seeded,
 thinly sliced into rounds and crisped in ice water
 (see note, page 37)
½ green bell pepper, peeled, seeded,
 thinly sliced into rounds and crisped in ice water
 (see note, page 37)
1 small red onion, thinly sliced and separated into rings,
 soaked for 30 minutes in ice water, then drained

In a bowl, mix the tomato chunks
with 1 tablespoon olive oil, salt, pepper and sugar.
Let stand.

Peel the potatoes while they are hot.
Sauté the bacon in a small saucepan;
when bacon is crisp, add ¼ cup vinegar, salt, pepper
and the mustard to the pan.
Cook, stirring, for 30 seconds.
Add the scallions, ⅓ cup olive oil and
the chicken stock or beef bouillon; heat thoroughly.
Stir in the parsley.
Slice the potatoes and place them in a bowl.
Pour the heated dressing over them.
Let stand.

In a bowl, combine the chopped peppers, onion,
remaining ¼ cup vinegar, garlic, ½ cup olive oil
and the mixed herbs.
Stir well.
Add the oil from the anchovy can
as well as the oil from the tuna can.
Stir in the chopped anchovies.
Mix well and adjust the seasonings.
Reserve for the dressing.

LORD SNOWDON

Remove and discard the tough outer leaves
of the romaine lettuce.
Cut out and discard the core from the leaves.
Arrange the romaine, watercress and string beans
in piles at either end of the serving platter.
Line the center with leaves of Boston lettuce.
Heap the potatoes in the center of the platter.
On either side of the potatoes,
make nests of drained tomatoes and tuna.
Decorate with hard-boiled eggs, olives,
crisscrossing lines of anchovies
and the coarsely chopped greens.
Spread the rings of peppers and onions
over the potato salad.
Spoon the dressing over all but the potatoes.

Serves 6.

Serving Suggestions:

Salad Niçoise makes a cold lunch with bread, cheese, a
piece of fruit and one of the better Provençale red wines
such as Château Vignelaure. To expand to a main meal, you
might begin with thin slices of Marinated Salmon with Dill
Sauce (page 24) and conclude with Bourbon Pie (page 438).

With appreciation.

Gerald R. Ford

GERALD R. FORD

6/3/80

Chicken with Shrimp

Chicken with shellfish is a classic—to wit, poularde poêlée docteur, which was a roast chicken with crayfish made famous at Lapérouse. Here, a chicken, barely warm, is combined with shrimp and a creamy sauce. The chicken cannot be made ahead; chicken contains so much gelatin that it hardens when refrigerated and never recovers the desired texture.

One 4-pound tender roasting chicken
⅓ cup dry white wine
3 cloves garlic, unpeeled
2 sprigs fresh tarragon
Kosher salt
Freshly ground black pepper
2½ tablespoons white wine vinegar
½ cup dry vermouth
1½ pounds medium-sized shrimp, shelled and deveined
3 egg yolks
3 tablespoons imported green-herb Dijon mustard (see page 518)
1 cup walnut oil
½ cup virgin olive oil
1 cup heavy cream, whipped
Arugula, watercress and dandelion leaves, stems removed
½ cup toasted pepita seeds
24 thin 3-inch celery sticks
Six ¼-inch-thick zucchini rounds, hollowed

Heat the oven to 350°F.

Remove the excess fat from the chicken.
Chop the fat
and heat it with the white wine and garlic cloves
in an ovenproof skillet large enough to hold the chicken.

Meanwhile, run your fingers between the skin and flesh
over the breast of the chicken to loosen the skin.
Be careful not to tear the skin.
Slip a sprig of tarragon under the skin
on each side of the breast.
Season the back and cavity
with salt and freshly ground black pepper.
Truss the chicken,
then lay it on its side in the hot fat in the skillet.
Place the pan in the oven to let the chicken brown
for 6 minutes.
Turn the chicken on its other side
and brown for a further 6 minutes,
basting with the pan juices.
Turn the chicken on its back and continue to roast
until the bird is golden brown and tender,
about 50 minutes, or until done.
Remove the chicken from the pan,
untie the trussing strings and allow to cool.

Meanwhile, in a clean skillet,
reduce 1½ tablespoons wine vinegar to a glaze.
Add the vermouth, 1 teaspoon kosher salt
and a few grindings black pepper.
Bring to a boil.
Cook the shrimp in the vermouth for 4 minutes
over medium heat, tossing constantly.
Transfer cooked shrimp to a side dish.

Cut up the chicken with the skin on.
Remove and discard all the bones.
Cut the chicken into 1 x 1½-inch pieces.

Prepare the sauce in a wooden bowl.
Whisk the egg yolks until thick.
Add the mustard, 1 teaspoon kosher salt
and a generous amount of fresh pepper; beat well to
combine.
Add the remaining tablespoon vinegar,
then the oils in a slow steady stream, beating constantly.
Beat in half the whipped cream.
Gently fold in the remaining cream.

In another bowl, combine the chicken, shrimp
and some of the sauce, just enough to coat the pieces.
Mix lightly, taking care not to separate the skin
from the chicken flesh.
Spread the greens in a shallow serving dish.
Pile the mixture on half the greens
and sprinkle with the pepita seeds.
Serve remaining sauce on the side.

Push 4 celery sticks
through each of the 6 zucchini rounds.
Use these to garnish the other half of the platter.

Serves 6.

Serving Suggestions:
A Cold Tomato Bisque with Basil Sorbet (page 166) as a first
course, and for dessert a Fruit Tart (page 464), would make
this a super meal.

— eating your
wonderful food
makes you feel all
four seasons in one!

LUISE RAINER

Cold Salmon

Cold poached salmon in summer is a classic. Classics often need reinvigoration. Here, a summery tomato-tarragon sauce does the job brilliantly.

2 pounds salmon, trimmed of skin and bones
1 small onion, thinly sliced
2 cups dry white wine
2 cups water
1 tablespoon sea salt
Freshly ground white pepper
Crisp mixed greens—watercress sprigs, sorrel leaves,
    arugula and Boston lettuce

Cut the salmon on the bias into
six 5-ounce (approximately) slices.
Oil a large flameproof skillet.
Arrange the salmon slices side by side in the skillet.
Add the onion.
Pour the wine and water over the fish.
Sprinkle with salt and pepper.
Bring the liquid almost to the boil.
Remove from the heat
and allow the fish to cool a little in the cooking liquid.
Transfer the fish to a serving dish.
Do not chill or refrigerate.
This dish is best served at room temperature.

To serve, spoon some Tomato and Tarragon Sauce over the salmon.
Garnish with crisp mixed greens and Dilled Cucumbers (see recipe, page 396).

Serves 6.

my thanks to all —

Tomato and Tarragon Sauce

1 pound ripe tomatoes, peeled and quartered
3 sprigs tarragon leaves,
    fresh or preserved in vinegar, drained and rinsed
2 cloves garlic
4 shallots, halved
2 tablespoons tarragon vinegar
½ cup dry white wine
4 egg yolks
3 tablespoons imported Dijon mustard
1 teaspoon kosher salt
Freshly ground black pepper
Juice of ½ lemon
1 cup virgin olive oil
½ cup heavy cream

In a heavy, non-aluminum saucepan,
combine the tomatoes, tarragon, garlic, shallots,
vinegar and wine. Bring to a boil; lower the heat
and allow to bubble gently, uncovered, for 30 minutes,
or until thick and almost all the liquid has evaporated.

Push the resulting sauce through a fine strainer.

In a mixing bowl, beat the egg yolks
with the mustard until thick.
Add salt, pepper and lemon juice, beating well.
Still beating, add the oil in a slow steady stream.
Stir in the tomato mixture.

In a separate chilled bowl set over ice, whisk the cream
until soft peaks form, then fold into the tomato mixture.

Serving Suggestions:

Cold poached salmon is a delicious and easy dish to
prepare for a crowd. For a festive meal, begin with the
Galantine of Capon (page 50) and finish with the Figs with
Whipped Cream (page 458). Here again, we have a salad
and a fish that would be happy with a white wine.

DAN RATHER

The Main Course / 193

April 21, 1977

Striped Bass with Trout Mousse

This gala dish is served at The Four Seasons accompanied by Tarragon Mayonnaise. It is time-consuming but well worth the effort, especially for company. If you don't have time to do it all at once, prepare the fish the night before up to the point when it is wrapped in aluminum foil. The mayonnaise, too, can be made ahead except for adding the whipped cream.

The fish is served at room temperature so allow about 3 hours before eating to start the final preparations. Seppi feels strongly that refrigeration after cooking will change the taste of the fish so do not refrigerate at that time. Provided your kitchen is not too hot, the fish should be fine for up to 3 hours after cooking.

One 2½- to 3-pound striped bass,
   cleaned, scaled, boned, with head and tail intact
½ pound salmon fillets, skin removed
Two ¾-pound trout, filleted, skin removed
2 egg whites
½ cup heavy cream
Kosher salt
Freshly ground black pepper
1 teaspoon brandy
½ teaspoon powdered saffron
2 heads romaine lettuce
Olive oil
½ cucumber, unpeeled (see note)
1 head Boston lettuce
12 cherry tomatoes
1 bunch fresh tarragon

Wash the striped bass well under cold running water. Remove any blood clots and small bones. Rinse again.

Cut the salmon fillets into 1-inch cubes; set aside.

Cut the trout into chunks.
Process in a food processor until finely chopped.
Beat in the egg whites.
With the machine running, slowly pour in the cream.
Process until very smooth.
Add salt, pepper, brandy and saffron.
Scrape into a mixing bowl, then add the cubed salmon.
Mix well and refrigerate.

Bring a large pot of water to a boil.
Plunge about twenty-four large romaine lettuce leaves,
a few at a time, into boiling water for 3 seconds.
Then drop them immediately into ice water
(otherwise the leaves will blacken).

When all the leaves are blanched,
completely cut out and discard the hard veins.
Pat the leaves dry.

Place a large piece of plastic wrap
on your work surface.
If it is not large enough to wrap the stuffed fish,
use two overlapping pieces.
Brush the center of the wrap with olive oil.
Do not brush the outer edges or it will be difficult to seal.
Spread blanched romaine leaves, slightly overlapping,
across the oiled wrap.
You will need enough lettuce to wrap the body of the fish
but not the head and tail.

Arrange the fish on the lettuce bed
skin side down and open.
Sprinkle the fish with salt and pepper;
spread the trout-salmon mixture down the center.

With both hands, pick up the far side of the wrap
and bring it toward you to wrap the fish
and reconstruct its shape.
Roll the ends of the wrap together to seal well,
but do not seal tightly
or you will force the mousse out of the fish.

Place the wrapped fish on a large piece of aluminum foil
and wrap the fish completely in the foil,
sealing the edges very well.
You may refrigerate the fish at this time.

When ready to cook the fish, heat the oven to 375°F. Place the fish
in a baking dish large enough to hold the fish flat.
Fill the pan with ½ inch water, place in oven and
bake for 35 minutes.

Remove the fish from the oven and from the baking pan.
Let rest, wrapped, at room temperature for at least 2 hours.
Do not refrigerate.

When you are ready to serve,
open the aluminum foil and plastic wrap.
Carefully remove the fish from the wrappings
and place it on a platter.

Thinly slice the cucumber on the diagonal.
Arrange the cucumber slices overlapping in a row
alongside the fish.
Alongside the cucumber,
alternate leaves of romaine and Boston lettuce.
Place cherry tomatoes among the lettuce leaves.
Top the fish with sprigs of tarragon.

Bring the platter to the table
and slice the fish crosswise into six even slices,
each about 1 inch thick.
Serve with Tarragon Mayonnaise (recipe follows).

Serves 6.

Note:
If cucumber has a waxed peel, use another garnish
such as zucchini.

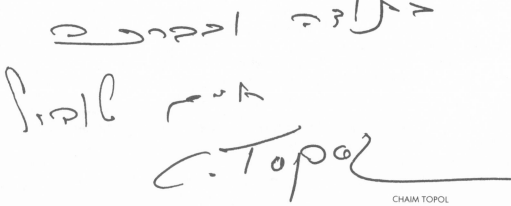

CHAIM TOPOL

Tarragon Mayonnaise

2 tablespoons imported Dijon mustard
3 egg yolks
Kosher salt
Freshly ground black pepper
½ cup walnut oil
½ cup olive oil
1 tablespoon tarragon vinegar
¼ teaspoon lemon juice
¼ cup firmly packed fresh tarragon leaves
¼ cup heavy cream, whipped

Place the mustard, egg yolks, salt and pepper
in the work bowl of a food processor
fitted with a steel blade.
Process 1 minute.
Combine the walnut and olive oils
in a measuring cup.
With the machine running, dribble the oil
through the food tube.
Once the mixture begins to thicken,
add the oil a little faster.
When the mixture is fairly thick,
add the vinegar and lemon juice.
Then pour in the remaining oil.
Add the tarragon and process until it is chopped.
Fold in the whipped cream.

Serving Suggestions:

Once you have even contemplated making this dish, you
probably will want a simple first course; Avocado with
Tomato and Basil in Vinaigrette (page 34) would be perfect.
If, however, you have leftover energy, a Sorrel Vichyssoise
(page 138) and Apple Pithiviers (page 452) for dessert
complete the meal in style. After you have done all the work
on this fish, it probably merits your best Montrachet.

For the Four Seasons

For Truman Capote

TRUMAN CAPOTE

Muhammad Ali aug. 26-75

MUHAMMAD ALI

Death is so near, and time for friendly actions is so limited

Seafood

It is perhaps—if one had to pick an area—in seafood and fish that Chef Renggli and The Four Seasons excel. Long before the nouvelle cuisine focused attention on seafood, we prided ourselves on the care it receives in our kitchen. One of the benefits of learning to do really marvelous fish and seafood dishes is that by altering the size of the portions you can serve these dishes equally well as first- and main-course dishes. As they are described in the recipes in this section, the portions are meant to be main-course portions. However, anywhere from one-half to two-thirds of the quantity would make an excellent first-course portion.

Mousse of Trout in Leeks

This invention of Chef Renggli's was used for the Barrel Tasting dinner of March 1978 and was served with a Chardonnay from Burgess Cellars—the 1975 Winery Lake.

Although working with leek leaves is painstaking, the result is extremely attractive and well worth the effort. It took Chef Renggli some time to create this combination of mousse and leeks so that it would be easy to cut and eat.

1 ½ pounds (about 6) skinless, boneless
  rainbow trout fillets
3 or 4 very large leeks
Kosher salt
2 egg whites
1 cup heavy cream
5 tablespoons Fish Stock (see recipe, page 505)

Cut the trout into 1-inch cubes and chill.
The fish must be very cold.

You will need twelve large outer leek leaves,
each about 9 inches long.
Cut the root ends and green tops off the leeks.
Make a lengthwise cut in each leek,
stopping at the middle.
Separate the leaves and wash well.
Keep twelve leaves for this recipe and
reserve the rest of the leeks for another use.

In a large kettle,
bring enough water to a boil to cover the leek leaves.
Add salt to taste and the leaves.
Let simmer for about 2 minutes, then drain.
Run leaves under cold water until well chilled.
Drain; pat dry.

Heat the oven to 400°F.

Sprinkle the trout cubes with salt.
Place them in a food processor
fitted with the metal blade.
Process until smooth.
With the machine running,
pour the egg whites through the feed tube;
then pour in the cream.

Open up the leek leaves
and arrange them on a flat surface.
Place a mound (about 3 tablespoons) of trout mousse
near the base of each leaf.
Roll up each leaf to enclose the mousse.
Be sure to roll the leeks up against the grain
or the finished paupiettes will be very difficult to cut.

Arrange the rolls, seam side down,
in a buttered 14 x 8-inch metal baking dish.
Pour the fish stock around the rolls.
Put the pan on top of the stove.
When the pan liquid comes to a boil,
place the dish in the oven.
Bake 15 minutes, or less,
until the mousse is cooked through.

Drain off the liquid and reserve.
Cover the fish and keep warm,
while making the shallot butter.

Shallot Butter

2 tablespoons white wine vinegar
2 tablespoons water
2 tablespoons finely chopped shallots
½ pound lightly salted butter, at room temperature

Combine the vinegar and water with
the reserved cooking liquid in a saucepan
and bring to a boil.
Add the shallots and
cook until most of the liquid has evaporated.
Add the butter, bit by bit, to the saucepan,
beating rapidly with a wire whisk over low heat.
The sauce must be thoroughly hot but it must not boil.
When ready, the sauce should be thick and creamy.

JOYCE BROTHERS

Serving

Freshly ground black pepper
2 tablespoons olive oil

Place two fish rolls on each of six plates.
Top with shallot butter.
Grind some pepper over the rolls and
drizzle on olive oil.

Serves 6.

Serving Suggestions:

Start this meal with a vegetable soup such as the Purée of
Seasonal Vegetables (page 148) and end with a sweet
Walnut Tart (page 442). For a heartier meal you might begin
with this elegant trout mousse and continue with Capon Four
Seasons (page 251), ending perhaps with the Pear Mousse
with Poached Pears (page 459). In such a meal, you could
either choose to start with a light, acidic white wine and go
on to a richer red, or you could begin immediately with a
full-bodied white like some of the Chardonnays from Napa
and continue with it throughout the meal.

For the spaciousness around me

and the fulness inside me — gratitude !

JOHN SIMON

A very hard act to follow, specially

on a stomach filled with delight —

LEO LERMAN

Escalope of Salmon with Caviar

This extremely festive dish ranges from luxurious to sublime depending on the kind of caviar you use. At the low end you can use lumpfish caviar in two contrasting colors; and at the most extravagant, fresh salmon caviar contrasted with a good beluga malossol. As you need only one teaspoon of each for each portion, this is not so wildly out of reach. As for any caviar remaining, we recommend taking a large spoon and finishing it yourself at a moment when life seems to have fewer rewards than usual.

4 large shallots, finely chopped
1 cup dry vermouth
1¾ cups heavy cream
2 tablespoons Glace de Poisson (fish glaze)
   (see recipe, page 506)
Kosher salt
3 tablespoons crème fraîche
2 tablespoons lightly salted butter
Twelve 3-ounce ¼-inch-thick boneless fresh salmon slices
Freshly ground black pepper
1½ tablespoons olive oil
6 blanched strips of the green of scallions,
   each about 2½ inches long
2 tablespoons red caviar
2 tablespoons black caviar

Place the shallots and the vermouth
in a heavy saucepan.
Cook over high heat to reduce to a glaze.
Add the cream and the glace de poisson.
Cook, whisking, for 2 minutes over medium heat.
Lower the heat and let the sauce simmer for 5 minutes.

Strain the sauce into a clean saucepan
and stir in salt to taste.
Off the heat, stir in the crème fraîche.
Gradually add the butter,
moving the pan on and off the heat, whisking constantly.
Set aside, keeping the sauce warm
but not allowing it to boil.

Lightly season the salmon with salt and pepper.
Heat the olive oil in a large, nonstick skillet.
Add the salmon and
sauté over medium heat for 45 seconds on each side,
or just until barely cooked.

For each serving, place some sauce on each plate
and top with two salmon slices.
Place a blanched scallion strip diagonally
across the two slices of fish.
Dot one side with red caviar
and the other side with black caviar.
Serve at once.

Serves 6.

Serving Suggestions:

In serving this dish as a first course, you may find that one
slice of salmon is enough. Follow with Braised Calf's Liver
(page 291). Either way, serve a dry but fruity Alsatian
Riesling, such as Clos-Sainte-Hune, with the salmon.

JACQUELINE ONASSIS

Grilled Salmon with Cucumbers

This simply prepared dish owes a great deal to the Japanese influence and is a forerunner of today's nouvelle cuisine.

Four 8-ounce salmon fillets, skin left on
Kosher salt
¼ cup soy sauce
1 large cucumber

Turn the fillets skin side up and cut slits crosswise through the skin at a slight angle. Space the slits ½ inch apart and run them across the whole fillet, leaving a 1-inch margin on either side. Rub a generous amount of kosher salt over the skin.

Pour the soy sauce into a dish and add the salmon, skin side up. Let rest for 2 to 3 hours at room temperature.

Peel the cucumber and cut it into 4½-inch lengths. From the lengths, cut four pieces 1½ inches wide, ½ inch thick and 4½ inches long. If possible, cut from the side rather than the middle so each piece is curved.

Place a cucumber piece flat on your work surface. Make a slit parallel to the long side, ½ inch down, stopping ½ inch before one end. Starting from the uncut end, make a second slit parallel to the first, ½ inch down and stopping ½ inch before the other end.

Lift the cut ends and gently place one underneath the other. Repeat with the other cucumber pieces and set aside.

Heat the broiler, and heat the oven to 400°F.

Place the salmon, skin side up, under the broiler for 4 minutes.
Then, place the salmon in the preheated oven for 3 minutes with the cucumbers.
Garnish each serving of salmon with one cucumber piece.

Serves 4.

Serving Suggestions:
Soy and other Chinese condiments tend to create difficulties when you are choosing a wine, particularly with rich fishes high in fat content such as the salmon. If you serve small portions as a first course, then an unusual but compatible selection is a medium-dry sherry. If the salmon is a main course, which we recommend, a white Graves or the equivalent Sauvignon Blanc would be in order. You might then want to begin with an Avocado Soup with Avocado Sorbet (page 144) if the weather is warm or a Pumpkin Bisque (page 151) if the day is cold.

I'll think of something better to write in this book the next time I'm here.

Joseph Heller

JOSEPH HELLER

11/16/78

Escalope of Red Snapper with Spinach and Mushrooms

Twelve 3-ounce ¼-inch boneless red snapper slices
1½ pounds fresh spinach, washed, stems removed
Kosher salt
14 ounces lightly salted butter
2 tablespoons chopped shallots
3 large cloves garlic
Freshly ground black pepper
1 cup unsalted Fish Stock (see recipe, page 505)
Juice of ½ lemon
12 medium-sized mushrooms, peeled and quartered

Pick over the fish slices for small bones
and remove them with tweezers.

Blanch the spinach leaves in boiling salted water
for 1 minute.
Drain and rinse under cold running water.
Drain well; wrap in a kitchen towel
and squeeze out all the excess moisture.

Heat 6 ounces butter in a heavy skillet.
When it begins to foam and turn nut-brown,
add the shallots and garlic, then the spinach.
Sauté briskly, stirring with a fork, for 1 minute.
Discard the garlic.
Place the spinach
along the center of a long serving dish.
Keep hot.

Season the fish with salt and pepper.
In a 10-inch skillet, heat ¼ cup fish stock.
Add four fish scallops, laying them side by side.
Cook, uncovered, over high heat for 1 minute,
shaking the skillet
to keep the fish from sticking to the bottom of the pan.
Turn the fish and continue to cook for 30 seconds longer.
The fish must be very white, firm, and barely flake.
Arrange the fish slices overlapping on the spinach.

Add another ¼ cup stock to the skillet
and cook four more scallops in the same way.
Place them on the spinach.
For the last four scallops,
add the remaining ½ cup stock to the skillet.
Cook as directed above.
Place the cooked fish on the spinach; keep warm.

Over high heat, reduce the cooking juices to half.
Cut 4 ounces butter into pieces.
Gradually whisk the butter pieces
into the reduced cooking juices,
moving the pan on and off the heat,
until the sauce is thick and foamy.
Stir in the lemon juice, adjust the seasoning,
and spoon over the fish on the platter.

In a medium-sized skillet,
heat the remaining 4 ounces butter.
When it turns nut-brown, add the mushrooms
and sauté them over brisk heat,
stirring until the mushrooms are light brown,
about 1 minute.
The mushrooms must remain firm
and not be allowed to lose their water.
Do not season them.
Garnish the dish with the mushrooms and serve at once.

Serves 6.

Serving Suggestions:

The combination of mushrooms, fish slices and spinach
makes an attractive plate and a light dish which could be the
star of a lunch served with a simple salad and dessert. We
suggest a light Italian white wine, such as Vernaccia.

Baked Red Snapper and Scallop Tartare

Do not let the gentle, bland look of these patties confuse you.
The green peppercorns give them zest and bite.

¾ pound scallops
1¼ pounds skinless red snapper fillets
6 tablespoons lightly salted butter, at room temperature,
    cut into chunks
1 tablespoon plus 24 green peppercorns
    packed in salt water, drained
1 tablespoon kosher salt
2 tablespoons brandy
Very fine fresh bread crumbs
½ cup heavy cream

Heat the oven to 350°F.

Put the scallops, snapper fillets and butter
through the blade of a meat grinder with ¼-inch holes.
Smash 1 tablespoon green peppercorns to a paste
with the flat of a knife.
With your hands, gently mix the smashed peppercorns,
salt and brandy into the ground fish.
Work quickly; the mixture gets pasty if overworked.

Divide the mixture into four equal parts
and shape each into an oval about 5 inches long
and 2½ inches wide.
Lightly coat each one with the bread crumbs,
gently pressing them in.

Place the patties in a buttered 8 x 12-inch baking dish without letting them touch.
Pour the cream into the dish.
Try not to pour the cream directly on the fish.
Press about 6 whole green peppercorns
into the top of each patty.

Bake in the preheated oven for 25 minutes.
Serve hot with some of the pan liquid.

Serves 4.

Serving Suggestions:
We suggest a vegetable dramatic enough to appear as a separate course in the Italian style. If the season is right, turn to our Asparagus section (pages 389 to 394) and use one of these recipes either as a first or a vegetable course. If asparagus are not in season, begin with the Purée of Seasonal Vegetables (page 148), and then follow the fish with a light, perhaps lemon juice-dressed, salad and finish up with a Bourbon Pie (page 438). With your meal, serve a Muscadet.

Would it be fair for a gourmet
to ask for a _fifth_ Season?

David Wayne

DAVID WAYNE

Fillet of Pompano with Citrus Fruits and Pistachio Nuts

2 grapefruits
2 navel oranges
Three 1½- to 1¾-pound pompanos, filleted, skin left on
Kosher salt
Freshly ground black pepper
All-purpose flour
2 tablespoons clarified butter
9 tablespoons lightly salted butter
Juice of ½ lemon
Juice of ½ lime
3 tablespoons shelled, blanched and peeled pistachio nuts
6 thin lime slices
6 thin lemon slices

Remove the peel and pith
from the grapefruits and oranges.
Then remove each section one by one,
by separating with a small knife
alongside the membranes.
Set aside.

Heat the oven to 450°F.

Season the pompanos lightly with salt and pepper.
Spread the flour on waxed paper;
add the fish and
press down gently to coat with flour on both sides.
Shake off the excess flour.

Heat 1 tablespoon clarified butter
and 1 tablespoon salted butter in
each of two nonstick skillets.
Add three fish fillets to each.
Sauté the fish until golden brown,
about 2 minutes on each side, shaking the skillets gently.

Arrange the fillets overlapping on a heatproof platter.
Pour off the fat from one of the skillets;
add 3 tablespoons salted butter and swirl it around.
Whisk in the lemon and lime juices.
Off the heat, whisk in 2 tablespoons salted butter.
Pour the pan juices over the fish.
Arrange the prepared orange and grapefruit sections
overlapping alongside the fish on the platter.
Set in the preheated oven for 5 minutes.

Sauté the pistachios
in the remaining 2 tablespoons salted butter for 1 minute.
Garnish the fish with lemon and lime slices
and sprinkle with the pistachios.

Serves 6.

Serving Suggestions:

The wine selection requires some thought because of the
citrus fruit garnish. Consider a young white or perhaps an
unusual rosé such as a Sancerre. If you have the time to
prepare it, the Galantine of Capon (page 50) or the
Vegetable Terrine, Pepper Sauce (page 66) are first courses
that blend well with the rosé. For dessert, the Walnut Tart
(page 442) or the same tart made with pecans would round
out a satisfying meal.

REGINA RESNIK BLATAS

Baked Striped Bass with Fennel

This dish, which goes back a long way in The Four Seasons history, is the American version of the classic loup of the South of France, which is traditionally cooked over flaming fennel. Our preparation, which both poaches and flames the fish and then reinforces the fennel taste with Pernod, seems to have the best of all possible worlds.

One 5-pound striped bass, cleaned and scaled,
    head and tail intact
1 bunch dried fennel stalks
Sea salt
1 carrot, roughly cut up
1 leek, green part only, roughly cut up
1 celery rib, roughly cut up
8 sprigs dill
1 clove garlic, crushed
½ onion, roughly cut up
6 parsley stems
1 teaspoon freshly cracked black pepper
2 cups dry white wine
2 cups Fish Stock (see recipe, page 505) or water
1 teaspoon Tarragon Purée (see recipe, page 225)
2 cups heavy cream
2 tablespoons Pernod

Heat oven to 500°F.

Wash the fish well; remove the blood clots.
Rinse again.
Place the fish
in a baking dish large enough to hold the fish flat.
Stuff the cavity with half the fennel stalks
and sprinkle with 1 tablespoon sea salt.

Add the carrot, leek, celery, dill, garlic, onion,
parsley stems, pepper, white wine and stock to the pan.
Bring the liquids to a boil over high heat
on top of the stove,
then place in the preheated oven to bake for 25 minutes.
Remove the pan from the oven
and strain the cooking liquid into a clean bowl.
Cover the fish and keep warm.

Place 2 cups of the strained cooking juices
in a saucepan.
(Save extra liquid for fish soups or sauces.)
Bring to a boil over high heat
and cook until reduced to a glaze.
Stir in the tarragon purée and the cream.
Cook until reduced to 1½ cups.
Adjust the seasoning.
Place in a sauceboat.

Place the remaining fennel stalks
on a flameproof serving platter.
Place the fish over the fennel.
Heat the Pernod, add it to the platter and flame.
Cover the pan to extinguish the flames.

Serve at once.
To serve, start at the head and roll back the skin.
Then, lift off slices of fish.
When you have served the top side,
remove the bone and begin serving the second side.
Season each serving with freshly ground pepper;
spoon some sauce over the fish.

Serves 6.

Serving Suggestions:

At the restaurant we flame the bass in the dining room
before our guests. To serve it so splendidly at home, heat the
platter over an alcohol burner on a side table before
flaming and use a bunch of parsley to douse the flames.
Take a hint from the South of France and serve with an
inexpensive Provençal Blanc de Blancs.

Steamed Striped Bass with Shrimp and Clams

This is one of those dramatic fish dishes where the package of fish and seafood is opened at the table to give forth its perfume. It is a triumphant moment for the cook and one of pleasure for the guests.

One 5-pound striped bass, cleaned and scaled
Sea salt
¾ cup snipped parsley sprigs
½ cup fresh dill sprigs
2 teaspoons freshly cracked black pepper
12 medium shrimp, peeled and deveined
18 small clams on the half shell with their liquor
1 cup carrots, cut into julienne strips
2 celery ribs, cut into julienne strips
1 onion, thinly sliced
1 large leek, washed and cut into julienne strips
1 cup Sauternes

Heat the oven to 400°F.

Wash the fish well under cold running water.
Remove any blood clots.
Rinse again.

Line your work surface
with two sheets of aluminum foil (preferably heavy duty)
large enough to completely seal the fish.
Fold the two sheets together to make a tight seal.

Score one side of the fish at 1-inch intervals,
going about ½ inch down through the skin
and into the flesh of the fish.

Place the fish, scored side up,
in the center of the foil.
Sprinkle salt over the scored flesh.

Stuff the cavity with half the parsley,
all the dill and half the pepper.
Add the shrimp and the clams, still on the half shell.
Pat the fish into shape
and spread the carrot, celery, onion and leek on top
with the remaining parsley and pepper.

Lift up the foil sides and begin sealing the fish in.
When the sides are high enough to prevent leakage,
pour in the Sauternes.
Finish sealing well.

Add water to a 12 x 8-inch roasting pan
to a depth of 1 inch, about 4 quarts.

Place the fish in the pan
and bring the water to a boil.
Place in the preheated oven and bake for 50 minutes.

Let the fish rest for 10 minutes before serving.
Bring to the table in the foil wrapping and
open the package in front of your guests.

Serves 6.

Serving Suggestions:

Accompany the striped bass with a dry Graves, such as an
Haut-Brion Blanc, and precede it with one of The Four
Seasons pastas, then finish up with the Pineapple Compote
(page 456).

Fillet of Striped Bass in Phyllo Leaves

This delicious dish, developed for a Barrel Tasting dinner, was served in tiny portions kept moist by the stuffing and by the phyllo wrapping. It was served with a Dry Creek Vineyard Chardonnay. We think that any dry white wine with a rich body would be presented at its best by this dish.

For home service, we recommend the variation suggested in the note—a whole fish, looking most festive at the table.

1 packed cup cooked spinach leaves, squeezed dry
  (4 cups uncooked spinach)
12 oysters, shucked (liquor reserved)
Freshly ground black pepper
Kosher salt
2 tablespoons Pernod
2 tablespoons lightly salted butter
2 cloves garlic, lightly smashed
1 large shallot, finely chopped
1 teaspoon finely chopped fresh tarragon
2 tablespoons finely chopped fresh parsley
Juice of ½ lemon, strained
5- to 6-pound striped bass, filleted, skin left on
¾ cup clarified butter
12 sheets (about ½ pound) phyllo dough
Dry bread crumbs

Heat the oven to 375°F.

Virgil Thomson

VIRGIL THOMSON

Chop the spinach with the oysters.
Fold in the oyster liquor, pepper,
1 teaspoon salt and Pernod.
Set aside.
Heat the butter in a medium-sized skillet.
Add the garlic cloves, shallot, tarragon and parsley
and sauté gently for 1 minute, stirring.
Add the spinach-oyster mixture
and sauté briskly for 20 seconds, stirring.
Set aside and let cool.
Stir in the lemon juice.
Discard the garlic.

Cut each fillet crosswise into three equal parts.
Trim each portion into a rectangle and make three slits
across the grain of the flesh, cutting to,
but not through, the skin.

Fill each slit
with about a teaspoon of the spinach-oyster mixture.
Divide the remaining mixture into six equal portions
and spread over each piece of fish.

Brush one sheet of phyllo pastry
with clarified butter
and sprinkle lightly with bread crumbs
(this prevents the pastry from becoming soggy).
Lay a second sheet over the first;
butter and sprinkle with bread crumbs again.
Place a piece of bass 4 inches up from the bottom
of the pastry, skin side down.
Bring up the lower part of the pastry to cover the fish.
Carefully roll the pastry up,
ending with the fish skin side down.
Trim the excess pastry.
Place the package on a lightly buttered baking sheet,
seam side down.
Brush the top with butter and sprinkle with bread crumbs.
Repeat the procedure with the remaining fish and pastry.

Bake in the preheated oven
for 15 to 20 minutes, or until golden brown.

Remove the fish to a heated serving platter.
Serve hot accompanied by Baked Fennel Parmesan
(see recipe, page 371).

Serves 6.

Note:
If you prefer, cook the fish whole. Cut off the head and tail and remove the bones, leaving the two fillets attached. Stuff the fish with the spinach-oyster mixture and wrap completely with the phyllo dough. You will only need four sheets of phyllo and 6 tablespoons clarified butter. Measure the fish at its thickest point and cook it 10 minutes per inch of thickness plus 5 minutes longer, since it is stuffed.

Serving Suggestions:
We did not serve this with a sauce at the Barrel Tasting dinner, but we feel that a light sauce such as Shallot Butter (page 201) might be very good with it. This fish, with its light dough and spinach, needs no side dish. If used as a main course, you might want to begin with Duckling Consommé (page 158) and serve after it a festive salad such as Seasonal Greens with Cracklings (page 38); then you would still have room for a rich dessert such as Walnut Tart (page 442). If serving the fish as a first course, follow it with a simple roast such as the Barbecued Leg of Lamb (page 307) or Saddle of Lamb Baked in Salt (page 304), then a light and simple salad before a festive sorbet such as Kiwi and Champagne (page 476). With this beautifully prepared dish, you might try a spicy Gewürztraminer from Alsace or California.

The Best Duck did ever had! Thank you

John Travolta

JOHN TRAVOLTA

5/7/80

Baked Striped Bass on Sea Salt with Black Pepper

This is a dramatic preparation, tasty and light.

One 3½-pound striped bass
Coarsely cracked black peppercorns
½ cup plus 1 tablespoon virgin olive oil
10 to 12 cups (about 2 pounds) sea salt
½ cup very finely chopped fresh dill
½ cup very finely chopped parsley
Juice of 1 lemon

Heat the oven to 350°F.

Place the fish on its side
and measure its thickest point in the center.
Figure your baking time at 10 minutes per inch.
If the fish is 2½ inches thick, for example,
bake for 25 minutes.

Clean the fish.
Cut out the gills and wings but leave the scales intact.

Spread the pepper in a layer on waxed paper.
Brush the fish with 1 tablespoon olive oil
and place it so one side is over the pepper.
Press it so the pepper adheres to the fish on that side only.

Line an ovenproof platter just large enough
to hold the fish with the salt.
Place the fish, pepper side up, over the salt.
Pat the salt around the fish to coat to the backbone.
Do not put any salt over the pepper-coated side.

Place in the oven
and bake for the appropriate time.
Just before the fish is done,
make the sauce by mixing the dill, parsley,
½ cup olive oil, lemon juice and salt to taste.

To serve, start at the head end and roll back the skin.
Then, lift off pieces of fish.
When you have served the top side,
remove the bone and begin serving the second side,
leaving the bottom skin on the platter.
Serve with the herb sauce.

Serves 4.

Serving Suggestions:

Put a small amount of the sauce on top of each portion for decorative purposes. If your guests like lots of sauce, you may wish to make more and put it on the table in a separate dish. Boiled or steamed rice is nice with this, and you might wish to prefix the meal with Calf's Brain Flan with Fried Capers (page 80). The wine should be light and fresh, like a Seyval from New York State.

[handwritten inscription in Hebrew/cursive]

10·I·1976

SIMCHA DINITZ

Fillets of Bass with Mussels and Oysters

This is the kind of recipe that tends to discourage the cook from trying it, as it calls for both fish stock and fish velouté. However, it is less of a problem than it appears, since the velouté is made from the fish stock, and the fish stock is rapidly prepared. Extra fish stock can be frozen in cubes, sealed up in a plastic bag and kept for future use.

Three 2¼-pound sea bass, filleted, skin removed
18 mussels, shucked
18 oysters, shucked
Kosher salt
Freshly ground black pepper
¼ cup Fish Stock (see recipe, page 505)
2 cups Fish Velouté (see recipe, page 507)
1 cup heavy cream
⅔ cup Champagne

Heat the oven to 375°F.

Score the boned side of each fillet at equal intervals, about 1 inch apart.
Pat dry.
Place the fillets side by side
in a large buttered baking dish or individual gratin dishes.
Place the mussels and oysters over the fish.
Sprinkle the fish with salt and pepper.
Moisten with the fish stock;
cover loosely with buttered parchment paper,
buttered side down.
Set aside.

Place the velouté, cream and Champagne in a saucepan. Cook over high heat until reduced to 2 cups.

Bake the fish in the preheated oven for 10 minutes.
Pour the fish liquid into the reduced cream mixture.
Keep the fish warm
as you reduce the sauce again to 2 cups.
Correct the seasoning with salt and pepper to taste.
Spoon some sauce over the fish and serve at once.

Serves 6.

Serving Suggestions:
Since this recipe provides half of a filleted fish per person,
the fillets can either be served directly onto the plates or
placed side by side on a platter. Use a broad spatula to
pick up the fillets without breaking them.
If you serve the fish as the center of the meal you might
want to start with Purée of Seasonal Vegetables (page 148).
Follow with a light salad, then a wonderful soufflé, such as
Cappuccino Soufflé (page 491). This is the kind of elegant
meal that can be served with just one wine, such as a well-
rounded dry Chenin Blanc from Sonoma, and no one the
poorer or wiser.

#1
is for celebrating at the Four Seasons!
More Power! to you —
Michael Korda

MICHAEL KORDA

Shrimp and Scallops Sautéed with Tarragon

This dish should be made in summer or early fall when tarragon is plentiful and not too expensive. If made in early fall, it has the added advantage of using shrimp when they are at their best.

¼ pound lightly salted butter
1 pound medium shrimp, shelled and deveined
1 pound bay scallops
2 tablespoons brandy
1 tablespoon Tarragon Purée (recipe follows)
2 cups Fish Velouté (see recipe, page 507)
½ cup heavy cream
Kosher salt
Freshly ground black pepper

Heat 4 tablespoons butter in a heavy skillet;
add the shrimp and sauté 3 to 5 minutes,
or until pink and cooked.
With a slotted spoon, remove the shrimp to a dish.
Keep warm.

Add the scallops and remaining 4 tablespoons butter
to the same skillet.
Sauté the scallops for several minutes, until cooked.
Remove with a slotted spoon and add to the shrimp.

Over high heat,
reduce the skillet cooking juices until reduced.
Stir in the brandy, tarragon purée, fish velouté and cream.
Cook over high heat, swirling the pan, for 30 seconds.
Lower the heat
and stir in the accumulated juices
from the shrimp and scallops;
fold in the scallops and shrimp.
Season to taste then reheat gently, stirring.
Serve with Steamed Rice (see recipe, page 243).

Serves 6.

Tarragon Purée

4 tablespoons lightly salted butter
1 cup fresh tarragon leaves

Heat the butter in a skillet.
Add the tarragon leaves and stir to coat well.
Cover the pan
and let the tarragon cook gently for 30 minutes,
or until completely soft.
Purée the mixture in a food processor
or through a sieve.

Serving Suggestions:

We think these tastes, textures and colors go well with a
Grand Cru Chablis.

LESLIE CARON

June 18, 1977

Shrimp and Scallops with Vermouth and Grapes

Green grapes with fish or white meat chicken provide the classic Véronique. Here the combination of shrimp, scallops and vermouth gives the dish an energy lacking in the classic.

½ cup heavy cream
½ cup dry vermouth
Freshly ground black pepper
3 tablespoons lightly salted butter
¾ pound shrimp, shelled and deveined
¾ pound bay scallops
¾ cup Fish Velouté (see recipe, page 507)
¾ cup seedless green grapes
    (if unavailable, use seeded grapes, halved,
    seeds removed)

Heat ¼ cup heavy cream, ¼ cup vermouth and pepper to taste in a 10-inch skillet.
Cook until mixture is reduced to a glaze.
Add the butter.
When hot, add shrimp.
Stir and cook over high heat
just until the shrimp turn opaque.

Add the bay scallops and continue cooking, shaking the pan, until the scallops are cooked, about 5 minutes.
With a slotted spoon,
remove the shrimp and scallops to a serving dish.
Keep warm.

Add the remaining ¼ cup vermouth
to the cooking liquid in the pan.
Cook over high heat until the liquid is nearly evaporated.
Add the velouté, stirring constantly.
Add the remaining ¼ cup heavy cream, still stirring.

Check for seasoning.
Add the grapes and toss to heat.

Grind fresh black pepper on top.
Cook for 30 seconds.
Pour over the shrimp and scallops in the serving dish.

Serves 4.

Serving Suggestions:
You might want to try a Kabinet Moselle of a good year with
this dish. It is light, fragrant, and redolent enough of grapes
to complement the grapes in the sauce. For a first course, the
Ham Mousse with Peaches (page 29) or, also in summer,
Wild Mushrooms with Herbs (page 77) would be delicious.
If late enough in the summer for the crisp new apples to
have made their appearance, try the Apple Pithiviers
(page 452) for dessert.

For Tom, Paul —
and
With appreciation
from Harold

HAROLD ROBBINS

Court Bouillon of Shrimp, Scallops and Oysters

Court bouillon is the classic friend of fish. Here, it is an entire presentation, truffled and luxurious.

2 cups Fish Stock (see recipe, page 505)
12 tablespoons lightly salted butter, chilled
5 tablespoons dry white wine
1 carrot, cut into julienne strips
1 celery rib, cut into julienne strips
1 leek, washed and cut into julienne strips
1 pound shrimp, shelled and deveined
1 pound bay scallops
Sea salt
Freshly ground white pepper
18 oysters, shucked (liquor reserved)
1 large black truffle, thinly sliced

Place the fish stock in a saucepan
and cook over high heat until it is reduced to 1 cup.
In a separate saucepan,
bring 4 tablespoons butter and 4 tablespoons wine
to a boil.
Add the julienne of carrot, celery and leek;
cook, covered, over low heat for 5 minutes,
shaking the pan often.
Remove from the heat.

In a small saucepan,
heat the remaining tablespoon of white wine.
Cut the remaining 8 tablespoons butter
into about ten pieces.
Using a wire whisk,
gradually beat the butter pieces into the wine.

Heat the reduced fish stock in a wide skillet.
Add the shrimp, then the scallops.
Season to taste with salt and pepper.
Simmer, stirring, for 1 minute.
Add the oysters, the oyster liquor
and the julienned vegetables.
Simmer gently for 1 minute longer
to allow the flavors to blend.
Transfer to a serving dish,
scatter the truffle slices on top
and sprinkle with a few drops of truffle liquid.
Pour the reserved wine-butter sauce over the seafood
and swirl to combine.
Serve hot with Steamed Rice (see recipe page 243).

Serves 6.

Serving Suggestions:

This is best served right from the skillet with a deep spoon.
Simple crudités first and Fresh Fruit Salad (page 454) to end
would make this a visually appealing, flavorsome but not
overly filling meal. We suggest a rosé for the wine.

Ow! matchless Four Seasons! Fours like that, what a Year —

Olivier

SIR LAURENCE OLIVIER

A Skewer of Shrimp and Sea Scallops

The marinated shrimp pairs well with scallops, chicken and chipolatas to make this simple grilled dish a constantly popular choice, and one version or another is usually on the Bar Room menu. With it, a salad and a glass of white wine, or a glass of bubbling mineral water for the diet-conscious, create a satisfying lunch.

Marinated Shrimp

24 large shrimp, shelled and deveined
½ cup minced parsley
2 garlic cloves, minced
Juice of 1 lemon
¼ cup olive oil
¼ cup bread crumbs
¼ teaspoon ground mace
¼ teaspoon dried oregano
1 teaspoon Hungarian sweet paprika
1 teaspoon kosher salt
Freshly ground black pepper

Place the shrimp in a large bowl
and add the rest of the ingredients,
seasoning liberally with black pepper.
Mix together until the shrimp are evenly coated.
Cover and marinate overnight
in refrigerator before using.

Assembly
24 (about 1½ pounds) sea scallops

Wrap four shrimp around four scallops
on each of six skewers, as follows:
skewer the fat end of a shrimp, then a scallop.
Then, holding these firmly in place,
pull the tail end of the shrimp over the scallop until taut
and skewer the tail end.
This assures that the shrimp
will be curved snugly around the scallop.
Repeat with all the shrimp and scallops.
Grill for 2 minutes, turn and grill 1 minute longer.

Serves 6.

Variation with Shrimp and Chicken and Bacon:
Three 3-ounce whole, boneless chicken breasts,
*   skin removed*
24 marinated shrimp
12 bacon strips, cut crosswise in halves

Slice each chicken breast
into eight lengthwise strips
for a total of twenty-four strips.
Following the curve of the shrimp,
wrap a strip of the chicken around each shrimp.
Then, stretch a piece of bacon
around the entire circumference of the chicken,
overlapping the bacon ends.
Place four of these on each of six skewers,
being sure to catch the bacon ends in the skewer.
Grill as for Shrimp and Sea Scallops.

Variation with Shrimp and Chipolatas:
Twenty-four 2- to 3-inch chipolatas
24 marinated shrimp

Blanch the chipolatas in boiling water to cover
until plumped and almost done, about 4 to 5 minutes.
Alternate four shrimp and four chipolatas
on each of the six skewers
so the skewer pierces the shrimp and chipolatas
crosswise through the middle.
Grill as for Shrimp and Sea Scallops.

Broiled Swordfish with Olive Butter

This rich black olive butter is Chef Renggli's tribute to that fine Mediterranean fruit. It combines well with the sturdy broiled swordfish steak.

1 cup kalamata olives
¼ pound lightly salted butter
Kosher salt
Freshly ground black pepper
Four 8-ounce swordfish steaks

Push the olives through a fine drum sieve.
This will give you a smooth purée
without skin or pits.

Cream the butter until very soft.
Whisk in the olive purée.
Season to taste
with a generous amount of salt and pepper.

Heat your broiler.
Broil the swordfish
for a total of 10 minutes per inch thickness.
Just before serving,
spread a layer of the olive butter over the fish.
Put it back under the broiler just to glaze.

Serves 4.

Serving Suggestions:

At an elegant dinner, start this meal with Sweetbreads and Spinach Millefeuille (page 127). Less formally—perhaps for lunch—begin with a Chilled Gazpacho (page 143). For the informal meal, end with a Mango and Lemon Sorbet (page 476). The more formal meal could end with an Almond Bavaroise (page 433). Elegant or simple, choose a direct, clean, slightly hard-edged white wine, such as a Chardonnay from Macon or Mendocino.

Fillet of Sole with Shrimp

A very Four Seasons rendition of a classic dish. Serve with a classic Chablis or a California Chardonnay.

Vegetables

4 tablespoons lightly salted butter
3 cups washed, sliced leeks
Kosher salt
Freshly ground black pepper
1 cup cooked spinach leaves,
  drained well and squeezed dry

Heat 2 tablespoons butter in a saucepan.
Add the leek slices and season with salt and pepper.
Sauté, stirring, for 5 minutes.
In another pan,
heat the remaining butter until lightly brown.
Add the spinach and cook until wilted.
Add to the leeks and stir to combine.

Pour the leeks and spinach in a gratin dish
and spread evenly over the bottom.

Sole

4 fillets of sole (Boston, grey, lemon or Dover),
  similar in size
Kosher salt
Freshly ground white pepper
⅓ cup dry vermouth

Preheat the oven to 400°F.

Butter a baking dish.
Sprinkle the fillets with salt and white pepper.
Roll up tightly from the tail, the skin side inside.
Cut the rolls in half crosswise through the middle
and place them snugly in the dish, flat ends down.
Pour vermouth over the fish.
Cover with foil.
Bake in the preheated oven for 15 minutes.
With a slotted spoon, arrange the sole rolls,
flat side up, neatly over the vegetables
in the gratin dish.
Keep warm.

Sauce

Juice of 1 lemon
1 cup Fish Stock (see recipe, page 505)
1 tablespoon heavy cream
¼ pound lightly salted butter, cut into pieces

Place the lemon juice in a saucepan.
Bring to a boil until reduced to a glaze.
Add the fish stock
and reduce the liquid to 1½ tablespoons.
Stir in the heavy cream and the butter,
whisking until smooth.
Keep warm.

Shrimp

2 tablespoons olive oil
1 pound large shrimp, shelled and deveined
Kosher salt
Freshly ground black pepper
2 tablespoons brandy

Heat the oil in a skillet.
Add the shrimp and salt and pepper to taste.
Cook, stirring, until the shrimp turn opaque.
Add the brandy and stir to blend.

Spoon the shrimp over the sole in the gratin dish.
Spoon the sauce over the top.

Serves 4.

Sautéed Soft Shell Crabs

There are moments when the season prescribes and the cook simply fulfills. Soft shell crabs are one of the delights of spring and early summer, and this simple recipe tampers with them least of all.

¼ pound lightly salted butter
Eight 1¾-ounce soft shell crabs, patted dry
Juice of 1 lemon
2 tablespoons Fish Stock (see recipe, page 505) or water
Sea salt
Freshly ground black pepper

Heat the butter in a deep 10-inch skillet
over high heat until lightly browned.
Add the crabs, skin side down,
and sauté quickly for 1 minute.
Turn and sauté 1 minute longer.
Remove to a heated serving dish.

Pour off most of the butter in the skillet.
Deglaze the pan with the lemon juice,
scraping the bottom of the pan with a wooden spoon.
Stir in the fish stock.
Spoon the pan juices over the crabs.
Season with very little salt and plenty of pepper.
Serve immediately.

Serves 2.

Serving Suggestions:
This recipe for two needs only bread, salad and fruit and a well chilled bottle of Champagne to make a memorable meal.

April 7, 1980

What Transit strike ?!:

Mary Tyler Moore

MARY TYLER MOORE

Chicken and Capon

Chicken is easily available and relatively inexpensive. As more and more of it is served in our homes, it is interesting to look to better restaurants for the recipes and techniques they have created to make chicken festive. Sometimes an expensive ingredient such as shrimp is added, but on balance the dish will still be less expensive than the equivalent beef or veal.

While almost every Frenchman or Italian drinks red wine with chicken dishes, Germans will drink beer or one of their marvelously fruity white wines—assuming the dish is hot. Cold chicken dishes take lighter, drier, fruitier—not sweet—chilled white wines. Light, fruity, chilled Beaujolais also goes well. Some of the dishes in this section are homey and are best served with beer or ale. This is particularly true of the curry, but also can apply to the Chicken Pot Pie.

Lime Broiled Breast of Chicken

This is an example of a simply and quickly prepared chicken dish definitely removed from the ordinary. Toasting coriander seeds, as with other warm spices, brings out their taste and also crisps them so that they are easier to crush.

Six 10-ounce whole boneless chicken breasts, skin removed
Kosher salt
Freshly ground black pepper
Olive oil
3 tablespoons imported green-herb Dijon mustard
  (see page 518)
3 tablespoons honey
½ teaspoon toasted coriander seeds, crushed
24 very thin slices fresh lime, peeled

Heat a grill and heat an oven to 375°F.

Season the chicken breasts with salt and pepper; rub with oil.
Thread two half-breasts lengthwise on each of six skewers.
Broil them on the grill 3 minutes on each side.

Remove the chicken from the skewers and arrange the pieces side by side in a buttered baking dish.
Mix the mustard, honey and coriander seeds in a small bowl.
Spread the mixture over the chicken and top with thin slices of fresh lime.
Bake 8 minutes in the preheated oven.

Serve at once with Lemon Compote (recipe follows) as a dip.

Serves 12.

Lemon Compote

½ cup sugar
10 peeled lemons, seeds removed, very thinly sliced
Pinch of red pepper flakes

Heat a heavy saucepan.
When hot, add the sugar and let caramelize lightly.
Quickly stir in ¼ cup water and the sliced lemons.
Cook, stirring, over low heat
to soften any hardened sugar.
Add the pepper flakes.
Cook for just 1 minute,
or the lemons will begin to break apart.
Pour into a dish to cool.

Serving Suggestions:

The colors of this dish are so attractive that simple white rice
is all you need on the plate. To start, perhaps one of the
vegetable soups. If you are in a hurry, smoked fish would
make a pleasant introduction and a Chocolate Rum Sorbet
(page 844) follows nicely. This is a dish that can be
presented as simply or as elegantly as the requirements for
your party dictate. Any table setting from stoneware and
stainless steel to porcelain and sterling silver would work.

there are four seasons in everyone's life — I'm happy that some of mine have been spent here —

love

Rod McKuen

ROD McKUEN

1962 – 1976 — ant

Breast of Chicken with Glazed Apples

Chicken with apples and cream is a classic preparation. Seppi's personal version calls for the apples to be cooked separately so that both chicken and apples maintain perfect texture.

Breast of Chicken

1 cup Chicken Stock (see recipe, page 497)
¼ cup heavy cream
Kosher salt
Freshly ground black pepper
Lemon juice
5 tablespoons lightly salted butter
3 tablespoons imported green-peppercorn Dijon mustard
2 egg yolks
3 tablespoons finely chopped fresh mixed herbs
   (lemon thyme, parsley, chervil, chives, etc.)
2 whole boneless chicken breasts, skin removed, split
All-purpose flour
Fresh bread crumbs
3 tablespoons clarified butter

Place the chicken stock in a small saucepan.
Cook until reduced to about 2 tablespoons.
Stir in the cream and salt and pepper to taste.
Add a drop of lemon juice.
Whisk in 4 tablespoons butter in chunks.
Keep warm.

In a small bowl, blend the mustard and egg yolks.
Stir in the herbs.

Season the chicken pieces
on both sides with salt and pepper.
Dip them in flour to coat lightly; shake off the excess.
Brush with the mustard mixture.
Then coat very well with the bread crumbs.

Heat the clarified butter in a 10-inch skillet.
When hot,
add 1 tablespoon lightly salted butter and the coated chicken.
Cook for about 4 minutes, or until nicely browned.
Turn and cook 3 minutes on the other side.

Let rest for 5 minutes before slicing.
Cut each piece on the diagonal into four slices.
Place some sauce on each of four serving plates.
Fan the chicken slices over the sauce
on one side of the plate and
the Glazed Apples (recipe follows) on the other side.

Serves 4.

Glazed Apples

2 large firm apples
4 teaspoons, approximately, softened lightly salted butter
4 teaspoons, approximately, sugar

Preheat the broiler.

Peel the apples, halve them and remove the cores.
Cut each half crosswise into ⅛-inch-thick slices.
Keep them in the apple shape.

Butter an ovenproof dish large enough
to hold the apple halves.
Place each half on the dish, flat side down.
Hold your hands on either side of one half
and shift the slices by moving one hand toward you
and one away from you so the slices are on the slant.
Repeat with the other halves.

Spread about 1 teaspoon softened butter
across the top of each half;
then sprinkle with about 1 teaspoon sugar.

Place under the broiler
until the apples are soft and brown, about 5 minutes.

Serves 4.

Serving Suggestions:
For a special evening, Duck Liver Flan (page 83) might be a
great way to start. End with Hazelnut Cake (page 447).

Chicken and Shrimp Curry

Curries have long been popular in America where their pronounced taste is particularly favored for luncheons and light suppers. Chef Renggli has developed a recipe which is halfway between the English sahib's cream curry and the true curries of the Orient. All recipes serve six.

Curry

1 tablespoon olive oil
1 teaspoon coriander seeds,
   toasted in a dry skillet for 5 minutes
½ teaspoon white peppercorns
2 whole cloves
¼ teaspoon red pepper flakes
1 teaspoon cumin seeds
2 tablespoons curry powder
1 teaspoon chopped fresh ginger
½ clove garlic
⅛ whole nutmeg
2 teaspoons kosher salt
1 quart Chicken Stock (see recipe, page 497)
1 cup dry white wine
2 cups heavy cream
4 tablespoons lightly salted butter
¼ cup all-purpose flour
¼ cup clarified butter
Four 8-ounce whole boneless chicken breasts,
   cut into 1½ x ¼-inch chunks
1½ pounds medium shrimp, peeled and deveined

In a skillet, heat the oil.
When hot, add the coriander seeds, white peppercorns, cloves, red pepper flakes and cumin seeds.
Stir to avoid burning,
then add the curry powder, tossing to blend.
Place in a spice mill or coffee grinder
with the ginger, garlic, nutmeg and salt.
Grind to a powder; set aside.

In a deep saucepan,
boil the stock and wine together until they reduce to 2 cups.
In a separate pan, reduce the cream to 1 cup.

In a clean pan, melt the lightly salted butter.
Add the flour and cook, stirring, for 2 minutes,
without letting the mixture brown.
Mix in the prepared curry mixture.
Add the reduced stock and cream.
Bring to a boil over medium heat, stirring.
When sauce is thick and smooth,
strain through a fine sieve into a clean saucepan.

Heat 2 tablespoons clarified butter in a large skillet
and in it sauté the chicken, tossing,
until seared on all sides.
Heat the remaining 2 tablespoons clarified butter
in another skillet; sauté the shrimp for 1 minute.
Add the shrimp to the chicken
and sauté together for 2 to 3 minutes, stirring.
Spoon the sauce over the shrimp and chicken mixture.
Bring to a boil, stirring.

Serve at once with Flavored Steamed Rice, Sambal,
Peach Chutney and Marinated Fruits (recipes follow).

Flavored Steamed Rice

3 tablespoons jasmine tea leaves
2 cups long-grain rice
2 small pieces orange rind

Place the tea leaves and ½ cup water
in a small saucepan; bring the water to a boil
and strain it into 3 quarts hot water.
Bring that water to a boil and add the rice and orange rind.
Cover the pot and simmer for 10 minutes.

Drain the rice and discard the rind.
Place the rice in the top of a double boiler.
Cover the top and steam the rice
over simmering water for 30 minutes.
Fluff rice with a fork just before serving.

Variation:

Make plain steamed rice by eliminating the tea leaves and
orange rind.

Sambal

1 quart vegetable oil
1 large onion, sliced crosswise paper thin
3 ounces shredded unsweetened coconut
3½ ounces gado-gado
¼ pound unroasted peanuts, shelled
1½ teaspoons soy sauce
2 ounces blanched almonds, sliced

Heat the oil in a deep saucepan to about 325°F.
Separate the onion slices into rings;
drop them into the oil, and fry, stirring,
for 5 minutes or until golden brown.
Lift rings out with a slotted spoon
and spread on absorbent paper to dry.

Lower the heat and add the coconut to the oil.
Raise the heat to about 325°F. and, as with the onions,
fry, stirring, until the coconut is a pale golden color.
Remove and add to the onions.
Sprinkle the onions and coconut with gado-gado.

Add the peanuts to the oil and
cook for 2 minutes, stirring;
drain them, then fry in a dry skillet with the soy sauce,
tossing to coat each peanut.
Add to the onions and coconut.

Lightly fry the almonds in the oil until golden.
Remove and add to the onion mixture.
Toss well to combine; let rest 1 hour before serving.
When the mixture is completely dry,
it can be stored in an airtight tin.

Marinated Fruits

1 small cucumber, peeled, seeded and cut into small cubes
1 banana, cut into thin slices
2 kiwi, peeled and cut into thin slices
1 cup fresh pineapple, cut into ½-inch cubes
2 tablespoons soy sauce
1 tablespoon olive oil
Freshly ground black pepper

In a bowl, mix everything together until well blended,
and serve immediately.

Peach Chutney

6 firm yellow peaches
¾ cup sugar
½ cup cider vinegar
¼ teaspoon chopped garlic
¾ cup water
2 teaspoons chopped fresh ginger
⅓ cup cubed preserved ginger
2 tablespoons lime juice
2 teaspoons curry powder
1 cup seedless raisins
1½ teaspoons kosher salt
¼ teaspoon freshly ground black pepper
½ teaspoon red pepper flakes
5 ounces finely chopped onion

Peel and pit the peaches; cut each into eight wedges.

Place the sugar, vinegar, garlic
and water in a saucepan.
Stir over low heat until the sugar has dissolved.
Bring liquid to a boil
and cook 5 minutes until syrupy.
Add the peaches.
Simmer 10 minutes.
Remove the peaches with a slotted spoon and reserve.

Add the remaining ingredients to the syrup.
Boil slowly for 10 minutes,
or until mixture thickens slightly.
Return the peaches to the pan, bring to a boil,
then pour into a 1-quart jar.
Keep for a few days in the refrigerator before serving.

Makes 1 quart.

Serving Suggestions:

Ending this meal with fruit in season and a good cheese
would make a more than pleasant evening. However,
should you want to have a more classic meal, begin with a
clear Oyster Broth (page 155) and serve a salad of
Avocado with Tomato and Basil Vinaigrette (page 34) after
the curry, to continue with the unctuous and spicy tastes. For
dessert, we suggest a sorbet or any of the fruit desserts.

Bar Room Chicken Pot Pie

A Bar Room favorite, this is an elegant version of simple family food. It might also be a pleasant surprise at a dinner for jaded gastronomes.

Preparing the Vegetables

2 medium carrots
2 small turnips
2 medium kohlrabis
1 small celery root
4 small pearl onions, peeled
4 large, firm fresh mushroom caps

Prepare the carrots, turnips, kohlrabis
and celery root as follows:
Peel them and
cut them into 2-inch lengths, ¾ to 1 inch wide.
Trim the ends so you have
1½-inch ovals ("turned" vegetables).
You will need eight pieces of each vegetable.

Bring a pot of lightly salted water to a boil.
Add all the vegetables
except the turnips and mushroom caps.
Cook for about 5 minutes.
Add the turnips and cook for about 1 minute longer.
Drain well and cool.

Preparing the Sauce

6 tablespoons lightly salted butter
6½ tablespoons all-purpose flour
3½ cups Chicken Stock (see recipe, page 497)
Pinch freshly grated nutmeg
Pinch mace
¾ teaspoon kosher salt
Freshly ground white pepper
½ cup heavy cream

Heat the butter in a 2-quart saucepan.
Add the flour and blend well.
Cook for 2 minutes without letting the mixture brown.
Add 1 cup chicken stock and stir until smooth.
Stir in the remaining 2½ cups stock.
Cook, stirring, for 10 minutes.
Season to taste with nutmeg, mace, salt and pepper.
Stir in the cream; set aside.

Preparing the Chicken

One 4½-pound chicken
2 tablespoons lightly salted butter
Kosher salt
Freshly ground white pepper
1 tablespoon brandy
¼ cup dry white wine

Skin and bone the chicken,
reserving the breast and leg meat for this dish.
Cut each piece of meat into four pieces.
Set aside.

In a 10-inch skillet, heat the butter.
Add the chicken pieces and toss to sear on all sides.
Sprinkle with salt and pepper
and cook over medium-high heat for 5 minutes.
Add the brandy and wine.
Bring to a boil, turning the chicken pieces to coat.
Remove the chicken pieces to a side dish.
Stir the cooking juices into the sauce.

Assembly

4 sprigs fresh tarragon or marjoram
2½ pounds Puff Pastry (see recipe, page 523)
Egg glaze (1 egg mixed with 1 teaspoon water)

Butter four 2-cup gratin dishes each about 7 inches long.
Fill each with equal proportions
of dark and white meat chicken with their cooking juices.
Add two turned carrots, two turned turnips,
two turned kohlrabis, two turned celery roots, one onion
and one mushroom cap to each dish.
Spoon about 1 cup sauce over each serving.
Top each with a sprig of tarragon.
Let the filling cool for 10 minutes before topping with the crust.

On a floured board, roll the puff pastry
into a ¼-inch-thick rectangle.
Cut the pastry into four pieces
the size of the tops of the gratin dishes.
Roll them again
so they are about 1 inch larger than the dish
on all sides.
Brush the dough with egg glaze.
Fit each piece, egg side down, over a gratin dish.
With your fingers,
press the dough around the sides of the dish to adhere.
Brush the top with egg glaze and refrigerate 1 hour.

Heat the oven to 475°F.

Place the prepared dishes on a baking sheet
and bake in the preheated oven for 10 minutes.
Lower the heat to 350°F.; bake 15 to 20 minutes longer.

Serves 4.

Note:

If you wish to make the recipe a day ahead of time, prepare
the filling and place in the gratin dishes, then cover with
plastic wrap.
Roll out the dough and proceed with the recipe a few hours
before you plan to serve it.

Serving Suggestions:

One of the advantages of this dish is that it is a whole main
course and vegetables in one. If you want a fuller menu,
start with thinly sliced smoked salmon and follow with
Pineapple Compote (page 456) or homemade ice cream
(pages 481 to 486).

Best

George Burns

GEORGE BURNS

Fillet of Chicken, Oysters and Crayfish

This is the kind of dish that is generally much easier to prepare in a restaurant than at home. It is not a question of expense or difficulty of technique but that the restaurant has a ready supply of chickens from which to get the little fillets and oysters that this recipe requires. These delicacies are too often neglected when people prepare chicken. The fillets, attached to the breasts, become overcooked and tend to straggle off in any case. The oysters, protected as they are by the backbone and pelvic structure, often get ignored entirely. When you plan to serve this dish, you might prepare chicken a day or so before and jealously guard the fillets and oysters. Or remove the fillets and oysters from the chickens and then freeze the cut-up chicken pieces for future use.

Fresh shiitake mushrooms are just beginning to appear in our markets and are a great treat if you can find them. The crayfish tails can be omitted and the quantity of chicken fillets and chicken oysters increased by two each. Or, you can substitute shrimp for the crayfish (see note, page 87).

2 tablespoons Lobster Butter (see recipe, page 515)
6 chicken fillets (see note)
6 chicken oysters (see note)
1 shallot, minced
¼ pound cooked, shelled crayfish tails
2 tablespoons Cognac
¼ cup dry white wine
Kosher salt
Freshly ground black pepper
6 oysters, shucked (liquor reserved)
⅓ cup fresh shiitake mushrooms, sliced (see note)
1 cup heavy cream reduced to ½ cup

In a skillet, heat the lobster butter.
Add the chicken fillets,
chicken oysters and the minced shallot.
Sauté for 1 minute.
Add the crayfish tails and continue cooking
just long enough to heat them through.
Pour into a hot serving dish and keep warm.

Add the Cognac to the same skillet and reduce to half.
Add the wine and salt and pepper to taste.
Cook for 1 minute.
Add the oysters with their liquor and the mushrooms;
simmer for another 30 seconds.
Stir in the reduced cream
and continue simmering for about 1 minute longer.
Return the chicken and crayfish to the sauce.
Toss together thoroughly and return to the serving dish.

Serves 2.

Note:

A chicken fillet is the small flap of meat on the underside of
a chicken suprême (a boned half). You can easily detach the
fillet from the suprême with a knife or your fingers. The
chicken oysters are the small nuggets of tender meat found
on either side of the backbone of the chicken, just above the
thighs. They can be removed with a knife, scraping against
the bone.

If the fresh shiitake mushrooms are not available, use
dried shiitake soaked in warm water to cover until soft. Drain
them, squeeze dry and discard the hard stem before using.

Serving Suggestions:

Having reconnoitered to find the variety of ingredients
required here, you may want to go one step further and
make Fettuccine (page 93) to accompany the dish. A good
beginning is one of the Savory Soufflés (pages 129 to 134).
A light green salad followed by Bar Room Chocolate Cake
(page 428) would splendidly complete the meal.

Capon Four Seasons

Here is another of those dishes so typical of The Four Seasons style, where a simple family preparation is elevated by its excellence to festive heights. For a larger group, use a large capon and increase the cooking time and all other ingredients proportionately.

One 4-pound tender capon
1 large black truffle, thinly sliced
2 tablespoons brandy
Sea salt
½ teaspoon freshly cracked black pepper
2 tablespoons lightly salted butter
4 cloves garlic, unpeeled
2 celery ribs, cut into ¼-inch slices
1 onion, quartered
4 leeks, trimmed and washed, 2 halved, 2 left whole
1 carrot, cut into 1-inch pieces
Fresh sprigs Italian parsley
Fresh sprigs rosemary
1 cup dry white wine
8 pearl onions
8 "turned" carrots (see note)
8 "turned" parsnips (see note)
8 small new potatoes, peeled
½ cup crème fraîche

Trim the capon wings
by cutting off the tips at the last joint.
Reserve the wing trimmings.

Heat the oven to 350°F.

Loosen the skin
over the breast and thighs of the capon with your fingers,
being careful not to tear the skin.
Slip the truffle slices under the breast and thigh skin.
Rub the cavity of the bird with brandy, salt and pepper.

Meanwhile, in a casserole
large enough to hold the capon,
heat the butter with the garlic, celery,
onion, the two halved leeks, carrot, fresh herbs,
white wine and 1 cup water.
Add the reserved wing tips.
Bring liquid to a boil and add the capon.
Cover and set in the oven to cook for 50 minutes,
or until tender and cooked through.

While the capon cooks,
bring two pots of salted water to a boil.
To one, add the pearl onions,
turned carrots, parsnips and remaining two leeks.
Cook until the vegetables are just barely done.
Drain.
Halve the leeks lengthwise.

In the second pot, cook the potatoes
until done.

Remove the capon from the pan
and cut it into serving pieces.
Strain the cooking juices into a clean saucepan.
Bring to a boil and skim off the fat
and any scum that rises to the top.
Whisk in the crème fraîche.
Readjust seasonings to taste.
Pour the sauce over the capon
and surround with the fresh cooked vegetables.

Serves 4.

Note:

For directions on turning vegetables, see the recipe for
Chicken Pot Pie, page 246.

Serving Suggestions:

The dish brings with it all the vegetables and sauce it needs.
In summer you might start the meal with a Sorrel Vichyssoise
(page 138) and in winter, Essence of Red Snapper with
Vesiga (page 162). Depending on the appetites of your
guests, you might finish the meal with Crêpes Soufflés (page
449) or a Fresh Fruit Salad (page 454).

Chicken Paillard

This simple recipe is Seppi's favorite way to cook chicken breasts. He prepares breasts this way for chicken salad, which is why his has a fuller flavor than most.

4 whole boneless, skinned chicken breasts
  from four 2½-pound broilers, left in one piece
Kosher salt
Freshly ground black pepper

Heat a grill until hot.

Place the chicken, skinned side down, over the grill.
Cook to sear, about 30 seconds.
Lift the chicken with tongs and rotate it 45 degrees
to sear a diamond pattern into the flesh.
Cook another 30 seconds.
Turn over and cook 4 minutes longer.

Serve with the seared side up.
Season with salt and pepper.

Serves 4.

Serving Suggestions:

Set out on individual plates or lined up on a platter, these breasts make a perfect light lunch or dinner for people who do not wish to overeat. Baked Endive (page 372) would round out this dinner. Or in summer, when the vegetables are at their peak, try Eggplant, Zucchini and Tomato Gratin (page 387). At the same time peaches should be ripe and you could start with a Cold Peach Soup (page 146) and end with Melon and Port Sorbet (page 475). For those who wish to eat lightly, the chicken, a salad and fruit would be sufficient.

Thank you — Siobhán McKenna

SIOBHÁN McKENNA

Capon
Baked in Salt

For a gala presentation, try this salt-baked capon. The technique is as old as baking bread in clay. Developed when ovens were less good than those of today, it still has the advantage of cooking the bird evenly and retaining its juices. For maximum effect, remove the salt crust at the table, then place the capon on a waiting platter where it can be carved.

One 4-pound capon
3 tablespoons lightly salted butter,
    cut into 1/8-inch slices
1/2 teaspoon freshly ground black pepper
1/2 teaspoon kosher salt
5 garlic cloves, unpeeled
1 teaspoon dried sage
1 teaspoon dried rosemary
2 tablespoons Armagnac
1 tablespoon red peppercorns
3 slices fatback
3 1/2 cups kosher salt
3 1/2 cups sea salt
3 1/2 cups all-purpose flour
1 3/4 cups dry white wine, approximate
2 teaspoons olive oil

   Heat the oven to 350°F.

   Cut off the last joint of the wings (reserve for stock) and remove the excess fat inside the bird.
Cut off the tail.
Loosen the skin over the legs and breast with your fingers, being careful not to tear the skin.
Slip the butter slices under the breast and leg skin.
Season under the skin
with salt and freshly ground pepper.

Lightly crush the garlic with the side of a heavy knife.
Place it inside the capon
with sage, rosemary and Armagnac.

Sprinkle the red peppercorns over the breast
and cover with the fatback.
Tie the legs together.

Make a thick paste of the salts, flour and wine.

Pour the olive oil into a baking dish
just large enough to hold the bird.
Spread a layer of the paste about 1 inch thick
on the bottom.
Place the bird, breast side up, on the salt layer.
Cover the top with the paste,
working it all around to completely encase the bird.
Pinch the seams to seal.
Press the paste onto the capon so it adheres to the bird
and you can see the bird shape,
especially the legs.
Wet your hands and rub them over the paste
so it is smooth all over.

Place in the preheated oven
and bake for 1½ hours.
Remove from the oven and let stand 10 minutes
before removing the salt shell to serve.

Serves 4.

Serving Suggestions:

With so much drama, you might want to serve a Steamed
Vegetable Platter (page 384) which can be placed in the
middle of the table, your guests helping themselves. In
summer, begin with a Red Snapper Madrilene (page 141). In
winter, try the Ramekin of Oysters and Periwinkles
(page 104). If you start with a cold fish course, end with a
gala Apple Pithiviers (page 452). If you start with a hot first
course, end with Pears Poached in Red Wine (page 461).

L. Wertm. tanks!

LINA WERTMÜLLER

It's always so d'eaminable —
and have nice to share a page
with such a brilliant lady —
Bess '81 Myerson

BESS MYERSON

Duck

Most cookbooks do not have a separate section on duck; but, usually, include these recipes in a section on poultry and other birds. However, duck is one of the most popular foods in restaurants and The Four Seasons has made a specialty of this favorite bird. Basically, two techniques are given for cooking duck: one, The Four Seasons Crisp Duck; the other, that given in the recipe for Green Pepper Duck. The Crisp Duck is a time-consuming recipe but gives extraordinary results, and we give you a choice of different sauces and garnishes. The sauces are based on a basic duck sauce. We also include vegetable and fruit dishes that we have found to go particularly well with duck. Perhaps the most popular of The Four Seasons duck recipes is the Crisp Duck with Black Pepper Sauce.

If you have less time to spend and wish to delight in duck, try the Green Pepper Duck. Here, the skin is used in crisp strips as a garnish instead of being crisply laid out in its original position on top of the bird. The advantage of this preparation is that it removes all the fat. If you follow our method for carving duck, you will find that with one duck you will be able to serve three or four instead of two.

In general, duck can be accompanied by the same wines as red meat. It is lovely served with a full-bodied red wine, such as a California Zinfandel. A classic combination is a full-bodied Chambertin with duck.

Depending on the style of dinner you wish to give, you can be flexible with first courses, permitting fish or soups, hot or cold. The only restriction is that if you are using fruit sauces or the apple garnitures, you should avoid more fruit in the meal.

To eat is one thing —

to eat well, another —

but, to eat well —

and with grace — superb! —

Many Thanks

ELIZABETH ASHLEY

The Four Seasons Crisp Duck

Master Recipe

Begin the preparation three days before serving.

Preparation

Two 4½-pound ducks (if frozen, thoroughly defrosted),
    necks removed and reserved for the sauce

Cut off the wings at the second joint
and reserve for the sauce.
Cut or pull away all the fat from the ducks' cavities.
Clear a rack in your refrigerator
and place the ducks on it,
breast sides up and a few inches apart.
It is important that air be allowed to circulate freely
around the ducks so the skin will dry.
You can place a large baking pan
on another rack below the rack with the birds
to catch drippings.
Leave the birds for 3 days.

Marinade

1 ounce fresh ginger, peeled and thinly sliced
2 cloves garlic, unpeeled and halved
Rind of ½ orange, cut into thin strips
2 teaspoons crushed coriander seeds
1½ teaspoons black peppercorns
1 cup soy sauce
2 tablespoons honey

Place all the ingredients in a jar.
Shake well to combine
and refrigerate for 3 days, shaking daily.

Roasting

¼ cup loose jasmine tea leaves
1 tablespoon Szechuan pepper (optional)

About 3 hours before you plan to serve the ducks,
remove them and the marinade from the refrigerator.
In handling the ducks, avoid pressing on the breasts
since this will leave dark spots after roasting.
With the point of a small sharp knife,
prick the skin all over, except the breasts.

Place a rack over a shallow pan
and place the ducks on the rack.
Strain the marinade through a sieve into a bowl.
Brush the marinade liberally
over the entire skin surface of both ducks.
Spoon the remaining marinade into the ducks' cavities.
Let the ducks dry, breast side up, on the rack for 15 minutes.
Scrape any marinade drippings
from the pan into the cavities.

Adjust the oven racks so that one is at the lowest level
and the other is directly above the first.

Heat the oven to 350°F.

Fill a large roasting pan with
3 quarts of water and the tea leaves.
Place the pan on the lower oven rack.
Position the ducks
directly on the higher oven rack over the roasting pan.
(Do not let the ducks touch each other.)
Leave the ducks to roast undisturbed for 1½ hours.
When the ducks are cooked,
the skin should be shiny, dark caramel in color
and very crisp.

Remove the ducks, still on the rack, to your work area.
Insert a kitchen fork into the neck cavity
of one duck and tip it over a bowl to collect the juices.
Repeat with the second duck.
Set the juices aside for the sauce.

Place the ducks on the carving board and
sprinkle with the Szechuan pepper.
Let stand 10 minutes before carving.

Carving

Place one duck on your carving board, breast up,
with the legs facing you.
Have ready a fork and carving knife.
Rest the fork against the left wing
to steady the duck on the board.
With the knife,
make an incision through the skin just above the right leg.
Press the knife blade to the right,
forcing the leg away from the body
and exposing the thigh joint.
Work your knife through the thigh joint
and cut down to the board, separating the thigh and leg
from the body.

Keeping the fork in the same position,
cut off the other leg and thigh in the same way.
Scrape away the fat.
With the tip of your knife,
find the joint between the thigh and leg
and separate the leg from the thigh.

Turn the bird around so the neck end faces you.
Place the tip of your knife
at the far end of the duck against the bone,
just to the right of the center bone.
Bring the knife toward you, following the breastbone
until you reach the wishbone.

Feel with the point of the knife for the wing joint.
Bring down the blade
to cut through the wing joint to the board.
As you cut, keep the knife against the rib cage,
separating the wing and breast in one piece.
Scrape away all the fat.

Repeat this step on the left side of the duck.
Cut the wings from the breast pieces.

Repeat entire procedure with the second duck.

Serving

Spoon a layer of Orange Sauce
over the bottom of a warmed serving platter.
Arrange a pair of drumsticks,
wing bones and thighs at each end of the platter.
Place the breasts in the center and surround the meat
with one of the fresh fruit garnishes which follow.
Sprinkle with the sugared orange rind
(see Orange Sauce recipe).

Place the remaining orange sauce in a sauceboat and
serve on the side.

Serves 4.

Variation:

Serve the duck with the Black Pepper Sauce (see recipe,
page 268) in place of the orange sauce. In that case, omit
the fruit garnish and sugared orange rind.

Basic Duck Sauce

1 tablespoon vegetable oil
Necks and wing tips from 2 ducks
1 celery rib, chopped
1 carrot, chopped
1 onion, chopped
1 bay leaf
3 large mushrooms, halved
4 cloves garlic
1 tablespoon freshly crushed black peppercorns
6 whole cloves
2 tablespoons tomato purée
2 tablespoons all-purpose flour
1 cup dry red wine
4 cups Brown Veal Stock (see recipe, page 498)
Cavity juices reserved from 2 crisp ducks
    (see preceding recipe)

Heat the oven to 400°F.

In a large skillet, heat the oil.
Add the duck pieces and brown over high heat,
stirring, for 5 minutes.
Place the skillet in the preheated oven
to cook the duck pieces for 25 minutes, stirring occasionally.

Add the celery, carrot, onion, bay leaf, mushrooms,
garlic cloves, pepper and cloves.
Let brown in the oven for another 5 minutes.

Place the skillet on top of the stove.
Stir the tomato purée in the middle of the pan.
Sprinkle the flour over the mixture and stir.
Add the red wine and brown stock;
stir and bring to a boil.
Reduce the heat and simmer 3 hours.

Stir in the cavity juices and cook 10 minutes longer.

Strain the sauce through a fine mesh strainer
into a medium saucepan.
Press against the solids with a ladle
to remove as much liquid as possible.
Heat the sauce.
Skim any fat.
Cook until thick.

Makes about 1½ cups.

Orange Sauce

2 oranges
1½ cups Basic Duck Sauce (see preceding recipe)
Sugar
2 tablespoons Grand Marnier
2 tablespoons currant jelly
2 tablespoons lightly salted butter
Kosher salt
Freshly ground black pepper

Remove the rind from the oranges with a stripper.
If you don't have a stripper, use a vegetable peeler
and then cut the rind into thin julienne strips.
Place in a pot with water to cover.
Bring to a boil and cook for about 3 minutes,
or until soft.
Drain.

Squeeze the oranges and place the juice in a pot.
Cook over high heat
until reduced to about one-fourth the volume.

Place the basic duck sauce in another pot
and bring to a boil.
Lower the heat and simmer
while you prepare the rest of the sauce.

Place ½ cup sugar and 1 cup water in a pot.
Bring to a boil and add the julienned rind.
Cook over high heat for about 5 minutes,
or until the syrup begins to caramelize,
turning light brown.

Have a dish ready with a layer of sugar in it
about ½ inch thick.
Remove the rinds from the pan
and toss in the sugar to coat completely.
Set the rinds aside to cool.

Continue cooking the syrup
until it reduces to a dark caramel syrup.
Stir in the Grand Marnier and currant jelly,
then the reduced orange juice.
Whisk until smooth.

Pour in the basic duck sauce and whisk until smooth.
Cook for a few minutes to thicken slightly.
Whisk in the butter
and season to taste with salt and pepper.

BILL RODGERS

Fig Garnish
for Crisp Duck

Vegetable oil
4 dates
4 to 6 walnut halves
1 tablespoon raisins
1 tablespoon candied fruits
8 ripe figs
2 cups all-purpose flour
1½ cups beer
Kosher salt
Sugar
Ground cinnamon

Heat the oil in a deep pot to 375°F.

Place the dates, walnuts, raisins and candied fruits
in the work bowl of a food processor.
Process until coarsely chopped.

With your finger,
work a hole in the center of each fig
through the bottom, leaving the stems intact.
Divide the nut-and-fruit mixture into eight portions
and stuff one portion into each fig.

Mix the flour and beer to make a batter.
Season with salt and sugar to taste,
about 1 teaspoon of each.
Dip the figs in the batter.
Add them, one by one, to the oil,
holding the stems until the batter begins to set.
Drop completely into the oil and cook until crisp.
Drain well,
then roll in a mixture of cinnamon and sugar.

N.Y. City Marathon 79' – 2:11:42

Orange Garnish
for Crisp Duck

2 oranges
2 tablespoons lightly salted butter
2 tablespoons sugar
2 tablespoons brandy

Peel the oranges completely.
Cut them into quarters and then cut out the cores.
Set aside.

When ready to serve the ducks, prepare the garnish.
Using a chafing dish at the table
(or a skillet in the kitchen), heat the butter with the sugar.
When the sugar melts and begins to brown,
add the reserved orange quarters.
Allow them to heat through, turning once.
Off the heat, pour in the brandy,
scraping the bottom of the pan with a spoon.
Place the orange quarters and their sauce
alongside the duck pieces.

Peach Garnish
for Crisp Duck

2 ripe, but firm, fresh peaches
1 tablespoon lightly salted butter
2 tablespoons brandy
¼ cup grenadine

Bring a small pot of water to a boil.
Drop in the peaches
and cook for about 30 seconds to loosen the skin.
Drain well and peel.
Cut the peaches in half and remove the pits.

Heat the butter in an 8-inch skillet.
Add the peaches, cut side down, and cook for a few seconds.
Pour in the brandy and flame.
When the flames die down, add the grenadine
and cook over high heat for about 30 seconds.
Turn the peach halves and cook another 30 seconds.
The sauce should be syrupy.

With a slotted spoon,
remove the peach halves, cut side up, to a serving platter.
Spoon the sauce into the peach cavities.

Plum Garnish
for Crisp Duck

8 ripe, but firm, fresh Italian prune plums
1 tablespoon lightly salted butter
2 tablespoons brandy
¼ cup grenadine

Cut the plums in half and remove the pits. Do not peel.

Make the sauce and cook the plums
as for the Peach Garnish (see preceding recipe).

Cherry Garnish
for Crisp Duck

1 tablespoon lightly salted butter
3 tablespoons sugar
1 pound Bing cherries, pitted (preferably with a pitter)
¼ cup cherry brandy

Heat the butter in an 8-inch skillet.
Add the sugar and stir to blend.
When the sugar dissolves, add the cherries.

Add the brandy and flame.
When the flames die down, cook for about 3 minutes.
Remove the cherries with a slotted spoon
to the serving platter.

Continue cooking the sauce over high heat until syrupy.
Spoon the sauce over the cherries.

Black Pepper Sauce

½ cup dry red wine
2 large shallots, chopped
2 teaspoons freshly crushed red or black peppercorns
1 ½ cups Basic Duck Sauce (see recipe, page 262)
3 tablespoons lightly salted butter
Freshly ground black pepper

Place the wine, shallots and peppercorns
in a 1-quart saucepan.
Bring the liquid to a boil and reduce to a glaze.
Pour in the duck sauce and whisk to blend.

Stir in the butter.
Strain the sauce into a sauceboat
and grind some fresh pepper over the top.

Green Pepper Duck

Two 4½-pound ducks
Kosher salt
One 1-pound celery root, peeled and chopped
1 carrot, chopped
1 parsnip, chopped
1 celery rib, chopped
1 leek, chopped
6 cloves garlic
1 bunch parsley stems
1 teaspoon fresh summer savory
   or ½ teaspoon dried savory
3 fresh sage leaves or ⅛ teaspoon dried sage
1 tablespoon freshly crushed black peppercorns
1 bottle (about 3 cups) dry white wine
2 cups vegetable oil, approximate
1½ cups heavy cream
1½ tablespoons green peppercorns
   packed in salt water, drained and crushed
Freshly ground Szechuan pepper

Heat the oven to 325°F.

Cut the wing tips from the ducks and reserve them, with the necks.
Pull out any excess fat and discard.
Season the ducks all over with salt.

Place the wing tips and necks with the vegetables, herbs and black pepper in a casserole or roasting pan.
Place the ducks on top.
Pour in the bottle of wine
and place the casserole in the preheated oven
to cook for 1 hour.
Cover the pan with foil and cook for 1 hour longer.

Remove the ducks from the pan,
pouring the cavity juices back into the pan.
Cover the ducks loosely with foil and keep warm.

SAM NEWHOUSE

Place a sieve lined with a dampened kitchen towel
or several layers of cheesecloth over a saucepan.
Pour the contents of the casserole through,
pressing down on the solids
to release as much liquid as possible.
Skim off as much fat as possible.
Discard the solids.
Cook the stock until it reduces to a glaze,
about 3 tablespoons.
Chill it until it is solid.

While the glaze chills,
heat the vegetable oil in a deep pot to 375°F.

Place the ducks on your work surface.
Cut around the legs and thighs in large circles,
cutting through the thigh joints.
Peel back the skin and scrape off the fat.
Cut the legs and thighs into two pieces through the joints.

Cut off the breast skin the entire length of the ducks.
Reserve.
Slice the breast meat away from the bones.
Place the legs, thighs and breast meat in a baking dish.
Cover loosely with foil.
Return to the oven to heat through, about 10 minutes.

In a small saucepan, bring the cream to a boil.
Beat in the duck glaze and green peppercorns.
Keep warm.

Cut the duck skin into ¼-inch-wide strips.
Fry these in the hot oil until crisp.
Drain well and sprinkle with Szechuan pepper.

Pour the sauce over the duck
and garnish with the fried skins.

Serves 4.

Stuffed Apples with Red Cabbage

One 1½-pound red cabbage, shredded
2 tablespoons red wine vinegar
2 tablespoons sugar
5 McIntosh apples
2 tablespoons lard
1 cup finely chopped onions
2 ounces salt pork
1 tablespoon Arborio or long-grain rice
1 cup dry red wine
1 cup Chicken Stock (see recipe, page 497)
1 cinnamon stick
1 bay leaf
Freshly ground black pepper
⅓ cup red currant jelly
1 tablespoon butter

Place shredded cabbage in a large bowl.
Sprinkle with vinegar and sugar; toss.
Press a plate down over the cabbage and
refrigerate overnight.

The next day, peel and core
one of the apples and cut it into eight pieces.

Heat the oven to 350°F.

Heat the lard in a large ovenproof saucepan.
Add the onions and cook over medium-high heat
until transparent, about 3 minutes.
Add the salt pork, rice and cut-up apple.
Stir to blend.
Add the wine, chicken stock, cinnamon stick and bay leaf.
Bring to a boil.

Stir in the cabbage with its juices and
season with black pepper.
Do not add salt;
the salt pork should season the mixture sufficiently.

Cover the pan and place in the preheated oven
for 1½ hours.
Remove the pan from the oven and
raise the oven temperature to 375°F.
Remove the salt pork, bay leaf and cinnamon stick
from the mixture; discard them.
Stir the jelly into the mixture and cook it,
uncovered, over medium heat on top of the stove
until most of the liquid becomes syrupy.

Meanwhile, prepare the four remaining apples.
Remove the stems and
cut about ½ inch evenly off the tops.
Using a melon baller, remove the core and
scoop out most of the pulp,
leaving about a ½-inch border of pulp on all sides.
Peel the apples halfway down.

Spoon the cooked cabbage mixture into the apple shells.
Dot the tops with butter.
Place them in a shallow buttered baking dish.
Bake in the preheated oven for 15 to 20 minutes,
or until the apples are cooked,
but still hold their shape.

Serves 4.

With the best Wishes

11-3

EMIL ZATOPEK

New York, OCT. - 22-1979

Apple Roesti

8 tablespoons lightly salted butter
Twelve ¼-inch slices dry French or sourdough bread
4 green apples, peeled, cored and sliced ⅛ inch thick
¼ cup plus 3 tablespoons sugar
½ teaspoon ground cinnamon

In an 8-inch skillet,
heat 6 tablespoons butter until foamy.
Add the bread slices
and cook until crisp and brown on the bottom.
Turn and cook until crisp and brown
on the second side.
Set aside.

In a 12-inch well-seasoned or nonstick skillet,
heat 2 tablespoons butter.
Add all the apple slices in a thick layer.
Sprinkle ¼ cup sugar and the cinnamon over the apples.
Cook over medium-high heat, without stirring,
until the apples get brown and soft, about 10 minutes.

Sprinkle the remaining 3 tablespoons sugar
over the top of the apples.
Place a large plate over the skillet.
Turn the plate and skillet over together,
then slide the apples back into the pan,
sugared side down.

Spread the bread slices over the apples in a layer
and press them to adhere to the apples.
While constantly moving the pan, cook until the sugar
caramelizes.

Place the serving plate over the skillet
and turn the skillet and plate over together.
Serve hot.

Serves 4.

7/23/75

Dear Tom and Paul,
I love your courage,
your spirit,
your dedication.

Which makes me love your restaurant.
But most of all, I love you both.

George Lois

Veal

As pork and duck are the prevailing meats of China, lamb of the Near East, and beef of America, veal, along with the ubiquitous chicken, is the prevailing meat of Europe. In this country, good veal is both more expensive and harder to find. Veal is a meat that is gentle in taste, but it should not be tasteless. It is tender, but should not be mushy; it is pale, but should not be gray. Traditionally, the nearer it is to white—milk fed —the better the quality. However, there is good veal in America today; it is pale pink in color. At The Four Seasons, most of the veal dishes are light preparations not meant to overwhelm the taste of the meat. A few of the dishes in this chapter are not for the veal itself, but for its specialty meats. While many Americans think of veal as a white meat taking white wine, our own prejudice is usually for a light red wine with veal. However, there is no doubt that with the more elegant dishes you may wish to have a superb white such as a great Montrachet or California Chardonnay.

Fillet of Veal with Crabmeat and Wild Mushrooms

If you are not a hunter of mushrooms, this is not a dish that you will often prepare. Should you, however, find this pair—the classic golden salamander-yellow chanterelle and the royal trompette member of its family, with its black-purple, midnight-deep color—you will know that you have a dish worthy of that special moment.

Goodness knows, having found the summer mushrooms, fresh herbs are the least of your problems.

4 tablespoons clarified butter
9 tablespoons lightly salted butter,
   cut into 1-tablespoon pieces
Six 8-ounce rounds veal tenderloin
½ cup dry white wine
1½ tablespoons Glace de Viande (meat glaze)
   (see recipe, page 502)
Freshly ground black pepper
½ pound whole fresh chanterelles
10 ounces royal trompette mushrooms, quartered
⅓ cup finely chopped mixed fresh herbs
   (chervil, tarragon, parsley and chives)
Kosher salt
1 pound lump crabmeat, picked over

In a 10-inch skillet, heat 2 tablespoons of clarified butter with 1 tablespoon salted butter.
Add the veal and sauté, turning once,
until the meat is cooked and golden brown, about 5 minutes.
With tongs, remove the veal to a side dish.
Keep warm.
Discard the butter.

Deglaze the pan with the wine,
scraping the bottom to loosen any bits.
Stir in the meat glaze and season with pepper.
Return the veal to the pan and
coat with the syrupy pan juices.
Arrange the meat overlapping on a serving platter.
Cover and keep warm in a low oven.

To the remaining pan juice,
add the remaining 8 tablespoons of butter pieces,
whisking constantly.
It may be necessary to move the pan on and off the heat
to keep the butter hot but not liquid.
Pour the sauce over the meat
and keep warm in the low oven.

In a clean skillet,
heat the remaining 2 tablespoons clarified butter.
Add the chanterelles and sauté for 2 minutes, tossing.
Add the other mushrooms and
toss together over high heat 1 minute longer.
Sprinkle in the herbs; fold in the crabmeat and
season with salt and pepper to taste.
Heat through.
Spread the mixture over the veal and serve hot.

Serves 6.

Serving Suggestions:

This rich and spectacular dish requires nothing beside it,
little before it, and the lightest of desserts after it. If you,
however, feel impelled to garnish the dish, a few fresh
noodles would not intrude. Before the veal, something as
simple as the Avocado with Tomato and Basil Vinaigrette
(page 34) would be entirely adequate, and a fruit sorbet
(see pages 474 to 477) would be a light dessert. If you feel
that you wish to continue the drama of the evening, finish
with a Cream Cheese and Riesling Soufflé (page 489).

Fillet of Veal with Fiddlehead Ferns

Whereas the previous veal was for late summer with its rare glories, this recipe is for early spring when the fiddlehead ferns, their tops still tightly closed, begin to push up along the sides of roads and deep in forests.

Before you attempt to cut the ferns yourself, make sure that you read a good guidebook; other ferns besides the fiddlehead have the same conformation at the top. The difference lies in the patterning of the spores. No fern that we know of will actually harm you. On the other hand, they will not be interesting or pleasant to eat if they are not the real fiddleheads. When picking fiddleheads, make sure that they are tight and unopened. Once the leaves begin to spread and develop, they are no longer palatable. In some markets, fiddleheads can be bought fresh.

One 12- to 14-ounce veal kidney
Six 6- to 8-ounce boneless veal loin fillets
1 pound fresh or frozen fiddlehead ferns
Kosher salt
Freshly ground black pepper
2 tablespoons clarified butter
½ pound lightly salted butter
½ cup dry white wine
3 tablespoons Glace de Viande (meat glaze)
   (see recipe, page 502)
½ teaspoon red wine vinegar
¼ pound small mushrooms, peeled and thinly sliced

Carefully trim all the fat off the kidney, removing the thin skin which surrounds it. (Save fat for the Chicken Liver Mousse, see recipe, page 27.) Cut the kidney into very thin slices.

Loosely wrap each piece of veal in a damp kitchen towel
and flatten it to half the width with a mallet
or the flat side of a cleaver.

If using fresh fiddlehead ferns,
bring a pot of water to the boil
and blanch the ferns in it for 1 minute.
If using frozen ferns, soak them in water until thawed.
Either way, dry them well in a kitchen towel
to squeeze out the excess moisture.
Spread them out on a towel and reshape.
Set aside.

Season the veal with salt and pepper.
Heat the clarified butter
and 2 tablespoons salted butter in a sauté pan
over high heat.
Sauté the veal in the butter for 5 minutes,
turning the meat once with tongs.
Arrange the veal slices overlapping on a serving dish;
keep hot.

Pour off the fat from the skillet
and deglaze with the white wine,
scraping the bottom with a wooden spoon.
Blend in the glace de viande.
Set aside.

Heat 2 tablespoons salted butter in a small skillet
over high heat until golden brown.
Add the kidney slices and sauté them,
stirring, for 30 seconds.
Sprinkle on the vinegar and remove from the heat.

In another skillet,
heat another 2 tablespoons of salted butter
over brisk heat until golden brown.
Sauté the mushrooms, stirring, for 1 minute.
Add them to the kidneys.
Keep warm.

In the same skillet, heat 2 tablespoons salted butter.
Add the fiddlehead ferns and gently sauté for 1 minute,
or just until heated through.
Salt lightly.

Gradually whisk the remaining butter,
a tablespoon at a time, into the reserved veal pan juices,
moving the pan on and off the heat as needed,
until the sauce is light and fluffy.
Stir in the mushroom and kidney cooking juices,
reserving the mushrooms and kidneys.
Adjust the seasoning with a little black pepper.
Strain the sauce over the veal.
Scatter the mushrooms and kidneys on top.
Garnish each with two or three Fried Sage leaves
(recipe follows).
Serve at once with the fiddlehead ferns on the side
in a small dish.

Serves 6.

Fried Sage

Vegetable oil
⅔ cup all-purpose flour
½ cup beer
18 fresh sage leaves
Kosher salt

Heat the oil in a deep pot to 375°F.

Mix the flour and beer to make a batter.
Dip the sage leaves into the batter
and drop them, a few at a time, into the hot oil.
Fry about 1 minute, or until golden brown.

Drain well and season with salt.
Serve immediately.

Serves 6.

Serving Suggestions:

The inclusion of veal kidney in this dish gives it a stronger
and more complex taste than you might expect. Look for a
light Cru Bourgeois of Bordeaux to accompany this or a
Chianti Riserva. A vegetable is not necessary here. Leave the
ferns to star, but serve enough bread for those who wish to
enjoy the sauce. You might begin with a Sorrel Vichyssoise
(page 138), since sorrel, like sage, is one of the first greens
of spring. If the first course has no cream, you might indulge
your guests in Crêpes Soufflés (page 449) for dessert.

Tournedos of Veal with Oyster Purée

We feel you may be somewhat startled by the idea of this dish and can only hope that you will try it, as we truly believe it to be exceptional. Fresh shiitake mushrooms, just beginning to appear on the market, are a flavorful, domesticated mushroom that can enrich our fund of basic ingredients.

8 slices bacon
3 tablespoons olive oil
8 fresh shiitake mushrooms, caps only
Kosher salt
Freshly ground black pepper
Eight 2- to 3-ounce boneless veal fillets,
    each about 2 inches thick
12 oysters, shucked
2 tablespoons lightly salted butter
⅓ cup dry white wine
½ cup heavy cream

Heat the oven to 400°F.

Place the bacon on a baking sheet.
Sprinkle about 1 tablespoon of water over it
and bake for 5 minutes to slightly precook the bacon.
Remove from oven and set aside; turn the broiler on.

Spoon about 1 teaspoon of oil
inside each mushroom cap.
Season with salt and pepper; set aside.

Loosely wrap each piece of veal in a damp kitchen towel
and flatten to half with a mallet
or the flat side of a cleaver.
Season with salt and pepper on all sides.

Wrap a slice of bacon
around the edge of each piece of veal;
secure the ends in place with toothpicks.

Purée the oysters in a food processor.

Heat the butter in a 12-inch skillet.
When the foaming subsides, add the veal
and sauté over high heat until well browned on both sides.
Transfer the meat to a serving platter.
Remove the toothpicks; keep the meat warm.
Discard the butter.

Deglaze the pan with the white wine,
scraping the bottom with a wooden spoon.
Reduce the liquid to a glaze.
Add the oyster purée and simmer 2 minutes.

Add the cream to the skillet and bring to a boil.
Whisk constantly until well blended.
Pour in the meat juices that have collected
on the serving platter.
Stir and cook over medium-high heat for 1 minute.

Place the mushrooms, tops down, under the broiler
just until soft.
Place a mushroom cap, hollow side up, on each piece of veal
and spoon the oyster purée into the cap.

Serve with sautéed cherry tomatoes and sugar snap peas.

Serves 4.

Serving Suggestions:
This veal dish garnished with mushroom caps, served with
tomatoes and sugar snap peas, makes a beautiful and
complete plate. For the most festive of meals in mid-winter,
you might begin with one of the game terrines
(pages 55 to 65) or A Feuilleté of Vesiga with Chervil (page
121). Conclude either lightly with a Chocolate Rum Sorbet
(page 479) or, more grandly, with a Cappuccino Soufflé
(page 491), depending on your taste.
Your first course will determine your choice of white or
red wine for the veal. A game terrine would indicate a
progression of reds; the feuilleté would indicate a
progression of whites.

Veal Scallops, Lemon Butter

When good veal is available, you want a light and simple main course. This is it.

Eight 2½- to 3-ounce veal scallops
Kosher salt
Freshly ground black pepper
All-purpose flour
4 tablespoons lightly salted butter
1 recipe Lemon Butter Sauce (see page 514)

Season the veal with salt and pepper.
Dip in flour to lightly coat.

Heat the butter in a large skillet
(or use two skillets).
When the butter is foaming and lightly brown,
add the veal pieces.
Cook until meat is nicely browned on the bottom,
then turn and brown the other side.

Top with lemon butter sauce.

Serves 4.

*I memories a lovely day —
close to Thanksgiving
— thanks to all seasons*

Maureen O'Sullivan

MAUREEN O'SULLIVAN

Veal Scallops, Lemon Parmesan

This recipe takes the lemon and veal combination of the previous dish and, by invoking the classic veal Parmesan, goes on to greater heights.

Eight 2-ounce veal scallops
Kosher salt
Freshly ground black pepper
1½ cups fresh white bread crumbs
½ cup grated fresh Parmesan cheese
Grated rind of 1 lemon
All-purpose flour
2 eggs, beaten
4 tablespoons clarified butter
1 tablespoon vegetable oil
1 recipe Lemon Butter Sauce (see page 514)

Flatten the veal scallops
with a meat pounder to a ¼-inch thickness.
Season lightly with salt and pepper.

Mix the bread crumbs
with the Parmesan cheese and grated lemon rind
in a shallow dish.

Dust the veal scallops with flour,
shaking off the excess.
Dip them in the beaten eggs
and coat well with the bread-crumb mixture on both sides.

In a 10- to 12-inch skillet,
heat 2 tablespoons clarified butter.
When hot, add four breaded veal scallops
and brown quickly over medium-high heat,
turning once with tongs.

When the scallops are cooked,
remove to a warmed dish.
Add the remaining 2 tablespoons clarified butter
and 1 tablespoon vegetable oil to the skillet
and brown the remaining four breaded scallops
as described above.
Serve with lemon butter sauce.

Serves 4.

Variation

To make Scallops of Veal with Melon,
prepare the Scallops of Veal, Lemon Parmesan,
omitting the Parmesan cheese and grated lemon rind.

Garnish as follows:
Sauté eight rindless ½-inch wedges of cantaloupe
in 4 tablespoons butter until lightly browned;
set aside.
Add eight cherry tomatoes and sauté just to heat.

Top the veal with some lemon butter sauce
and garnish with the melon and tomatoes.

Serves 4.

Serving Suggestions:

As you can see from the variation, this is a basic and elegant
way of preparing veal which can be continually varied
according to your imagination. Other garnitures might be
cucumbers or zucchini. The rest of your meal will tell you
whether you want a white or red wine to serve with it.
Perhaps the fruit versions would be more comfortable with
the white wine; cheese versions with a red.

It was again, a
pleasure!

DINA MERRILL

The Main Course / 285

Veal Chop with Tomato, Basil and Mushrooms

This dish applies Chef Renggli's talent to an Italian-inspired combination of veal and tomato, basil and mushrooms.

Veal

Four 1½-inch-thick veal chops, fat trimmed off long bone
Kosher salt
Freshly ground black pepper
4 tablespoons lightly salted butter
2 or 3 sprigs fresh rosemary

Heat the oven to 425°F.

Season the chops with salt and pepper.
Heat the butter in a 10-inch skillet.
Add the rosemary.
When the butter begins to foam,
add the chops and place in the preheated oven.
Cook for 8 minutes.
Turn the chops and cook 8 minutes longer.
Remove the chops from the skillet and keep warm.

Sauce

½ cup dry white wine
2 tablespoons Glace de Viande (meat glaze)
  (see recipe, page 502)
½ cup heavy cream
3 tablespoons lightly salted butter

Pour the fat out of the skillet; deglaze with the wine, scraping the bottom of the pan with a wooden spoon.
Stir in the glace de viande.
When it melts, stir in the cream,
then the butter in pieces; keep warm.

Tomatoes
2 tablespoons olive oil
1 clove garlic, smashed
½ cup roughly chopped fresh basil leaves
2 beefsteak tomatoes, peeled, seeded and
    cut into 1-inch cubes
Kosher salt
Freshly ground black pepper

Heat the olive oil in an 8-inch skillet.
Add the garlic and cook for 1 minute.
Add the basil and discard the garlic.
Add the tomatoes and cook just to heat through.
Season to taste with salt and pepper.

Mushrooms
2 tablespoons olive oil
2 cups mushroom caps, quartered if large,
    left whole if small

Heat the oil in a 10-inch skillet.
When very hot,
add the mushrooms and cook just to brown.

Serving
Place a veal chop
in the center of each of four serving plates.
Spoon some sauce over the chops.
Place the tomatoes on one side of each chop
and mushrooms on the other side.

Serve with Roesti Potatoes (see recipe, page 412).

Serves 4.

Serving Suggestions:
To make this a centerpiece for a formal dinner, begin with a
savory soufflé (pages 129 to 134). For a simpler meal, try the
Onion Soup (page 149) as the first course. Finish
with salad, fruit or cheese for a simple dinner, or the Pine
Nut Galette (page 440) for a more elegant evening. This is
definitely a veal dish for red wine. You might look to
California or Italy: California for a Merlot from the Napa
Valley; Italy for a Venegazzu from the Veneto region.

Veal Paillard

Every day in the Bar Room at lunch, The Four Seasons serves numerous paillards. The most classic is probably the veal.

Four 8-ounce slices bottom round veal,
  cut on an angle
Vegetable oil
Kosher salt
Freshly ground black pepper

Heat a grill.

Oil eight sheets of waxed paper.
Place each veal slice on a sheet of paper
and top with a second sheet.
Pound the slices with a meat pounder
or the bottom of a heavy pot
until they are about ¼ inch thick.

Remove the top sheets of paper
and place the meat on the hot grill.
Remove the second sheets.
Cook the meat until it sears, about 30 seconds.
Turn over and sear the second side,
about 30 seconds.

Serve with the first side up
sprinkled with salt and pepper.

Serves 4.

IRENE WORTH

22 February 1978

Steamed Calf's Liver with Mushrooms and Shallots

The fat livers of France and Hungary are often served with sweet wines—anywhere from a Sauternes to a late-picked Moselle. Such wines, of course, are now being spectacularly produced in the Napa Valley. For those who do not like sweet wine, a robust red, such as a Pommard.

1½ tablespoons red wine vinegar
2 tablespoons Madeira wine
3 tablespoons lightly salted butter
1 clove garlic
½ cup thinly sliced shallots
½ pound finely chopped mushrooms
⅓ cup finely chopped parsley
Freshly ground black pepper
1½ cups Demi-Glace (see recipe, page 500)
Six 6-ounce slices calf's liver
6 trimmed scallions
Coarse sea salt
6 cornichons, halved lengthwise

In a medium-sized saucepan,
heat the vinegar and Madeira
until reduced to a glaze.
Add the butter and garlic to the pan.
Stir to blend.
When the butter has melted,
add the shallots and cook until soft.
Add the mushrooms, parsley and black pepper to taste.
Cook, stirring,
until all the liquid in the pan has evaporated and
the mushrooms are dry.

Remove and discard the garlic clove;
stir in the demi-glace.
Simmer gently for 5 minutes.
Readjust the seasoning and set aside.

Make a steamer as follows:
Use a cake rack which will fit into a roasting pan
with a tight-fitting cover.
The pan must be deep enough so the rack can be raised
about 1½ inches from the bottom.
Inverted custard cups are a good support for the rack.

Butter the cake rack and
place the liver slices on it in one layer.
Put a scallion on top of each slice.

Place 1 inch of water in the roasting pan.
Bring it to a boil.
When the water is boiling,
place inverted custard cups in the pan.
Make sure the tops of the cups are above
the level of the boiling water.
Place the cake rack on the cups
so it is supported above the steam.
Cover the pan and steam the liver for 1 minute.

Remove the cover, holding it away from you
so the steam does not scald your face.
Remove the scallions, turn the meat over with tongs,
replace the scallions, cover the pan again and
steam for another minute.

To serve, ladle about ⅓ cup of sauce
on each of six individual serving plates.
Place a liver slice over the sauce on each plate.
Season with salt and pepper to taste.
Garnish each plate
with a cooked scallion over the meat and
two cornichon halves in the sauce.

Serves 6.

Serving Suggestions:
You might think about starting this meal with Seasonal
Greens with Cracklings (page 38), and ending it with a
Grapefruit and Tequila Sorbet (page 475).

Braised Calf's Liver

A whole piece of calf's liver to be carved at the table is not something that comes to most people's minds. We feel that it makes a spectacular dish.

¼ cup olive oil
4 pounds onions, halved and cut into ¼-inch slices
3 pounds calf's liver, in one piece
20 fatback strips, ¼ inch square and 4 inches long,
    well chilled
1 cup Madeira wine
1 cup tawny port wine
Kosher salt
Freshly ground black pepper

Heat the olive oil
in a large ovenproof skillet or casserole.
Add the onions and
cook until very soft and lightly brown,
about 45 minutes.

While the onions cook, prepare the liver.
Using a larding needle,
work ten fatback strips across the top of the liver
in parallel lines, moving the needle in and out.
Alternate the ins and outs
so the pattern resembles a checkerboard.

Turn the liver over and do the same thing
on the other side with the remaining ten strips.

Cut off and reserve the excess fat.
Place it in a small skillet with 1 tablespoon water.
Cook until the fat renders.
Strain the fat into a 10-inch skillet
and add the rendered cubes to the onions.

Heat the oven to 400°F.

When the onions are soft,
add the Madeira and port and bring to a boil.
Heat the rendered fat in the skillet
and when hot, add the liver and
cook about 3 minutes on a side, until well browned.

Place the liver on top of the onions,
spooning some onions over the top of the liver.
Place in the oven.

After 15 minutes,
check to make sure the liver is moist,
spooning more onions over if necessary.
Braise an additional 15 minutes.
The liver will be rare.

Season the liver and onions with salt and pepper.
Remove the cooked liver to a board
to rest for 10 minutes before slicing.
Cook the onions on top of the stove
for a few minutes to thicken.

Cut the liver into thin slices on the diagonal
and serve with some of the onions on top.

Serves 6 to 8.

Serving Suggestions:

As we mentioned in the preceding recipe, sweet wines go
well with liver. Since this is a more robust dish, you might
serve a Chambertin or a rich California Zinfandel produced
by growers who do not want a particularly French
vinification. An equally special vegetable, such as the
Eggplant Flan (page 378), or a crisp one such as the
Sautéed Sugar Snap Peas (page 380), would be unusual
with this dish.

Veal Kidneys and Mushrooms

This is a classic dish we feel merits your attention: the vinegar and brandy counterbalance the taste of kidneys in such a way to make them pleasant to most palates, while the cream and glace de viande smooth and enrich it.

2 tablespoons clarified butter
3 or 4 finely minced shallots
2 veal kidneys, trimmed of excess fat
    and very thinly sliced
2 teaspoons sherry wine vinegar
2 tablespoons brandy
½ cup heavy cream
1 tablespoon Glace de Viande (meat glaze)
    (see recipe, page 502)
4 large mushroom caps, peeled and thinly sliced
Kosher salt
Freshly ground black pepper

Heat a 10-inch skillet until very hot.
Add the butter, shallots and kidney slices.
Stir to sear the slices and cook about 1 to 2 minutes.
Pour the contents of the skillet into a side dish.

Add the vinegar to the skillet, then the brandy.
Flame.
When the flames die down,
add the cream, then the glace de viande.
Whisk until smooth.

Pour out and discard the blood and other liquid
that has accumulated in the dish with the kidneys.
Return the kidneys to the pan and add the mushrooms.
Toss to coat.
Season with salt and pepper.

Serve hot.

Serves 4.

Serving Suggestions:
The sauce from this dish is special and we think you might
want some steamed rice to help your guests enjoy it.
Certainly, this is a red wine dish and probably even
deserves a good Bordeaux from St. Emilion or, similarly, a
Sonoma County Merlot.

*What a lovely way
to spend the 4 seasons;
to eat delicious food
and be surrounded by
delights to the eye!
I came, I saw and I too, overate!!

With all best wishes,
Arlene Dahl*

ARLENE DAHL

Lamb

Lamb is one of the best, but one of the most underused, meats in America. It is now widely available throughout the year and throughout the country. Lamb varies perhaps more than any other meat according to the amount of time it is cooked. It is not simply a question of being over- or underdone, but rather that lamb fat has a strong taste, and when lamb is cooked for a long period of time or at a high heat, the lamb fat decomposes, permeating the meat and any other food cooked with it. Therefore, in roasting and grilling lamb where a certain amount of fat is necessary to retain its moisture, we believe that a high heat for a brief period of time is the most satisfactory solution. When cooking small amounts of lamb with no surrounding fat, we recommend sautéing or stewing.

If there is a classic accompaniment to a fine red Bordeaux, it is a lamb roast. In our opinion, the increasingly excellent Cabernet Sauvignon or Merlot wines of the Napa Valley, the two major wine grapes of Bordeaux, also shine in this pairing. Some of the more highly seasoned dishes would be complemented by the heavier styles of California Zinfandels and the Petite Syrahs. Also, there are a few extraordinary Zinfandels vinified in the French manner. Look for wine of Clos du Val and Carneros Creek.

Chopped Lamb Steak with Pine Nuts

One of the least expensive cuts of lamb is the shoulder. Here it is pared of all the fat and gristle and then tenderized by grinding. The unusual seasonings in this recipe give it an excellent taste.

You might also keep this recipe in mind when you are obliged to buy a leg of lamb larger than you need. Ask the butcher to remove the chops at the end, bone them and remove all the fat. Then grind them and use as you would the ground shoulder.

2½ pounds boneless lamb shoulder, ground
¾ cup pine nuts
2 teaspoons curry powder
¼ teaspoon ground coriander
1 tablespoon kosher salt
1 teaspoon Hungarian sweet paprika
¾ cup ice water

Thoroughly, but gently, combine all the ingredients.
Do not overmix,
or the mixture will become pastelike
and toughen when cooked.

Divide the mixture into eight equal portions.
Form each portion into a 5-inch-long, egg-shaped patty.
Place on a plate;
cover and refrigerate 2 hours before cooking.
This will bring out the flavors and set the shape.

Heat the grill or broiler.

Grill or broil the lamb patties evenly
to desired doneness,
about 5 minutes on a side for medium-rare.

Serve with Green Tomato Chutney (see recipe, page 420).

Serves 4.

Note:

If you wish to sauté the patties, heat 2 tablespoons clarified butter in a large skillet. Add the patties and cook until brown on both sides and pink inside.

Serving Suggestions:

Since this dish has the seasoning of a curry, we recommend serving the Green Tomato Chutney with it. You might think of beer as an accompaniment, and either a green salad after or Seasonal Greens with Cracklings (page 38) before. For dessert, clear your palate with a fruit sorbet (pages 475 to 477).

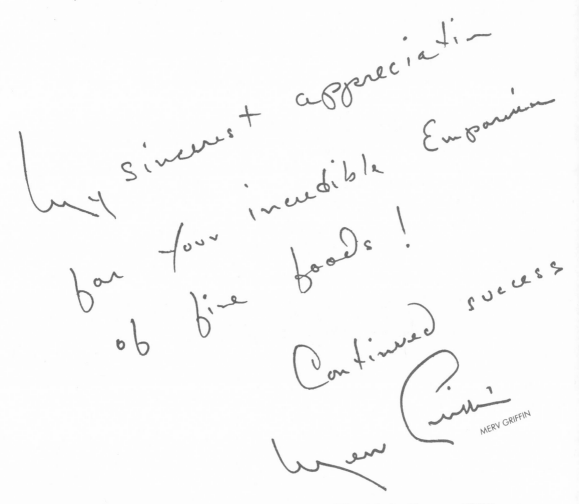

My sincerest appreciation for your incredible Emporium of fine foods! Continued success

MERV GRIFFIN

Medallions of Lamb with Coriander Butter

This simple-tasting but remarkable dish was featured as part of the Barrel Tasting of 1978 and was served with Eggplant Flans (page 378). Although there are many steps to making this menu, they can be done in stages. If you make the glaze and eggplant purée the day before your party, you will find your work that day considerably reduced. Lamb, coriander and eggplant make a warm-tasting and wonderful combination.

Making the Glaze

One 4- to 5-pound trimmed saddle of lamb
2 tablespoons lightly salted butter
2 celery ribs, cut into 2-inch pieces
1 medium carrot, cut into 2-inch pieces
1 medium onion, halved
1 sprig fresh rosemary or ¼ teaspoon dried rosemary
2 cloves garlic
½ cup dry white wine

Bone the saddle of lamb so you have
the two loins and the two fillets uncut.
Set the meat aside.
Save all the trimmings and bones.
Discard all the fat
and chop the bones into 2-inch pieces with a cleaver
(or ask the butcher to do it for you).

Melt the butter over high heat in a large skillet.
Add the trimmings and bones
and brown them 15 minutes, turning as necessary.
Drain off the fat.

Turn the heat down to medium
and add the celery, carrot, onion, rosemary,
garlic and 1 cup water.
Scrape the bottom of the pan
with a wooden spoon to deglaze.
Simmer for 10 minutes,
or until the water is almost evaporated.
Add another cup of water, scrape again with the spoon,
and continue simmering until the liquid is evaporated.
Add the wine, scrape again,
and simmer until the wine evaporates.
Add 3 cups water, scrape,
bring water to a boil over high heat.
Turn heat down to medium
and simmer until about 1½ cups of liquid are left,
about 1 hour.

Strain the liquid into a small saucepan.
Skim off the fat.
Over medium heat, reduce the liquid to ¼ cup.
It will be syrupy.
This is the glaze.
Reserve until needed.

Preparing the Lamb and Sauce

1 recipe Ground Spices (recipe follows)
2 tablespoons lightly salted butter
¼ cup dry white wine

Cut each loin crosswise into six pieces.
Wrap each piece in a damp kitchen towel
and flatten it with a meat pounder.

Sprinkle the ground spices
(less the tablespoon reserved for the coriander butter)
on the twelve pieces of loin and the two fillets.
Melt the butter in a skillet large enough
to hold all the meat in one layer.
When the butter browns, add all the meat to the pan.
Sauté the slices of loin for about 3 minutes on each side
until brown on the outside and pink on the inside.
Cook the fillets, being a little thicker,
about 4 minutes on each side.
Remove the meat from the pan, place on a platter,
and keep warm while preparing the sauce.

Pour the fat out of the skillet.
Return the skillet to medium-high heat,
add the wine and ½ cup water to deglaze,
scraping the bottom of the pan with a wooden spoon.
Add the reserved glaze.
Cook for 30 seconds,
or until the sauce is very hot and dark brown.

To serve the medallions,
slice each fillet diagonally into three pieces.
Place all the meat on one side of the platter
and the Eggplant Flans (see recipe, page 378)
on the other.
Top each piece of meat with some sauce
and a tablespoon of Coriander Butter (recipe follows),
which will melt slightly.
Put the rest of the coriander butter in a bowl
to serve on the side.

Serves 6.

WOW! Thank You!

Coriander Butter

1 tablespoon Ground Spices (recipe follows)
½ cup loosely packed fresh coriander leaves
3 large or 6 small shallots, halved
1 tablespoon imported Dijon mustard
2 tablespoons brandy
1 pound lightly salted butter, cut into 1-inch pieces

Place all the ingredients except the butter
in the work bowl of a food processor
fitted with a steel blade.
Process until the shallots and coriander are finely chopped.
Just before serving, add the butter and process
until the butter is soft.
If necessary, add more salt and pepper to taste.

Ground Spices

1 tablespoon coriander seeds, toasted in a dry skillet
   for 5 minutes
2 tablespoons sea salt
1 tablespoon black peppercorns

Grind the coriander, salt and pepper
in a blender or spice grinder.

Use 1 tablespoon for the Coriander Butter
(see recipe) and the rest to season
the medallions of lamb.

Serving Suggestions:

Certainly, this plate requires nothing else on it. You might
choose a dish from an earlier stage of the Barrel Tasting
dinner. The Mousse of Trout in Leeks (page 200) is a fitting
first course, and you might finish with the Cappuccino Soufflé
(page 491) from the same menu. The wine we served for the
dinner was Stag's Leap Wine Cellars Cabernet Sauvignon.
An alternate selection might be a Rioja from the early 1960s.

3·11·77

ANGELA LANSBURY

Sautéed Loin of Lamb

This dish is not dissimilar to the Medallions of Lamb with Coriander Butter in that it uses a boned saddle and uses the bones to create a well-seasoned base for the sauce. However, the bones are used to make a stock and not a glaze, and the seasoning is quite different. Serve this dish to friends who like garlic.

One 4- to 5-pound trimmed saddle of lamb
9 tablespoons lightly salted butter
10 large cloves garlic, unpeeled
1 celery rib, cut into 4 pieces
1 large carrot, cut into 4 pieces
½ cup plus 1 tablespoon dry white wine
Kosher salt
Freshly ground black pepper

Bone the saddle of lamb
so you have the two loins and the two fillets uncut.
Reserve the fillets for another dish.
Save all the bones.
Discard all the fat and chop the bones into 2-inch pieces
with a cleaver (or ask the butcher to do it for you).

In a wide skillet, melt 2 tablespoons of butter.
When hot, add the bones and meat trimmings
along with the garlic and cook until lightly brown.
Add the celery and carrot pieces.
Toss well with the lamb trimmings.
Sauté, tossing often, for 20 minutes,
or until nicely browned.
Strain to remove the fat.
Return the solids to the pan.
Deglaze the pan with ½ cup of wine,
scraping the bottom with a wooden spoon.
Add 1 quart of water and bring to a boil.

Skim the surface to remove any scum.
Reduce heat to a simmer.
Cook, uncovered, for 25 minutes.
Strain through a sieve into a clean bowl.
Reserve the garlic but discard the other solids.
Cool and skim off the fat; reserve.

Season the lamb with salt and pepper.
Heat a medium-sized, well-seasoned skillet;
add 3 tablespoons butter.
When the butter begins to foam,
add the lamb and brown nicely on all sides.
Cook about 6 minutes over brisk heat.
Transfer to a dish and keep moist and warm.

Heat the remaining tablespoon of wine
in a small, heavy saucepan.
When very hot, remove from the heat
and beat in the remaining 4 tablespoons butter,
bit by bit, until the mixture is thick and creamy.
Set aside, keeping warm.

Deglaze the skillet the lamb cooked in
with ¼ cup water, scraping the bottom
with a wooden spoon.
Add the reserved juices from the lamb trimmings
and reheat.
Turn the lamb in the sauce to glaze and reheat.
Transfer to a hot serving platter.
Surround with the reserved garlic cloves
and creamy butter mixture.
Spoon the skillet sauce over the lamb
and serve with Potatoes Paillasson (see recipe, page 416).

Serves 6.

Serving Suggestions:
A Crabmeat Mousse (page 33) as a first course would
provide a contrast of color, texture and taste. You might
serve some Glazed Yellow and White Turnips with Currants
(page 377) as well as the Potatoes Paillasson with the lamb,
and a Wild Honey Ice Cream (page 482) for dessert.

Saddle of Lamb Baked in Salt

While the salt may in fact be removed from the lamb in the kitchen as indicated, removing it at the table is spectacular. If you do it at the table, do it before serving your first course to give the saddle adequate time to rest before it is carved. The salt is not a conceit, but a flavoring and way of retaining all the meat juices.

One 4- to 5-pound trimmed saddle of lamb
Twelve ⅛-inch slices fatback, approximate
7 sprigs fresh rosemary or ⅓ teaspoon dried rosemary
7 sprigs fresh sage or ⅙ teaspoon dried sage
7 sprigs fresh lemon thyme or ⅓ teaspoon dried thyme
2 tablespoons red peppercorns
Kosher salt
Freshly ground black pepper
3 cups sea salt
1½ cups all-purpose flour
¾ cup dry white wine, approximate

Heat the oven to 425°F.

Trim off all the fat and the thin membrane
which covers the saddle
so the central bone is exposed.

In a roasting pan large enough
to hold the trimmed saddle,
make a layer of fatback slices large enough
to go under the whole saddle.
Top with 1 or 2 sprigs of each herb
and 1 tablespoon red peppercorns.
If using dried herbs, mix them and sprinkle a pinch
on the fatback, reserving the rest for the top.
Season the meat with salt and freshly ground pepper.

Place the saddle over the fatback, fillet side down.
Spread the remaining herbs and red peppercorns
generously over the top.
Cover with a layer of fatback.

Mix the sea salt, flour and wine until you have a paste.
If the mixture is too dry and crumbles,
add more wine.
Spread this mixture over the top to cover the fatback.
The sides should not be covered.

Place in the preheated oven
and roast for 45 minutes for rare meat.
When done, remove the saddle from the roasting pan.
Lift off and discard the salt crust and herbs.
If using dried herbs, scrape some of them off.
Let the meat rest 10 to 15 minutes before carving.

To carve, cut down along the center bone
to free the meat.
Then, holding the knife parallel to the cutting board,
cut thin slices across the loin.
Repeat with the second loin.
Turn the saddle over
and remove the fillets in whole pieces.
Slice these on the diagonal into about two or three slices
each.

Serves 4 to 6.

Serving Suggestions:

The direct yet simple taste of this lamb dish would go well
with almost any of the vegetables in the book. You might try
a green one, Snow Peas in Shoyu (page 381), and a heavier,
baked one such as Baked Knob Celery (page 374). A fine
California Cabernet would go well here.

John Houseman

JOHN HOUSEMAN

— Dec 23rd / 1977

Lamb Paillard

This is another—and probably the most unusual—in the Bar Room series of paillards. Our guests find it to be most satisfactory. Venison Paillard can be prepared in the same way.

2 loins of lamb, each about 10 inches long,
    trimmed of fat
Vegetable oil
Kosher salt
Freshly ground black pepper

Heat a grill until hot.

Cut each loin in half crosswise.
Place a piece flat on a work surface
and, with your knife parallel to the surface,
cut lengthwise through the middle of the piece,
stopping about ½ inch from the edge.
Open the piece up like a book.
Oil two sheets of parchment paper
and place the meat between them.
Pound the meat to a ¼-inch thickness with a meat pounder
or the bottom of a heavy pot.
Repeat with the remaining three pieces.

Peel off the top sheets of paper
and flip the meat onto the grill.
Peel off the second sheets.
After about 30 seconds, lift the meat with tongs
and rotate it 45 degrees.
Sear again, then turn over and sear the second side.
The whole cooking time should be about 2 minutes.
The lamb will be rare.

Serve with the first side up.
Season with salt and pepper.

Serves 4.

Serving Suggestions:
This is a wonderful light dish for lunch. The only vegetable needed is Bar Room Slaw (page 397).

Barbecued Leg of Lamb

The Mediterranean basin, and particularly Greece, Turkey and countries of the Near East, have largely lamb and chicken cuisines. This recipe takes some of their seasonings and some of their techniques and adds a few oriental touches. You have to marinate the lamb for two days; we think you will find that the fresh aromatic tastes are worth it.

Marinating the Lamb

½ medium onion, chopped
½ cup chopped fresh coriander leaves
One 1-inch cube fresh ginger, chopped
1 tablespoon coriander seeds, toasted in a dry skillet
   for 5 minutes and crushed
2 cloves garlic, halved
1 teaspoon black peppercorns, crushed
2 tablespoons sea salt
½ cup strained lemon juice
¼ cup olive oil
One 7-pound leg of lamb,
   boned and separated into its three parts

   Place all the ingredients except the lamb
in a bowl and mix.
Place the lamb in a glass dish
and spread the mixture over the lamb.
Cover the dish and let the lamb marinate
in the refrigerator for 2 days, turning once or twice.

Cooking the Lamb

3 large ripe tomatoes, cored and roughly cut up
1 cup dry white wine
3 tablespoons imported Dijon mustard
Kosher salt
Freshly ground black pepper
¼ pound lightly salted butter, cut into small pieces

   Drain the lamb and reserve the marinade.

Heat the grill to hot.

In a heavy saucepan,
bring the tomatoes and white wine to a boil.
Lower the heat and cook at a simmer for about 20 minutes,
or until the mixture is thick.
Rub the mixture and ¼ cup of the reserved marinade liquid
through a fine strainer into a heatproof bowl.
Set aside.

Wipe the lamb dry and set on a grill over hot coals.
Baste often with the remaining marinade
and turn after 10 minutes.
Cook 10 minutes on the other side.
Roll the lamb in the remaining marinade
and let rest 5 minutes before slicing.

Meanwhile, beat the mustard into
the reserved tomato mixture.
Season with salt and pepper.
Set the bowl over boiling water to heat.
When hot, beat in the butter bit by bit.
Serve with the lamb.

Serves 8.

Serving Suggestions:

Since this lamb dish comes with its own sauce which is
virtually a vegetable, you will, at most, want some rice or
good bread to serve with it. It might well be preceded by a
light soup or a fresh vegetable and followed—if you are
cooking this out of doors in the summer—by a fruit compote
or sorbet.

The Four Seasons
is one of my favorite
restaurants. The food and
the lovely atmosphere were
a real pleasure!

Roast Rack of Lamb with Leeks and Spinach

This is a thoroughly unusual preparation in that the bones are left in and Frenched, and more fat—more of the tail—is left on the chop than is usual in preparing the rack. This is so you will have more area to stuff. The stuffing itself is green and fresh in taste.

One 6-pound untrimmed double rack of lamb
8 tablespoons lightly salted butter
4 cups packed, sliced leeks, white and part of the green
4 garlic cloves
¼ teaspoon kosher salt
Freshly ground black pepper
Freshly grated nutmeg
4 cups (½ pound) packed fresh spinach,
   well washed and dried
1 cup Brown Veal Stock (see recipe, page 498)

Remove the thick fat layer around the rack
and split it into its two halves.
Trim the fat off the bone to within 1 inch of the eye.
Do not trim any closer,
or you won't have enough room for the stuffing.
Cut away all the fat between the trimmed bones.

With a long, thin knife,
cut behind the eye, against the bone,
through from one side of the rack to the other.
The hole should be to within ½ inch of the edge,
but be careful not to cut through; set aside.

Heat the oven to 400°F.

CYNTHIA GREGORY

In a large skillet, heat 4 tablespoons butter.
Add the leeks and garlic and cook over medium heat,
stirring often, for about 2 minutes.
Season with salt, pepper and nutmeg.
Add the spinach and sauté very slowly,
stirring frequently, for 5 minutes.
Drain the mixture in a colander and cool.
Discard the garlic cloves.

Divide the mixture in half
and stuff into the prepared holes of each rack.
Tie a string around the lamb
across the middle of the cavity.
Season the lamb well with salt and pepper.
Cover the exposed bones with foil to prevent burning.

Place the lamb in a roasting pan, fat side up.
Place in the oven and roast for 10 minutes.
Turn the racks over and roast an additional 15 minutes.

Remove the racks to the carving board
to rest for 5 to 10 minutes before carving.

Meanwhile, prepare the sauce.
Pour the fat out of the roasting pan
and pour in the veal stock,
scraping the bottom with a wooden spoon.
Strain the sauce into a small pan.
Skim off any excess fat and bring to a boil.
Whisk in the remaining 4 tablespoons butter.

Carve the racks into individual chops.
Spoon some sauce over the chops
and put the rest in a sauceboat.

Serves 4.

Serving Suggestions:

Since the stuffing of this dish consists of green vegetables,
another green vegetable would be redundant. A very
special accompaniment would be Gorgonzola Polenta
(page 408), preceded by a light first course like Duckling
Consommé (page 158). In season, Figs with Whipped
Cream (page 458) would be a very luxurious dessert.

Beef

Chef Renggli enjoys experimenting with cuts of beef other than the usual American steak. We think the results are quite special and yet still satisfy those who feel dinner isn't complete without beef.

Bar Room Sirloin Tartare

This dish is one of our most popular. It is thinly sliced rather than ground—rather like an Italian carpaccio. We serve this as a main course at luncheon.

Olive oil
Four 2-ounce pieces choice sirloin, trimmed of all fat
Kosher salt
Freshly ground black pepper

Brandied Mayonnaise
1 cup Mayonnaise (see recipe, page 517)
2 tablespoons imported Dijon mustard
3 tablespoons brandy
¼ cup chopped chives

Oil eight sheets of parchment paper
(the sheets must be larger than the intended serving plate).
Place each piece of meat between two sheets
and pound with a meat pounder or a heavy pot,
sliding it out from the center to the edges.
Do not let the edges get too thin.
Pound the meat until it is evenly paper thin.

Remove the top layer of paper and
place each piece of meat on a serving plate; peel off
remaining paper.
Trim to fit the plate; season with salt and pepper.

Mix the ingredients for the brandied mayonnaise
and serve on the side.

Serves 4.

Serving Suggestions:
We often serve this with Bar Room Slaw (page 397). A good beer or a light Tuscan Chianti, a fruity and young red wine, would be a fine accompaniment.

Steak Tartare

Oreste Carnevali, who has been with The Four Seasons for fourteen years and is headwaiter in the Pool Room, prepares a steak tartare that is a great favorite of those who lunch or sup in that room.

12 ounces bottom round, all fat removed, ground
2 egg yolks
4 anchovy fillets
18 capers
¼ cup finely chopped onion
2 tablespoons chopped fresh chives or parsley
Anchovy oil or olive oil
1 to 2 teaspoons Worchestershire sauce
2 teaspoons kosher salt
2 teaspoons freshly ground black pepper
1 tablespoon American spicy brown mustard
1 teaspoon red wine vinegar

Place the beef on a platter and shape into an oval.
Make two dents in the meat and place an egg yolk in each.

On a space next to the meat,
mash the anchovies to a paste with a fork against a spoon.
Next, mash the capers in the same way.
With two blunt knives,
mix together the meat, egg yolks, anchovies and capers.

Mash the onions lightly and mix them into the meat
with the chives and a drop of anchovy oil.
Mix in the remaining seasonings,
still using the blunt knives, until well blended.

Reshape the meat and
score the top with crisscross lines.

Serves 2.

Serving Suggestions:

As with the previous recipe, you will probably want a good salad, bread, and beer or perhaps a light red wine.
Today it is very popular to serve steak tartare for hors d'oeuvres on thin rounds of hard pumpernickel.

Hot or Cold Sirloin of Beef

There are times when nothing tastes as good or looks as spectacular as a large cut of roasted beef. This one, which is protected by a salt-and-flour paste, thus retaining natural juices and seasonings, is good served either hot or cold.

One 4-pound piece of boneless sirloin with ¼ inch
   of fat left on top
1 tablespoon freshly crushed black peppercorns
1 tablespoon freshly crushed white peppercorns
5 crushed allspice seeds
1 ½ cups kosher salt
1 ½ cups sea salt
1 ½ cups all-purpose flour

Heat the oven to 425°F.

Make shallow slits with a sharp knife
in a crisscrossing pattern across the fat.

Combine the peppers with the allspice
and rub into the top and bottom of the meat.

In a large bowl, combine the salts with the flour.
Add about 1 ¼ cups of cold water,
a little at a time, mixing thoroughly.
Mixture should be thick and pasty.

Place the meat, fat side down, in a roasting pan.
Cover the top with the salt mixture,
pressing it down over about 1 inch of the sides.
Do not coat the rest of the sides and the ends.
Place the roasting pan over high heat
on top of the stove until it sizzles.

Place the pan in the preheated oven for 15 minutes.
Turn the heat down to 400°F.
and cook an additional 30 minutes.
Remove and let the meat rest
until it reaches room temperature, about 30 minutes.

Remove the salt coating and discard.
Serve the meat at room temperature.
Do not refrigerate. Just before serving,
slice the meat on the bias into ¼-inch-thick slices.

Serve with Potato Salad (see recipe, page 403)
on a separate plate
and Beefsteak Tomato with Basil and Red Onions
(see recipe, page 401).

Serves 8.

Better than Bun & Burger — terrific!

JAMES COCO

Tournedos of Beef with Herb and Mustard Butter

This is one of those delicious recipes which is amazingly easy to prepare. In fact, the primary taste component, the seasoned butter, can be prepared ahead. It can even be made in quantities as much as a month ahead and frozen. This leaves you nothing to do but buy the meat and sauté it, taking the butter out of the freezer as you start the sautéing process.

1 pound plus 2 tablespoons lightly salted butter,
    softened to room temperature
6 tablespoons imported green-herb Dijon mustard (see page
    518)
2 sprigs fresh chervil
5 large fresh sage leaves
4 large fresh basil leaves
2 sprigs fresh tarragon
1 sprig fresh marjoram
¾ cup finely chopped parsley
3 tablespoons finely chopped shallots
2 tablespoons Armagnac
Freshly ground black pepper
Six 4-ounce beef tournedos
Kosher salt
6 tablespoons dry red wine
1 tablespoon Glace de Viande (meat glaze)
    (see recipe, page 502)

Place 1 pound butter and the mustard
in the work bowl of a food processor
fitted with the metal blade.
Process until smooth and light.
Add the herbs and shallots and
continue to process until completely blended and smooth.
Pour the Armagnac in through the feed tube
and continue processing until smooth.
Season well with black pepper, blending well.
Divide the seasoned butter into six even pieces.
Shape them into rounds and refrigerate until needed.

Wrap each tournedo in a damp kitchen towel.
Pound each with a mallet to flatten to half its thickness.
Lightly season the meat with salt and pepper.

In a skillet large enough to hold the six tournedos,
heat the remaining 2 tablespoons butter until browned.
Sauté the tournedos in the butter
to the desired state of doneness
(about 2 minutes a side for rare), turning with tongs.
Transfer the meat to a side dish and keep warm.

Remove any fat from the skillet.
Add the wine and meat glaze, whisking until smooth
and scraping the bits on the bottom of the pan
into the sauce.

For each serving, place a portion of the herb butter
in the middle of an individual serving plate.
Place a tournedo over the butter
and spoon a few spoonfuls of the skillet juices
over the meat.

Serves 6.

Serving Suggestions:
Almost any of our special vegetables (pages 363 to 394)
could go with this dish, depending on the season of the year.
A rich soup such as Cream of Artichokes (page 153) would
be an elegant precedent and a Bar Room Chocolate Cake
(page 428) a memorable end. The simple elegance of this
menu deserves a Chablis of a good year for the first course
and a fine red Bordeaux for the tournedos.

Tournedos of Beef with Six Peppers

This recipe, created by Chef Renggli for the Barrel Tasting Dinner of 1978, not only tastes good but also reflects Chef Renggli's respect for pepper in its many varieties.

1 teaspoon white peppercorns
1 teaspoon black peppercorns
¾ teaspoon Szechuan peppercorns
1 teaspoon grains of paradise peppercorns
¼ teaspoon crushed red pepper flakes
1 teaspoon green peppercorns packed in salt water,
    drained and crushed
1 teaspoon kosher salt
Twelve 3½-ounce beef tournedos
4 tablespoons lightly salted butter
¼ cup dry red wine
¼ cup Glace de Viande (meat glaze)
    (see recipe, page 502)
1½ tablespoons olive oil
2 red bell peppers, peeled, seeded, de-ribbed
    and cut into long, thin julienne (see note, page 37)
2 green bell peppers, peeled, seeded, de-ribbed
    and cut into long, thin julienne (see note, page 37)

Crack the white, black, Szechuan and grains of paradise peppercorns coarsely with the bottom of a heavy saucepan or skillet.
Mix with the pepper flakes, crushed green peppercorns and salt.
Sprinkle each tournedo very lightly with some of the above mixture on both sides.
There will be some mixture left over.

Heat two large, heavy skillets.
To each, add 2 tablespoons butter.
When the butter foams and begins to subside
and turn light brown, add the beef and cook,
2 minutes to a side for rare meat and longer for medium
or well done.
Remove to a side dish and keep warm.

Pour off the fat from the skillets
and deglaze each with 2 tablespoons red wine,
scraping the bottoms of the pans.
Add 2 tablespoons meat glaze to each, allowing it to melt,
and then whisking to combine the pan juices.
Return the meat to the skillets
and coat each piece with some of the syrupy pan juices.

In a separate skillet,
heat the oil and sauté the pepper strips for an instant.
Garnish each tournedo with a few strips.
Serve at once.

Serves 6.

Serving Suggestions:

This dish, garnished with the red and green bell peppers,
needs little else on the plate except some steamed new
potatoes or maybe rice, or a white vegetable purée. You
might want to begin this meal with one of our cold mousses
(pages 27 to 33) and end with a Raisin and Grappa Sorbet
(page 477). Accompany this dish with a wine with some
muscle such as a heavy Zinfandel, or Bull's Blood—the
Hungarian Egri Bikavér.

*thank you for the room with Air
and beautiful food and wines*

J. Fairchild

JOHN FAIRCHILD

Beef Paillard

This is one of the most popular paillards served in the Bar Room.

Four 1-inch-thick sirloin steaks, bone removed
Vegetable oil
Kosher salt
Freshly ground black pepper

Heat a grill.

Trim all the fat off the steaks.
Butterfly them by holding your knife parallel to the board
and slicing each one half through the long side
to about ½ inch from the edge.

Oil eight sheets of parchment paper.
Place each steak on a sheet of paper
and top with a second sheet.
Pound the steaks with a meat pounder
or the bottom of a heavy pot until they are paper thin.

Remove the top sheets of paper
and place the meat on the hot grill.
Remove the second sheets.
Cook the meat until it sears, about 30 seconds.
With tongs, lift it and rotate it 45 degrees.
Cook an additional 30 seconds.
Turn over and sear the second side, about 1 minute.

Serve with the first side up
sprinkled with salt and pepper.

Serves 4.

Serving Suggestions:
You might serve this with either the Bar Room Slaw
(page 397) or Zucchini with Pesto (page 367). As a light
lunch or after-the-theater supper, it doesn't require a first
course. We simply recommend fruit and cheese or a sorbet
for those who want it after. It would be hard to imagine a
pleasant red wine that you could not drink with this dish.

Boiled Beef

More of Chef Renggli's dishes are original than are conventional, but when he does do a classic dish such as a boiled beef, he does it up splendidly. A boiled beef has been on the menu of The Four Seasons, on and off, since it opened. We think this is a particularly nice one.

Preparing the Vegetables

In preparing the vegetables,
reserve the peels of the celery root, carrots and parsnips
with the leek greens and celery strings.
These will be the bouquet garni for the beef.

3 celery roots
3 carrots
3 parsnips
½ lemon
3 small leeks
3 celery ribs
1 small head cabbage

Wash the vegetables well.
Peel the celery roots, carrots and parsnips,
reserving the peels.
Rub lemon juice on the celery root to prevent discoloration.
Cut the vegetables into even oval shapes,
about 1½ inches long.
You will need six pieces of each vegetable.

Trim the leeks, saving the greens for the bouquet garni.
Cut the whites into six even pieces.
Peel the strings off the celery
and add to the bouquet garni.
Cut the celery into six even pieces.

Core the cabbage and place it in a saucepan.
Cover with cold water.
Bring the water to a boil
and cook the cabbage for 2 to 3 minutes.
Drain well.

Preparing the Beef

Two 6-inch marrow bones
2 pounds beef bones
3 large cloves garlic
1 onion, halved and burnt in a greaseless skillet
  over high heat
1 small bunch parsley stems
2 sprigs fresh marjoram or 1 teaspoon dried marjoram
6 whole cloves
2 bay leaves
1 whole nutmeg, broken into 4 pieces
Kosher salt
Freshly ground black pepper
5 pounds chicken steak (tafelspitz) with all but
  ¼ inch fat removed from the meat

Place the marrow and beef bones in a large pot.
Add cold water to cover.
Bring to a boil and blanch for 5 minutes.
Drain and wash well to rid the bones of the scum
that comes to the top. Remove the marrow from the bones
and reserve.

Place the bones, bouquet garni
and remaining ingredients, except the meat, in a clean pot.
Cover with cold water.
Bring slowly to a boil; skim well.
Reduce the heat to a simmer and add the meat.
Skim occasionally.
Cook for about 2 hours, or until the meat is fork tender,
turning the meat over after about 1 hour.

I enjoyed my first visit very much!
Julie Nixon Eisenhower

JULIE NIXON EISENHOWER

Remove the beef and set aside.
Place a strainer lined with a dampened kitchen towel
over a clean pot.
Pour the cooking liquid (beef broth) through.
Reserve the garlic cloves.
Discard the remaining solids.
Slice the marrow into six pieces; set aside.

Preparing the Cabbage Packets
1 bunch Italian parsley
Kosher salt
Freshly ground black pepper
Freshly grated nutmeg

Heat the oven to 400°F.

Remove the ribs from the blanched cabbage leaves.
Cut the leaves in half lengthwise.
Take twelve halves and overlap each pair
on your work surface.
In the center of each pair of leaves,
place some Italian parsley and half a reserved garlic clove.
Chop enough of the remaining cabbage
to make about 1 cup.
Divide it among the cabbage leaves.
Season each packet with salt, pepper and nutmeg.
Fold the bottom leaves over the fillings;
then fold in the sides and roll up.
Place the packets, one at a time,
in a clean kitchen towel.
Twist to squeeze out the liquid.

Place the packets in a baking dish
just large enough to hold them in one layer.
Spoon ½ cup of the reserved beef broth over the packets.
Cover with foil and
bake in the preheated oven for 12 minutes.

Cooking the Vegetables
Bring a large pot of lightly salted water to a boil.
Add the prepared celery root, carrot, parsnip, leek
and celery and cook for about 5 minutes,
or until just cooked through.
Drain.

Serving

Crushed black peppercorns
⅓ cup finely chopped chives

Heat the remaining beef broth and meat.
Season the broth to taste with pepper.
(To keep the broth clear,
wrap 1 tablespoon crushed peppercorns in a cloth.
Dip it in the broth for 10 seconds; squeeze.
If necessary, repeat.)
Place the broth in a tureen and sprinkle the chives on top.

Slice the meat and
place a slice with one piece of each prepared vegetable,
a marrow slice and one cabbage packet
in each of six individual soup bowls.
Spoon some broth over everything in each bowl.

Serve with sea salt, freshly grated horseradish
and an assortment of mustards,
such as Pommery, Düsseldorf and Dijon.

Serves 6.

Serving Suggestions:

Since this dish brings its first course and vegetables with it,
all you need to do is choose a salad and dessert. Boiled
beef, in one form or another, appears in almost every
European cuisine—from France to Switzerland, Italy, and
certainly Austria and Hungary, suggesting a multitude of
beverage choices for this dish. Consider a light Hungarian
red wine, such as Vilány; a first-growth Beaujolais, such as
Fleurie; or a California Gamay of a good year.

March 1976.

Thank you for all the fine times

Lillian Hellman

LILLIAN HELLMAN

Côte de Boeuf Four Seasons

Boeuf à la ficelle is a classic French dish made by suspending beef either by string or cheesecloth in a fine beef broth to gently poach until cooked but still rare. We had not previously seen it done with a côte de boeuf but think it works very well.

The sauce is somewhat unusual, more Italian than French in its derivation. It would also be excellent on the preceding Boiled Beef. The sauce should be started the day before, but you could also make it several days ahead.

1¾ pounds côte de boeuf (prime ribs of beef)
4 quarts strained Beef Bouillon (see recipe, page 503)
Sea salt
Côte de Boeuf Sauce (recipe follows)

The meat should be trimmed of most of the fat but the bone left intact.
The meat will cook suspended in the bouillon.
To do this, tie the meat like a package.
Then, tie the meat to a long skewer so the meat will be suspended about 8 inches below the skewer.

Bring the bouillon to a boil in a stockpot.
Lower heat to a simmer.
Suspend the meat in the pot
so the skewer rests across the top
and the meat is completely covered with stock.
Cook for 25 minutes (15 minutes to the pound) for rare meat.

Remove the meat and drain.
Let settle for 5 minutes before slicing.
Remove the bone and slice on the bias.
Place on a large platter sprinkled with sea salt.
Serve with the sauce on the side.

Serves 2.

Côte de Boeuf Sauce

2 red bell peppers, peeled, seeded, de-ribbed
    and cut into ¼-inch squares (see note, page 37)
2 green bell peppers, peeled, seeded, de-ribbed
    and cut into ¼-inch squares (see note, page 37)
1 tablespoon green peppercorns packed in salt water,
    drained
1 teaspoon green peppercorn juice
⅓ cup finely sliced shallots
2 bunches fresh chives, snipped
2 to 3 cloves garlic, blanched in boiling water
    for 1 minute, peeled and crushed
¼ cup chopped pine nuts
½ cup chopped parsley
¼ cup chopped capers
½ cup cornichons, cut into ¼-inch cubes
¼ cup imported green-herb Dijon mustard (see page 518)
1½ cups olive oil
Juice of 1 lemon

Combine the bell peppers, peppercorns,
peppercorn juice, shallots, chives, garlic, pine nuts,
parsley, capers and cornichons in a mixing bowl.
In a separate bowl, whisk the mustard
with the olive oil and lemon juice.
Fold in the vegetable and herb mixture.
Refrigerate overnight so the flavors meld.

Serve at room temperature with the Côte de Boeuf.

Serving Suggestions:

Boiled potatoes make a nice accompaniment to whatever
sauce is left. You will not need a salad but might want a fruit
dessert such as the Fruit Flan (page 466).

The energetic taste of the sauce requires a full
Romanée-Conti, a great St. Emilion Bordeaux or an older,
cherished California Cabernet.

Beef Roulade

Beef Roulade is native to our homeland, and though not typical of the restaurant's cuisine, it is one of the few dishes of ours that can be made ahead and be reheated—which is very practical.

6 slices bacon, cut in half crosswise
Twelve 4-ounce slices top round beef
Twelve 3 x 1-inch caraway rye bread spears
Twenty-four 3 x 1-inch dill pickle spears
Kosher salt
Freshly ground black pepper
Fresh thyme
Hungarian sweet paprika
All-purpose flour
2 tablespoons lightly salted butter
2 very large or 4 medium onions, cut into ½-inch dice
12 ounces (1½ cups) beer
2 bay leaves
4 whole cloves
Snipped chives

Heat the oven to 375°F.

Cook the bacon pieces in a skillet until wilted, 1 to 2 minutes; set aside.

Pound each slice of meat with a pounder to about ⅛ inch thick.
Place a bread spear on each piece of meat, about a third of the way up from the bottom.
Surround each piece of bread with two pickle spears.
Season each with salt, pepper and fresh thyme.
Top with a piece of wilted bacon.

Roll up each piece of meat as you would cabbage: lift the bottom piece of meat over the bread and pickles; fold in the side flaps and roll up tightly.
Tie each package with string going lengthwise and crosswise.
Season each package with salt, pepper and paprika on all sides; dredge them lightly in flour.

Heat the butter over medium-high heat
in a 12-inch skillet.
When it is hot, add the rolls in one layer.
When they are brown on the bottom, about 3 minutes,
turn them on their sides.
Continue cooking and rotating until brown on all sides.
Remove the browned rolls to an ovenproof casserole.

Add the onions to the fat remaining in the pan.
Cook them, stirring occasionally,
until they are nicely browned, about 10 minutes.
Scrape the onions over the beef in the casserole.
Pour in the beer.
Tie the bay leaves and cloves in a piece of cheesecloth
and add to the casserole.

Cover the casserole and
place in the preheated oven for 1 hour 15 minutes.
Remove the cover and cook 15 minutes longer.

Remove the rolls to a serving plate
and the sauce to a saucepan.
Skim off the fat from the sauce.
Remove the bay leaves and cloves.
Cook over medium heat, whisking well
to break up the onions and thicken the sauce.
Season heavily with pepper and lightly with salt to taste.

Pour the sauce over the roulades.
Top with the snipped chives.
Serve with Potato Galettes (see recipe, page 414).

Serves 6.

Serving Suggestions:
Consider a peasanty red wine or a beer with this dish. If you
feel like a first course, try a cold Fruit Salad with Curried
Mayonnaise (page 40), or, more formally, Vegetable
Terrine, Pepper Sauce (page 66).

Game

We do quite a bit of game at The Four Seasons not only because it was classically part of great dinners but because we feel these foods express particularly well the tastes of late fall and winter. Today, Cornish game hens, partridges, squab and quail are often domesticated animals. While they do not have the fullness of flavor that the wild ones have, they are more readily available and have a longer season. Historically, game has been eaten either very fresh or after being well hung— exposed to a flowing current of air for a week or more. Either way, the game should be tender. If you hunt, you will have no trouble getting your basic ingredients. If you do not, you may find our Notes on Ingredients of some help.

Germans eat a great deal of game, and with it they drink their superb white wines. In France, Italy, Spain and this country, we tend to drink red wine with our game, even game birds. Good choices are the Pomerols from Bordeaux or the great Cabernets from the Napa Valley. A robust beer is also a good solution.

Partridge with Champagne Cabbage

Sauerkraut and game birds are a classic combination. Often an old pheasant is cooked slowly in the sauerkraut to tenderize the meat. Here, a young, fresh partridge or a well-hung partridge is briskly roasted and then served with the Champagne Cabbage (page 332). Partridge cooked this way can be accompanied by other vegetables such as the Potatoes Paillasson (page 416).

Six 1-pound partridges
6 fresh sage leaves
18 juniper berries, toasted in a dry skillet for 5 minutes
1 McIntosh apple, peeled, cored and cut into sixths
Kosher salt
Freshly ground black pepper
6 thin slices of pancetta (if unavailable, use fatback)
2 tablespoons vegetable oil
1 onion, cut into ¼-inch cubes
1 carrot, peeled and cut into ¼-inch cubes
1 celery rib, cut into ¼-inch cubes
½ cup dry red wine
1½ cups Chicken Stock or Brown Veal Stock
  (see recipes, pages 497 and 498)
¼ pound lightly salted butter, cut into pieces

Heat the oven to 425°F.

Cut the heads and feet from the birds.
Trim the wings at the second joint.
Reserve the trimmings.

Divide the sage and juniper berries into six parts.
Stuff one part into each bird's cavity
with a piece of apple.
Season with salt and pepper.
Place a piece of pancetta over each bird's breast
and tie into place.

Heat the oil in an ovenproof pan.
When the oil is hot, add the bird trimmings
and the prepared partridge on their sides.
Roast in the oven for 10 minutes.
Turn the birds on the other side
and roast another 10 minutes.

Turn the birds breasts side up
and add the chopped onion, carrot and celery.
Roast another 10 minutes.
If the breasts are not brown,
raise the oven temperature to brown.
Remove the birds to a hot platter and keep warm.

Pour off the fat in the pan.
Add the red wine to deglaze,
scraping the bottom of the pan with a wooden spoon.
Pour in the stock and the cavity juices from the birds.
Simmer 10 minutes.
Strain the pan ingredients into a smaller pan.
Remove any remaining fat.
Whisk in the butter until the sauce is thick.

To serve, remove the strings from the birds
and split them open
on either side of the breastbone so they are easier to eat.

Line a large round platter
with Champagne Cabbage (recipe follows)
and place the partridges
over the cabbage in a circle, legs facing in.
Pour the sauce over the birds.

Serves 6.

MICHAEL BENNETT

Champagne Cabbage

2 pounds sauerkraut
7 ounces lard
1 large onion, thinly sliced
One 1-inch cube fresh ginger
1 large clove garlic
2 McIntosh apples, peeled, cored and thinly sliced
Kosher salt
Freshly ground black pepper
2 cups Champagne

Heat the oven to 350°F.

Place the sauerkraut in a colander
and wash under cold running water.
Drain, then squeeze out the excess moisture.

In a large ovenproof skillet, heat the lard.
Add the onion, ginger and garlic
and sauté until lightly golden in color.
Add the apple slices
and toss to coat everything with the hot fat.
Stir in the sauerkraut; season with salt and pepper to taste.
Pour in the Champagne and stir.

Cover and place in the preheated oven for 1 hour.
Discard the ginger.
Taste for seasoning and serve hot.

Serves 6.

Note:

Leftover Champagne cabbage may be used to make
Potato Galettes (see recipe, page 414).

Serving Suggestions:

Champagne cabbage calls for Champagne, and one with a
slight acidity would go well with the sauerkraut. If you serve
the partridge with another vegetable, we suggest a red
Bordeaux or a light California Cabernet. You might wish to
precede the partridge with a Purée of Scallops (page 69) or
a Mussels and Spinach Millefeuille (page 125). After salad
and a cheese, which will allow you a red wine, finish with
Pear Mousse with Poached Pears (page 459).

Roast Quail with Sage and Fried Grapes

The special flavor of quail makes it suitable for both lunch and dinner. This is the perfect dinner version.

12 quail
12 fresh sage leaves
6 thin slices pancetta, halved crosswise
36 juniper berries, toasted in a dry skillet for 5 minutes
Kosher salt
Freshly ground black pepper
14 tablespoons lightly salted butter
¼ cup gin
½ cup dry red wine
1½ cups Brown Veal Stock (see recipe, page 498)

Heat oven to 450°F.

Cut the heads and feet from the quail.
Trim the wings at the second joint.
Reserve the trimmings.

Place a sage leaf over each pancetta piece.
Roll them up together and stuff one roll into each quail,
together with two juniper berries and a pinch of salt.
Reserve the remaining berries for the sauce.
Cover the ends of the feet with foil.

Thread a toothpick through each quail's thigh joints.
Coat each breast with 1½ teaspoons butter.

Arrange the quail
in a large greased pan with the reserved trimmings.
Roast 12 minutes, breast side up, in the preheated oven.
Transfer the birds to a heated dish.
Keep hot while you finish the sauce.

Discard the pan fat.
Deglaze with the gin and red wine,
scraping the bottom to loosen any stuck bits.
Strain the mixture into a clean saucepan.
Pour in the stock and simmer for 10 minutes.
Whisk in the remaining 8 tablespoons butter,
then the reserved juniper berries.
Readjust the seasoning.
Pour the sauce on the serving dish
and arrange the quail on top.

Serve with Fried Grapes (recipe follows).

Serves 6.

Fried Grapes

3 cups seedless green grapes
All-purpose flour
2 eggs, beaten
Fresh bread crumbs
Vegetable oil

Rinse the grapes; do not dry.
Roll them in the flour.
Coat with egg and toss in the bread crumbs.
They must be well coated.

Fill a deep pot with oil.
Heat it to about 375°F.
Add the grapes and fry for 15 to 20 seconds.
They should be light golden in color.
Remove with a slotted spoon and drain on absorbent paper.

Place in a napkin-lined dish to serve.

Serves 6.

Serving Suggestions:

A Gattinara or Barbaresco—good, full red wines of Italy—
would blend nicely with the quail and sage tastes. It is not
necessary to add any vegetable to this plate, so you might
want to start with an exciting Mushroom and Knob Celery
Soufflé (page 132) or a Purée of Seasonal Vegetables
(page 148) and follow with a salad. For dessert, we suggest
one or a combination of sorbets (pages 473 to 479).

ANN LANDERS

Broiled Quail with Bacon and Mustard

A Bar Room favorite, these quail should be zesty and crisp on the outside, rare and tender on the inside. We find they go well with a fresh green salad and a light California Zinfandel. This is a good luncheon dish.

3½ ounces (½ cup) imported green-peppercorn
   Dijon mustard
½ teaspoon freshly cracked black peppercorns
2 tablespoons gin
1 tablespoon olive oil
12 quail, cleaned and trimmed
12 slices bacon

Preheat the broiler.

In a bowl, using a wooden spoon,
stir the mustard and pepper until combined.
Gradually blend in the gin, then the oil.

Cut one quail down the back
on both sides of the backbone.
Cut away the neck and backbone.
Spread the bird open, skin side up, on your work surface.
Press the breastbone firmly
against the surface to flatten.
Repeat with the remaining quail.

no Problems here! the food is delicious — the service divine! — April 9. '76

Brush the insides of each bird with about
1 teaspoon of the mustard mixture.
Top with a slice of bacon.
Rub a broiler pan with oil or soft butter.
Arrange the quail, bacon side up, in the pan.

Broil 4½ minutes, then turn with tongs
and brush each bird again with some of the mustard mixture.
Broil 2 to 3 minutes longer.

Remove with tongs to a heated plate.

Serves 6.

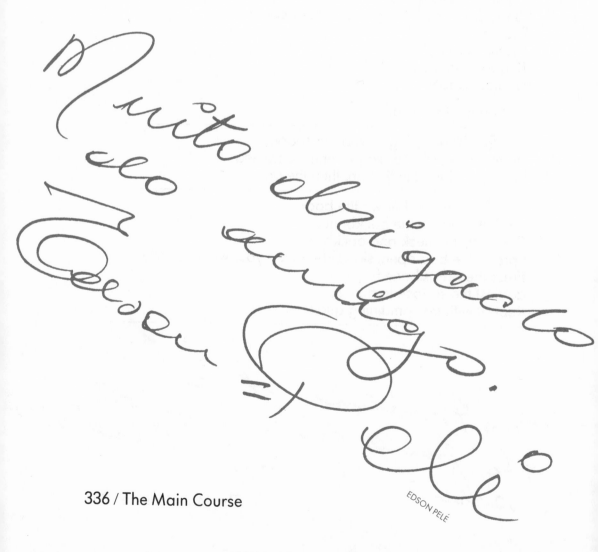

EDSON PELÉ

Cornish Game Hens with Oysters and Spinach

With a little searching, you can find fresh Cornish hens. These are infinitely better than the frozen, white-plastic-wrapped variety. Our unusual oyster stuffing may remind you of a stuffing from Colonial times, but the spinach and herbs make it lighter and more aromatic.

6 fresh 14- to 16-ounce Cornish game hens
13 tablespoons lightly salted butter
3 large shallots, cut into thin slices
1 packed cup coarsely chopped cooked spinach,
    squeezed dry
12 oysters, shucked
4 sprigs fresh tarragon, chopped
6 slices firm white bread, crusts trimmed
Kosher salt
Freshly ground black pepper
Freshly grated nutmeg
1 carrot, cut into ¼-inch cubes
1 onion, cut into ¼-inch cubes
1 celery rib, cut into ¼-inch cubes
½ cup dry white wine
1½ cups Brown Veal Stock (see recipe, page 498)

With scissors,
cut along on either side of the backbone of each hen.
Do not cut away the neck flap.
Use a paring knife to cut away the breastbone
as well as the ribs on each side.
Remove the thigh bones
but leave the drumsticks and wings intact.
Reserve all the bones for the sauce.

Heat the oven to 425°F.

Heat 2 tablespoons butter in a large skillet.
Add the shallots and sauté until tender.
Add the spinach and cook for about 3 minutes, stirring.

Roughly chop the oysters.
Place them in a bowl
with the spinach mixture and the tarragon.
Stir to blend well.

Cover the bread with cold water.
Let soak a few minutes, then squeeze dry.
Add to the spinach mixture.
Season to taste with salt, pepper and nutmeg.
Mix well and divide into six equal portions.

Season the birds inside and out with salt and pepper.
Stuff each bird with one portion of the mixture.
Using string, tie the bird to enclose the filling
and to keep the legs together.
Rub the skin of each bird with 1½ teaspoons butter.

Butter a roasting pan and add the birds,
on their sides, and the trimmings.
Roast for 10 minutes.
Turn the birds on the other side
and roast 10 minutes longer.
Turn the birds breast side up
and add the chopped carrot, onion and celery.
Roast another 15 minutes, or until the birds are cooked.

Remove the birds to a platter and keep warm.
Pour off the fat in the pan.
Add the wine and deglaze,
scraping the bottom with a wooden spoon.

Strain the pan ingredients into a small pan.
Add the stock and simmer for 10 minutes.
Remove any remaining fat.
Whisk in the remaining 8 tablespoons butter
until the sauce is thick.

Remove the strings from the birds
and serve with the sauce, placing some on the plates
and the rest in a sauceboat.

Serves 6.

Serving Suggestions:

In spring, a Risotto Primavera (page 98) and, in winter, a
Duck Liver Flan (page 83) would make perfect introductions
to this dish. Since the hens contain their own vegetables,
none need be provided. However, you might wish to serve a
salad after them. Complete the meal with a seasonal Fruit
Tart (page 464). For the wine, try one of the increasingly
interesting Napa Valley Pinot Noirs.

I love your restaurant!!!!
"in season".

Byron Janis

BYRON JANIS

10/4/77

Squab with Sweetbreads, Spinach and Crayfish

True squab are, of course, pigeons, wild pigeons being the most desirable. However, in descending order, domesticated pigeon will do, and you can even make this dish with what is called a squab chicken. The filling—stuffing seems too mundane a word for it—is unusual in its colors, ingredients and contrasting textures.

½ pair (about ½ pound) veal sweetbreads
Kosher salt
½ cup plus 1 tablespoon dry white wine
1¼ medium onions, the whole onion roughly cut up
14 tablespoons lightly salted butter
2 tablespoons minced shallots
6 medium (about ¼ pound) mushrooms, thinly sliced
2 sprigs chopped fresh tarragon
1 cup cooked, shelled crayfish tails (see note)
3 slices white bread, crusts trimmed
1 cup coarsely chopped cooked spinach
1 egg
Freshly ground black pepper
Six 12- to 14-ounce squabs, cleaned, livers reserved
1 carrot, roughly cut up
1 small celery rib
2 cups Brown Veal Stock (see recipe, page 498)

Soak the sweetbreads in several changes of cold water for 1 to 2 hours.
Carefully cut away
the connective tubes, gristle and fatty parts.

Place in a saucepan; cover with water.
Add salt, 1 tablespoon wine, and the onion quarter.
Cook at a simmer for 30 minutes.
Drain, discard the onion and cool the sweetbreads.
When cool, break them into 1-inch chunks,
and place them in a large mixing bowl.

Heat 2 tablespoons butter in a medium-sized skillet.
When the foaming subsides and the butter begins to brown,
add the shallots and mushrooms.
Sauté quickly, stirring, for 1 minute.
Add the tarragon and swirl to blend the flavors.
Remove the pan from the heat
and add the contents to the sweetbreads.
Add the crayfish.

Soak the bread in water to cover until soft.
Squeeze the bread and the spinach with your hands
or in a kitchen towel
to extract as much water as possible.
Add both to the mixing bowl.
Lightly beat the egg
and stir it into the mixture until blended.
Season with salt and pepper.
Divide into six equal portions.

With scissors,
cut along on either side of the backbone of each squab.
Do not cut away the neck flap.
Use a paring knife to cut away the breastbone
as well as the ribs on each side.
Remove the thigh bones
but leave the drumsticks and wings intact.
Reserve all the bones for the sauce.
Season the squabs' insides with salt and pepper.
Stuff each bird with a liver
and a sixth of the prepared filling mixture.
Using string, tie each bird to enclose the filling
and to keep the legs together.
Rub the skin of each bird
with 2 teaspoons butter, salt and pepper.
Refrigerate until ready to roast.

Heat the oven to 500°F.

Place the bones
with the carrot, remaining onion and celery in a pan.
Put in the oven for about 20 minutes.
When the bones are brown,
remove the pan from the oven and discard any fat.
Lower the oven temperature to 375°F.
Place the pan over a hot burner
and deglaze with ¼ cup white wine,
scraping the bottom with a wooden spoon.
Add the stock and bring to a boil.
Cook over high heat for 10 minutes,
or until the liquid has reduced by half.
Strain into a smaller pan, cool and skim the fat.
Reduce again until you have ½ cup; keep warm.

Roast the squabs in the preheated oven for 35 minutes,
10 minutes on each side and 15 minutes breast side up.
Remove squabs to a serving platter, cover loosely with foil
and return to the turned-off oven while you finish the sauce.

Pour the pan juices into the reduced stock
and skim off the fat.
Deglaze the pan with the remaining ¼ cup wine
and scrape that into the stock.
Cook over high heat until reduced to ½ cup.
Lower the heat
and beat in the remaining 8 tablespoons butter,
1 tablespoon at a time.

Remove the strings from the squabs
and serve hot with some of the sauce.

Serves 6.

Note:
If crayfish are not available, substitute ⅓ pound small,
cooked, shelled shrimp.

Serving Suggestions:
Since this dish is rich and varied, you might want a colorful
and simple first course, such as the Avocado with Tomato
and Basil Vinaigrette (page 34). For dessert try the Figs with
Whipped Cream (page 458). The combination of ingredients
in the stuffed squab deserves an exceptionally fine white
wine, perhaps a Meursault or a Chardonnay from Sonoma.

Scallops of Venison with Purée of Chestnuts

Many people tend to think of venison as a very heavy food. Here, trimmed into light scallops, it stays tender and pink and comparatively light. Be sure to allow enough time to prepare the sauce and chestnuts.

1 cup Game Sauce (see recipe, page 509)
Twelve 1½- to 2-ounce venison scallops, cut from the saddle
Kosher salt
Freshly ground black pepper
11 tablespoons lightly salted butter

Heat the game sauce in a small pan until it has reduced to ¾ cup.

Flatten the scallops with a meat pounder to a thickness of ¾ inch.
Season on both sides with salt and pepper.

Heat 8 tablespoons butter in two large skillets.
When the butter is foamy and brown, add the meat.
Sauté until browned on the bottom.
With tongs, turn the meat over and brown the second side.
The meat must remain pink in the middle.

Swirl the remaining 3 tablespoons butter into the game sauce.
Spoon some sauce on four individual plates.
Place three scallops on each plate.

Serve with Purée of Chestnuts (recipe follows).

Serves 4.

Purée of Chestnuts
3 pounds chestnuts, shelled and peeled
1 quart milk
½ stick cinnamon
One 2- to 3-inch orange peel
½ cup heavy cream
⅓ cup maple syrup
Pinch freshly grated white pepper
Pinch grated nutmeg

Place the chestnuts in a saucepan
with the milk and cinnamon stick.
Simmer over low heat for about 30 minutes.
Add the orange peel
and continue to simmer 1 hour longer,
or until the chestnuts are tender and sweet.

Remove and discard the orange peel and cinnamon.
Purée the chestnuts with the milk
in a food processor fitted with the metal blade.
With the machine running,
add the heavy cream and maple syrup in a stream.
Add the seasonings.
If you do not have a food processor,
purée the chestnuts through a food mill and beat the cream,
syrup and seasonings in with an electric mixer, or by hand.

Serves 4 to 6.

Serving Suggestions:
Venison is a fitting partner for the roundest and fullest red
wine in your cellar—a Burgundy from the Côte d'Or or a
Barolo from Piedmont aged with distinction. Consider
serving the Purée of Scallops (page 69) or A Feuilleté of Bay
Scallops (page 118) first. Finish triumphantly with Pear
Mousse with Poached Pears (page 459).

Roast Saddle of Venison

1 saddle of venison, hung for 2 to 3 weeks
Eighteen 3 x ¼-inch strips fatback, chilled

Heat the oven to 450°F.

Trim the flaps and all fat and membranes
from both the top and underside of the venison.
Using a larding needle,
lard the top of the saddle with crosswise strips of fatback,
going about ¼ inch deep.
Alternate the strips so the fat that shows on the top
is in a sort of checkerboard pattern.
Trim the extra fat protruding from the saddle and reserve.

Place the fatback trimmings
and any extra strips in a roasting pan; top with the saddle.
Roast in the preheated oven for 10 minutes.
Turn the venison and roast 10 to 15 minutes longer.
The meat will be medium-rare.
Let the meat rest for 10 minutes before carving.

Carve; serve with Game Sauce (see recipe, page 509).
Accompany the venison with Pear Baskets
and Cranberry Relish (see recipes, pages 421 to 422) or with
Purée of Chestnuts (see recipe, page 344).

Serves 6.

Variation:
If you prefer, bake the saddle of venison under a coating of
salt, following the recipe for Saddle of Lamb (page 304).

Serving Suggestions:
This is a dish to carve proudly at the table, as each slice
shows a neat pattern of meat and lard. For a light but
elegant first course, consider the Red Snapper and Salmon
Tartare (page 21). Conclude with a selection of sorbets. For
the venison, choose your biggest, best red wine.

Civet of Venison

It is a sad truth that deer yields more meat suitable for stewing than for roasting or sautéing. Luckily, some of the best venison dishes are stews, of which perhaps the best is this civet. A civet is a dish traditionally thickened by blood. In this country, you may find it difficult to buy blood, but the chocolate, which is used in game dishes in Spain, Austria and Germany, thickens and darkens the sauce very well. Remember, this is a dish that should marinate for two weeks.

4 pounds venison shoulder, cubed
1 recipe Civet Marinade (see recipe, page 508)
½ cup all-purpose flour
⅔ cup rendered duck or goose fat, or substitute oil
½ cup tomato purée
⅓ cup grappa
1 teaspoon unsweetened chocolate
⅓ cup beef blood (optional)

Garnish

½ cup belly bacon, diced, blanched for 1 minute
   in boiling water, dried and sautéed until crisp
½ cup pearl onions, peeled and cooked in butter until brown
½ cup mushrooms, quartered
   and sautéed in butter until browned
Finely chopped mixed fresh herbs
   (chervil, tarragon, parsley and chives)

Place the venison in a bowl.
Cover with civet marinade
and let marinate in the refrigerator for 2 weeks.
Remove the meat and reserve the marinade.
There should be about 2 cups marinade left.

Heat the oven to 350° F.

Dredge the venison with the flour.
Shake off the excess flour.
Divide the fat between two large frying pans
and sauté half the meat in each pan
until very well browned on all sides, about 10 minutes.
Scrape the meat into a large ovenproof casserole.

Pour half the reserved marinade into each frying pan
to deglaze, scraping the bottom with a wooden spoon.
Combine the liquids into one of the pans
after a minute or two.
Boil until the liquid is almost completely reduced,
about 10 minutes.
Stir in the tomato purée and simmer a moment longer.

Add the grappa and flame.
When the flames die down,
pour the contents of the pan over the venison.
Add 1 cup water to the same frying pan to deglaze.
Scrape the bottom
and add to the rest of the ingredients in the casserole.
Add another 3 cups water.
Bring the mixture to a boil on top of the stove,
cover and place in the oven for 2½ hours.

Strain the juices into a clean saucepan
and simmer them on top of the stove
until thick and rich, about 30 minutes.
Skim the fat from time to time.
While the sauce is simmering,
separate the venison cubes from the chopped vegetables
and seasonings in a strainer.
Discard the vegetables and seasonings.
Stir chocolate into the sauce.
When the sauce is ready, add the venison cubes.
Simmer together a few minutes to heat the venison through.
Stir in the blood.
Do not let the civet boil.

Turn into a casserole or deep serving dish.
Sprinkle with the bacon, onions, mushrooms
and mixed herbs.
Serve with Spätzle (see recipe, page 410).

Serves 8.

Serving Suggestions:
Select a light, relatively sauceless first course with this dish or
perhaps a clear soup such as Essence of Red Snapper with
Vesiga (page 162). For dessert, you might enjoy an Apple
Pithiviers (page 452). We hope you will serve a magnificent
red wine.

Civet of Mallard Duck

Like the civet of venison, this dish requires time for marination—but only one week rather than two. The sauce is also bound with chocolate and/or blood, giving it a rich brown color and a thick, complex taste.

Marinating the Ducks

Three 1½-pound mallard ducks
1 leek, washed and sliced
½ small celery root, peeled and sliced
3 shallots, quartered
2 garlic cloves, unpeeled and crushed
1 carrot, cut in thirds
10 juniper berries, toasted in a dry skillet for 5 minutes
1 teaspoon freshly crushed black peppercorns
1 large bay leaf
1 sprig fresh rosemary
2 tablespoons kosher salt
1 bottle (about 3 cups) red Bordeaux wine

With a sharp knife, remove the wings from the ducks.
Separate the wing tips from the rest of the wings.
Lift the breasts from each duck; bone and halve,
then cut each half into three pieces.
Separate the legs and thighs.
Bone the thighs and cut each into two pieces.
Cut the neck into three pieces.
Use the livers for another purpose.
Chop the carcasses and wing tips; reserve.

Mix together all the remaining ingredients.
Put the prepared duck pieces plus the hearts and bones
in a deep glazed earthenware, glass or stainless-steel bowl.
Pour the marinade over.
Toss until everything is well coated.
Cover the bowl and refrigerate for one week.

Cooking the Ducks

3 ounces fatback, cut into ½-inch cubes
¼ cup all-purpose flour
2 tablespoons grappa
Kosher salt
Freshly ground black pepper
One 2-inch piece orange peel
1 teaspoon grated unsweetened chocolate
2 tablespoons beef blood (optional)
2 tablespoons red currant jelly
½ cup heavy cream
2 egg yolks

Drain the bones, pieces of duck and vegetables.
Reserve the bones, duck, vegetables and marinade
in separate containers.

Heat the oven to 375°F.

Sauté the fatback in a large skillet
until it renders its fat and turns light brown.
Add the duck pieces without crowding the pan
and sauté 2 minutes.
Turn each piece and sauté 2 minutes longer.
With a slotted spoon,
transfer the duck pieces to a deep casserole.
Add the bones to the skillet and sauté until browned.
Add to the duck.
In the same fat, sauté the drained vegetables
until lightly browned, about 10 minutes.
Add to the duck.

Pour off all but 2 tablespoons fat.
Add the flour and cook, stirring, for 1 minute.
Add the grappa and orange peel.
Slowly stir in the reserved marinade.
Bring to a boil.
Pour over the contents in the deep casserole.
Cover and place in the preheated oven
to braise for 1 hour 45 minutes.

Remove the duck; skim off the fat;
strain the sauce into a saucepan,
pressing on the bones and vegetables
to extract all the liquid.
Bring it to a boil.
Season with salt and plenty of black pepper.
Whisk in the chocolate, beef blood and currant jelly.
Simmer over low heat for a few minutes;
do not let the sauce boil.
Remove the orange peel; readjust the seasonings.
Arrange the duck pieces in six 1-cup custard cups.
Divide the sauce among the cups.

Place the cream in a small saucepan
and cook until reduced to ¼ cup.
Beat the egg yolks in a small bowl,
then whisk in the hot cream.
Scrape the mixture back into the saucepan
and heat until it thickens.
Season to taste with salt and pepper.
Spoon some of the mixture on top of each cup.
Run under the broiler to glaze.

Serves 6.

Note:

The civet can be prepared a day or two in advance. Reheat in a bain-marie, then top with the glaze and run under a hot broiler to brown.

Serving Suggestions:

As this dish has a light glaze on it, you could serve a dark starch on the same plate such as Wild Rice with Pine Nuts (page 417). A cheerful contrast of color could be provided by Sautéed Sugar Snap Peas (page 380), if available, or Glazed Baby Carrots (page 376). Begin with a Crabmeat Mousse (page 33) and end with a soothing Coconut Caramel Pudding (page 434). This civet, although still robust, is somewhat lighter than the Civet of Venison (page 346). With the duck, try a fine Bordeaux from Saint-Estèphe or a young Zinfandel from California.

Epigrammes of Wild Boar

What, you may ask, is an epigram? An epigram is a short and witty, insightful statement, the kind of thing to which Oscar Wilde was much addicted. In culinary terms (and spelled "epigramme"), it is a small, extremely tasty bit of meat, cut in slices, breaded and sautéed or grilled. Our version is done with boar and flavored with mustard.

Marinating the Boar

One 4-pound leg of wild boar, bones removed and cut in two
½ cup red wine vinegar
1 bottle (about 3 cups) dry red wine
1 bunch parsley stems
½ onion, quartered
½ leek, washed and roughly cut up
1 celery root, peeled and roughly cut up
6 cloves garlic, halved
1 carrot, roughly cut up
5 bay leaves
10 whole cloves
10 juniper berries, toasted in a dry skillet for 5 minutes
1 ½ teaspoons freshly crushed black pepper
2 tablespoons kosher salt

In a glass bowl, place the boar and bones.
Add the remaining ingredients.
Cover the bowl and refrigerate 7 to 10 days,
turning the boar from time to time.

Cooking the Boar

3 tablespoons olive oil
½ cup tomato purée
⅓ cup all-purpose flour
1 quart Brown Veal Stock (see recipe, page 498)
3 tablespoons beef blood (optional)

Remove the meat and bones from the marinade and
wipe dry.
Drain the herbs and vegetables.
Reserve both liquid and solids.

Heat the oven to 375°F.

Heat the olive oil in a deep ovenproof saucepan
and brown the meat and bones evenly on all sides.
Remove the meat and set aside.
Add the drained herbs and vegetables
and continue to sauté, stirring,
until everything is nicely browned.
Stir in the tomato purée, then the flour.
Moisten with the brown stock and 1 cup reserved marinade.
Return the boar meat to the pan.
Bring to a boil, cover and set in the preheated oven
for 3 hours, or until the meat is tender.

Remove the pan from the oven
and separate the meat from the sauce.
Let the meat cool completely.
Strain the cooking juices into a clean saucepan
and bring to a boil.
Skim off any fat that rises to the surface.
Cook the sauce until it is reduced to a good consistency;
you should have about 3 cups.
Stir in the blood,
being careful not to let the sauce boil.

Finishing the Dish

All-purpose flour
1 cup imported green-herb Dijon mustard (page 518)
8 egg yolks
Fresh white bread crumbs
½ cup clarified butter

Carve the boar into slices about ¼ inch thick.
Dust each slice with flour.
Mix the mustard with the egg yolks.
Spread the mixture on both sides of each slice
and roll in the bread crumbs.
Heat the clarified butter in a large skillet until hot.
Add the slices
and sauté until they are golden on both sides.

Place some sauce on six individual plates
and top with several slices of boar.
Serve with Gorgonzola Polenta (see recipe, page 408)
on the side.

Serves 6.

Serving Suggestions:

A rare dinner such as this might begin with A Feuilleté of
Bay Scallops (page 118) and finish with a Frozen Chocolate
Soufflé (page 432). Clearly, this is a meal for Champagne
and your best Bordeaux or a fine Cabernet.

For Tom + Paul —
perfect example of
the American Dream —
Bill Safire

WILLIAM SAFIRE

Merci pour la bonne soupe.
Si nous pouvions dessiner
  comme vous faites la cuisine
  ce dessin serait un chef-
      d'oeuvre.

M, 26-III-'79.

Très amicalement

José Ferrer

The Four Seasons
Special Dinners

The Four Seasons Fall Foursome Dinner

October 3, 1979

Dom Ruinart, Blanc de Blancs, 1973	A Fall Savory
Johannisberger, Erntebringer Riesling Kabinett, Graf von Schönborn, 1975	Marinated Breast of Capon
Chardonnay, R. Mondavi, 1977	Ramekin of Oysters and Periwinkles
Corton-Charlemagne, Bonneau du Martray, 1975	Seafood Risotto
	Pumpkin Bisque
Pinot Noir, David Bruce, 1973	Wild Mushrooms with Herbs
Vosne-Romanée, J. Drouhin, 1973	Green Pepper Duck
	Seasonal Greens with Cracklings
Echézeaux, Romanée-Conti, 1974	A Cheese
Moët et Chandon Imperial Brut, 1971	Desserts
Calvados, Montgommery	Demi-Tasse

THE FOUR SEASONS

Foursome Dinners

A few years ago, to celebrate with our most loyal customers the beginning of each of the seasons of the year, we decided to have a gala dinner for no more than forty, all seated at one long table. These dinners have become a tradition and now, four times a year, we give Chef Renggli free rein to create menus for these Foursome Dinners that challenge and excite him. We then pay homage to his efforts by selecting perfectly balanced wines.

We thought you might enjoy seeing how Seppi planned his succession of courses and how we, in turn, planned a succession of accompanying wines. We feel it is a good example of how we like to think about the organization of a meal and the marriage of food and wine.

While you may not be able to find all the wines, our description should permit you to select comparable wines if you wish to create this evening at home. Of course, you can create your own dinner, or even prepare a briefer version of this one, by choosing only a few courses such as the Seafood Risotto, Pumpkin Bisque and Green Pepper Duck followed by cheese and a dessert.

The menu for a recent autumn dinner is opposite, our comments below. All the recipes can be found in the pages of the book.

Dom Ruinart Blanc de Blancs is a Champagne with a small production. The premier wine of this house, this six-year-old vintage wine was mature but not over-aged, round and soft without sweetness. This festive beginning was matched by the festiveness of quail as an unusual appetizer, the breasts and legs prepared separately as explained on pages 108 to 111.

We sat down to the lightest of the dishes on our menu, the Marinated Breast of Capon, breathtakingly beautiful in its flowerlike presentation. The barely cooked, delicately seasoned dish called for a fruity, fresh wine with a reasonable amount of acidity. We chose the Kabinett, normally the driest and lightest of the great German wines. Those of 1975 have a little more depth and perhaps a hint of sweetness because it was such a great year. This particular Kabinett is a fine wine from a pocket-sized vineyard.

Having excited people with a great Champagne and an elegant German wine, we then jumped to an American varietal wine from Napa

Valley with the strength of youth and the richness of all Mondavi wines, which was served with the Ramekin of Oysters and Periwinkles.

Having already served three white wines, we had the interesting problem of what to serve next. Following the rule that calls for moving from lighter to heavier, we decided on the richest of the French Burgundies to serve with the Seafood Risotto, which shows that a dish of Italian inspiration does not necessarily require an Italian wine. There is enough richness in the dish to stand up to the Burgundy, yet the creaminess of the risotto is not assaulted by too much acidity.

Great dinners usually have sorbets in the middle to clear the palate and permit diners to go from one part of the meal to another. Palates are often chilled by sorbets, which have become something of a cliché, so we often serve soup as our palate clearer instead. Soup is commonly served at the beginning of a meal. However, we find that one of the pleasures of our big dinners is to begin with marvelous wines which soups cannot often support.

For this dinner, we served a smooth Pumpkin Bisque. Pumpkin is a native American fruit at its best in the fall. We use the calabaza because it is less fibrous than the ordinary American variety. This subtly evocative but rich soup paved the way for a new series of tastes beginning with the wild mushrooms so typical of the fall. These have a meaty flavor but are lighter than a true meat, and they give the meal a rich taste without weight. The Pinot Noir, the great wine grape of Burgundy, has been less successful in California. However, this unusual wine of David Bruce which we served with the mushrooms has developed enough to show the potential of the wine, which is beginning to be made with more attention.

In a classic dinner, game would be served for this course, traditionally the dish with the heaviest taste. While not invented for this meal, the Green Pepper Duck fit marvelously with its crisp skin and rich, creamy sauce combining complex flavors.

With it, we served the Vosne-Romanée 1973, a red Burgundy of a seductive and drinkable year. The Romanée district is known for wines with a distinctive and full nose which suggests the earthy taste that follows. Some even say there is a hint of truffle.

For the salad course, Seppi played a game with the flavors by continuing with the duck flavorings in the cracklings on the salad. As always, we did not serve wine with the salad, believing no wine can stand up to the vinegar in the dressing.

Marvelous as the Romanée was, good as was the grower, it was interesting to compare it with the Echézeaux, the wine of the Domaine, which has been the most prestigious vineyard in Burgundy for hundreds of years. The comparison of the wines show the variations possible in a neighboring region. It is a tough wine able to stand up to cheese which is fatty. The St. Hubert we served merits and supports tough wines and, in fact, softens them.

Having reached this peak with the wines, we wanted a suitable end to the meal, but not a letdown, as with a great play which has a fifth act after the high point of drama in the fourth. Therefore, having begun with a Champagne, we decided to end with another Champagne to complement the desserts. The Moët et Chandon from a truly great year is a cousin to the Dom Ruinart. For dessert, we served an assortment of small portions of various desserts. Making this dinner at home, however, you will need no more than a sorbet or, at the very most, a fruit flan.

To round out the evening, we served Calvados, fragrant from fall apples, as our after-dinner drink.

The Four Seasons
Third Annual California Vintners
Barrel Tasting Dinner

March 20, 1978

Red Snapper and Salmon Tartare	Freemark Abbey: Chardonnay, 1977/1975
Mousse of Trout in Leeks	Burgess Cellars: Chardonnay, Winery Lake, 1977/1975
Fillet of Striped Bass in Phyllo Leaves	Dry Creek Vineyard: Chardonnay, 1977/1975
Sweetbreads with Saffron and Melon	Callaway Vineyard & Winery: Fumé Blanc, 1977/1976
Oyster Broth	

Quail Eggs with Chopped Sirloin	Mondavi Winery: Pinot Noir, 1977/1975
Lobster Ragout	Joseph Phelps Vineyard; Syrah, 1977/1976
Confit d'Oie	Simi Winery: Zinfandel, 1977/1974
Calf's Brains in Mustard Crumbs	The Clos du Val Wine Co.: Zinfandel, 1977/1974
Tournedos of Beef with Six Peppers	Montevina Wines: Zinfandel, 1977/1974
Grapefruit and Tequila Sorbet	

A Game Bird Terrine	Mirassou Vineyards: Cabernet Sauvignon, 1977/1974
Medallions of Lamb with Coriander Butter	Stag's Leap Wine Cellars: Cabernet Sauvignon, 1977/1974
Chèvre d'Authon	Chappellet Vineyards: Cabernet Sauvignon, 1977/1971
Cappuccino Soufflé	Firestone Vineyards: Johannisberg Riesling, 1977/1976
Chocolate Truffles and Fig Strip	Chateau St. Jean: Johannisberg Riesling, 1977/1976
Demi-Tasse	
Mignardises	

THE FOUR SEASONS

Barrel Tasting Dinners

We at The Four Seasons have always had a commitment to fine wines. Over the years we have been excited by the increasingly spectacular range of California wines. We wanted to share our enthusiasm with our friends and so we created the Barrel Tasting dinners, which have now become an institution. At these dinners our guests sample wines from the previous year's vintage, wines still in the barrel. However, since many people are unaccustomed to drinking new wines—and because new wines can be as ungainly as a colt or as ugly as the proverbial duckling—with each new wine, we serve a wine of the same lineage, but of an earlier year which is more mature.

Each annual Barrel Tasting dinner has been different in terms of the varieties of wines chosen, the vineyards represented and, of course, the food. In the first years we planned a different course for each pair of wines. Recently we decided to reduce the number of courses and serve two or three wines of the same varietal grape at the same time. In this way, guests can compare those wines with each other as well as with the new wines.

Because wines star at the Barrel Tasting dinners, the menu is developed to best show off the wine. In a dinner of such complexity it is always difficult to have an interesting progression without tiring the palate. Therefore small, almost miniature, portions are necessary. We always care how our food looks, but through such a long dinner, more art than usual is needed to keep the food appetizing and exciting.

The elaborate Barrel Tasting menu illustrated on the facing page involved fourteen pairs of wine, beginning with the Freemark Abbey Chardonnay, a beautifully balanced wine with great elegance and freshness. Our Red Snapper and Salmon Tartare allowed the freshness to show without overpowering the wine.

The next wine, a Chardonnay from Burgess Cellars, was full-bodied, soft and velvety, with a remarkable finish. The Mousse of Trout in Leek, with its delicate butter sauce, was what we felt was needed with it.

The last Chardonnay, Dry Creek, was bigger and more complex than the others, allowing it to balance the rich Striped Bass in Phyllo Leaves.

A Fumé Blanc from Callaway, fresh and youthful, complemented the rich Ramekin of Sweetbreads with Saffron and Melon.

After the puff pastry-topped Oyster Broth, we had an intermission to allow our guests to stretch and our staff to clear and completely reset the tables.

We then returned to the dining room and to Mondavi's Pinot Noir, a light wine with a delicate bouquet, which was set off to advantage by the chopped sirloin topped with a quivering quail egg.

The Phelps Syrah was on its way to becoming a very big wine and needed the richness of a Lobster Ragout.

The Simi, a typical Zinfandel with a raspberry bouquet, complemented the goose in the confit. Moving on to a bigger, nuttier, more complex Zinfandel made in the style of Bordeaux, we served the Clos du Val, a good companion to the light mustard flavor of the calf's brains.

The third Zinfandel, from Montevina, was a robust wine. We served it with a robust dish, the Tournedos with Six Peppers.

To clear the palate we had a refreshing grapefruit sorbet followed by another intermission.

Our first Cabernet Sauvignon was a soft wine from Mirassou with which we served a game bird terrine. The Stag's Leap Cabernet Sauvignon was silky and elegant, reminiscent of the style of Médoc. We served it with the Medaillons of Lamb with Eggplant Flan.

With the Chèvre d'Authon, we served the last Cabernet Sauvignon from Chappellet, well aged and complex.

Desserts began with the Firestone Vineyards Johannisberg Riesling, which is harvested late to make it fruity and fresh with a hint of sugar, lovely with the Cappuccino Soufflé. To end this long meal, we served Chocolate Truffles and a Fig Strip matched with the sweetest of the wines, Chateau St. Jean's Johannisberg Riesling, which resembles a German Beerenauslese. Recipes for all dishes mentioned in the menu are given in this book.

Harmony was the key throughout in this carefully orchestrated event, a truly matchless and memorable meal.

Vegetables

One of the hallmarks of a great restaurant is the attention and care vegetables and garnitures receive. At The Four Seasons, we have created a varied repertoire of unusual vegetable dishes. As much as anything else, the seasonal changes reflect our basic theme and point of view.

Many of our vegetable recipes are suitable as first courses, others are elegant enough to be served as separate courses following the main course. We hope you will have as much pleasure trying our vegetables as we have serving them.

Our recipes call for specific vegetables, but substitutions are often possible and are in keeping with The Four Seasons' philosophy—using the best ingredients available. The following lists suggest some of the different ways to prepare vegetables alone or in combination. When combining vegetables, keep in mind the eye appeal of different colors.

Thinly Sliced

Asparagus
Broccoli stems
Carrots
Celery
Chayote
Chinese cabbage
Fennel
Green bell peppers

Jîcama
Mushrooms
Red bell peppers
Snow peas
Turban squash
Turnips
Yellow squash
Zucchini

Turned

Beets
Broccoli stems
Butternut squash (top part)
Calabaza
Carrots
Celery root

Chayote
Daikon
Kohlrabi
Parsnips
White turnips
Yellow turnips

Julienned

Bean sprouts
Butternut squash (bottom part)
Carrots
Celery root
Chayote

Green cabbage
Parsnips
White turnips
Yellow squash
Zucchini

Puréed

Artichokes
Beets
Broccoli
Brussels sprouts
Calabaza
Carrots
Cauliflower
Celery root
Chayote
Chestnuts

Kohlrabi
Parsley
Parsnips
Peas
Salsify
Spinach
String beans
Sunchokes
Swiss chard
Yellow turnips

Combination Purées

Broccoli and celery root
Carrots and yellow split peas
Celery root and watercress

Kohlrabi and spinach
Sunchokes and parsley

Brussels Sprouts with Pine Nuts

Many people who have eaten soggy Brussels sprouts avoid them. It is a shame. Small, tight, properly cooked Brussels sprouts are one of the fine fall pleasures. You should make an effort to see them in their natural state as they grow in tight clusters up the stalk of the parent plant. They can only be described as amusing to pick.

Kosher salt
2 cups Brussels sprouts
1 tablespoon olive oil
2 ounces pancetta, finely chopped
    (if unavailable, substitute blanched bacon)
2 shallots, finely chopped
Freshly ground black pepper
Freshly grated nutmeg
1 tablespoon lightly salted butter
2 tablespoons pine nuts, crushed

Bring a pot of salted water to a boil.

Clean the Brussels sprouts
and mark the bottom of each with a ¼-inch-deep cross.
Boil in the salted water 5 to 8 minutes.
Cool immediately in cold water; drain well.

Heat the oil in a skillet.
Add the pancetta and sauté until the fat starts to melt.
Add the shallots and cook until they are transparent
and the pancetta is crisp.
Add the Brussels sprouts, pepper and nutmeg to taste.
Cook 5 minutes, stirring; transfer to a hot serving dish.

In a small skillet, heat the butter until it is brown.
Add the crushed pine nuts; sauté until golden brown
and sprinkle over the Brussels sprouts.

Serves 4.

Zucchini with Pesto

This dish resembles a pale green pasta with a green herb
sauce and is often served as a first course to our gourmet
dieters. We also use it as an accompaniment to simple meat
dishes. The pesto is, of course, a versatile sauce in its own
right and can also be used in soups, in stews, under the skin
of a chicken to be roasted, and in numerous other ways.
Ideally, this dish should be made in full summer when the
basil is available in quantity and the zucchini are growing
faster than you can think of ways to use it.

Pesto Sauce
⅓ cup shelled and peeled pistachio nuts
⅔ cup pine nuts
5 large cloves garlic
2 cups firmly packed basil
1 to 1½ cups olive oil

Place the pistachio nuts, pine nuts and garlic
in the work bowl of a food processor
fitted with the metal blade.
Process to a fine paste.
Add the basil and continue to process until puréed.
With the machine running,
pour in the olive oil in a thin stream.
When the mixture is thick and mounds like mayonnaise,
you have added enough oil.

Makes about 2½ cups of sauce.

Zucchini

2½ pounds large zucchini
2 tablespoons olive oil
Kosher salt
Freshly ground black pepper
Toasted pine nuts

Cut the zucchini into julienne strips with a mandoline, discarding the seeds.
Alternatively, cut the zucchini lengthwise in half and scoop out and discard the seeds.
Cut the halves lengthwise into slices ⅛ inch thick.
Stack these and cut them, lengthwise, into ⅛-inch strips.

Heat the oil in a 10-inch skillet and add the zucchini.
Sauté, tossing for 1 minute.
Stir in 2 tablespoons of pesto sauce and toss to coat.
Season to taste with salt and pepper.
Add the toasted pine nuts.
(Reserve the remaining sauce for another dish.)

Serves 6.

This is one of the most delightful places I've been in a long time. Keep serving!

Betty Ford

BETTY FORD

Zucchini Provençale

This recipe is similar to the previous one but uses a Provençale sauce, typical of the South of France.

Provençale Sauce

1½ tablespoons lightly salted butter
1 tablespoon olive oil
3 tablespoons chopped onion
1 large clove garlic, finely chopped
1 cup peeled, seeded and coarsely chopped tomatoes
1½ tablespoons finely chopped fresh basil
1½ tablespoons finely chopped parsley
1½ teaspoons kosher salt
Freshly ground black pepper

In a heavy saucepan, heat the butter and the oil.
Add the onion and cook, stirring, for 1 minute,
or until it is limp.
Add the garlic and continue to cook for another minute.
Add the tomatoes and cook until thick, stirring often.
Mix in the basil, parsley, salt and pepper; set aside.

Zucchini

2½ pounds large zucchini
2 tablespoons olive oil
Kosher salt
Freshly ground black pepper

Julienne the zucchini with a mandoline, discard seeds.
Alternatively, cut the zucchini lengthwise in half
and scoop out and discard the seeds.
Cut the halves lengthwise into slices ⅛ inch thick.
Stack these and cut them, lengthwise, into ⅛-inch strips.

Heat the oil in a 10-inch skillet and add the zucchini.
Sauté, tossing for 1 minute; stir in sauce.
Season to taste with salt and pepper.

Serves 6.

Brockflower Parmesan

Brockflower is a most unusual vegetable, purple when fresh, bright green when cooked. As its name indicates, it is halfway between broccoli and cauliflower in taste as well as look. Watching the color change is like a bit of magic. You may make the sauce ahead and reheat it just before serving.

3 tablespoons clarified butter
⅓ cup thinly sliced shallots
2 slices crustless white bread, torn into ⅜-inch pieces
2 eggs, boiled exactly 9 minutes, cooled, peeled
   and chopped
2 tablespoons finely chopped parsley
3 tablespoons freshly grated Parmesan cheese
Kosher salt
Freshly ground black pepper
3 heads brockflower, stems removed
2 tablespoons lightly salted butter

Heat the clarified butter in a heavy skillet.
Add the shallots and sauté until golden brown and crisp.
Remove with a slotted spoon, reserving the fat.

Strain the fat into a clean skillet; heat.
Add the bread and stir-fry until golden.
Add the eggs, parsley, cheese and the browned shallots.
Cook the mixture, stirring, for 1 minute,
or until rather dry.
Season with salt and pepper.

Cook the brockflower in a large pot
of boiling salted water for 6 minutes, or until tender.

Add the lightly salted butter to the shallot mixture.
Reheat, stirring.
Drain the brockflower; place in a hot bowl.
Pour the shallot mixture over and serve at once.

Serves 6.

Baked Fennel Parmesan

Fennel, often overlooked, adds an unusual note to a winter meal.

3 large heads fennel
2 cups milk
1 medium onion, sliced
2 tablespoons kosher salt
Freshly ground black pepper
¾ cup freshly grated Parmesan cheese
1 tablespoon lightly salted butter
2 tablespoons fresh bread crumbs
1 tablespoon olive oil

Trim the root end and leaves of the fennel.

Make a white stock in a deep kettle
with the milk, onion and 2 quarts water.
Slowly bring to a boil.
Add the fennel.
If it is not entirely covered with stock,
add water to cover.
Simmer 45 minutes, or until tender.
Drain well and reserve ¼ cup of the cooking liquid.

Heat the oven to 425°F.

Cut the fennel in halves and trim the core.
Arrange the pieces overlapping in a buttered baking dish.
Sprinkle with salt and pepper
and dot with Parmesan cheese mixed with the butter.
Scatter the bread crumbs over all.
Pour the reserved ¼ cup cooking liquid
around the border of the dish.
Place in the preheated oven to brown.
Before serving, drizzle olive oil over the dish.

Serves 6.

Baked Endive

The best endive comes from Belgium; the Belgians have a knack for growing it. It comes into season in mid-winter, just when we are looking for something fresh to serve.
Our creamy version presents it unlike any other we know.

1 cup milk
Kosher salt
1 medium onion, sliced
6 large, firm Belgian endives
Juice of ½ lemon
12 scallions, cooked for 3 minutes in boiling water, drained
Freshly ground black pepper
Freshly grated nutmeg
3 egg yolks
1 cup heavy cream
6 tablespoons freshly grated Parmesan cheese
3 tablespoons lightly salted butter, in 1 piece

In a saucepan, combine the milk, 1 quart water,
1 tablespoon salt and the sliced onion.
Bring to a boil, reduce the heat and simmer for 20 minutes.
Add the endives and lemon juice.
Simmer 12 minutes.
Carefully remove the endives and cool for 5 minutes,
or until cool enough to handle.

Heat the oven to 350°F.
and butter a 12-inch round, shallow baking dish.

Halve the endives lengthwise and cut away the cores.
Fold the tips underneath
and place the endives in a spoke-like pattern
in the prepared dish,
with the folded tips almost touching the rim.

Trim the scallions to 5-inch pieces
and place them between the endive halves.
Sprinkle with a little salt, fresh pepper and
a grating of nutmeg.

Beat the egg yolks, cream
and Parmesan cheese together in a bowl.
Pour the mixture over the vegetables.
Place the piece of butter in the center of the baking dish.

Set the dish in a large pan.
Add hot water to the pan
until it comes halfway up the side of the dish.
Bake on the middle rack of the preheated oven
for 20 minutes, or until golden brown.

Serves 6.

En souvenir du ☀

1er Lancement des   COURÈGES

Parfums COURREGES

aux U.S.A —

aux "4 SAISONS"

Amités et Mersis

Azrneigs

Vegetables / 373

Baked Knob Celery

Too often people ignore the virtues of knob celery or celery root and think of it only as cold and julienned in a fresh céleri rémoulade. Added to stews, particularly lamb and chicken, or to soups and vegetable mixtures, it provides an unusual and pungent note. When baked, as it is here, it is a delicious novelty.

6 (1½ pounds total) celery roots
Kosher salt
1 cup milk
2 cups Béchamel Sauce (see recipe, page 516)
2 ounces Gruyère cheese, grated
¼ cup fresh bread crumbs
1 tablespoon lightly salted butter
Freshly grated nutmeg
Freshly ground black pepper

Heat the oven to 375°F.

Peel the celery roots and cut them crosswise into ¼-inch-thick slices.

Fill a saucepan with 1½ cups cold water
and bring to a boil.
Season with salt.
Add the milk and celery root slices.
Bring back to a boil
and cook over medium heat for 10 minutes.
Drain.

Butter a 12- to 14-inch au gratin dish.
Spread 1 cup béchamel sauce over the bottom.
Sprinkle half the Gruyère cheese over the sauce.
Top with layers of the sliced celery root.
Cover with the remaining cup of béchamel sauce,
spreading evenly.
Sprinkle the remaining cheese over the sauce,
then sprinkle on the bread crumbs.
Dot with thin slices of butter.

Bake in the preheated oven for 20 minutes,
or until the top is golden.
Grate nutmeg and pepper over the top.

Serves 6.

Dear 4 Seasons —

Thank you

Lynn Redgrave

LYNN REDGRAVE

March 17th 78.

Glazed Baby Carrots

This is an unusual recipe for baby carrots well worth trying.

2 tablespoons lightly salted butter
2 pounds baby carrots, peeled and trimmed
2 tablespoons honey
Kosher salt
Freshly ground black pepper
3½ ounces ginger ale

Heat the butter in a saucepan.
Add the carrots and sauté for 1 minute.
Add the honey, salt and pepper; toss.
Pour in the ginger ale and bring to a boil.
Cover and cook for 3 minutes.
Remove the lid and
cook until the liquid turns into a glaze, about 5 minutes.

Serves 6.

Best Wishes

Nancy Lopez Melton

NANCY LOPEZ MELTON

10·4·79

Glazed Yellow and White Turnips with Currants

Yellow and white turnips have very different flavors.
Together with the currants they make a pretty and interesting
dish. This vegetable is strong enough for a heavy meat dish.

1 large (1-pound) yellow turnip,
    peeled and cut into ½-inch cubes
Kosher salt
3 whole cloves
7 ounces ginger ale
2 tablespoons clover honey
3 tablespoons lightly salted butter
3 medium (1 pound total) white turnips,
    peeled and cut into ½-inch cubes
Freshly ground black pepper
¼ cup dried currants,
    soaked in warm water to cover for 30 minutes

Place the yellow turnips, salt and cloves in a saucepan.
Pour in the ginger ale and bring to a boil.
Cover, reduce heat; simmer 15 minutes until tender.
Remove the cover and boil away the remaining liquid.
Remove and discard the cloves.
Set the yellow turnips aside, covered.

Melt honey and 1 tablespoon butter in a saucepan.
Add the white turnips, salt and pepper.
Cook over low heat until tender, about 4 minutes.

Combine the white and yellow turnip mixtures
in a warm baking dish.
Drain the currants
and stir in the remaining 2 tablespoons butter.

Serves 6.

Eggplant Flan

At least one kind of eggplant—Italian, Chinese, Japanese, or our own purple supersized vegetable—is available year-round. Each has its own taste and will give a slightly different, but delicious, result. You might serve the flan with a simply cooked lamb dish or poached chicken. While this is clearly a vegetable dish, if you add a light tomato sauce, it would make a superb first course.

3 slices bacon
3 shallots
1 small clove garlic
½ cup fresh coriander leaves
2 tablespoons olive oil
½ pound eggplant, peeled and cut into 1-inch cubes
¼ cup dry white wine
1 cup milk
3 eggs
1 egg yolk
½ cup heavy cream
Kosher salt
Freshly ground black pepper
Dash freshly grated nutmeg

Heat oven to 375°F.

Process the bacon, shallots, garlic and coriander in a food processor until coarsely chopped.

Place chopped ingredients in an ovenproof casserole.
Add the olive oil, eggplant and wine.
Stir to mix;
cover and bake in the preheated oven for 45 minutes.
Remove the casserole from the oven;
lower oven temperature to 300°F.

With a spatula, scrape the baked mixture
into the work bowl of a food processor and
process until smooth.
Rub the mixture through a drum sieve or fine strainer
to remove the seeds and make a silky purée.
If you don't have a processor,
put the mixture directly through a sieve.

Mix the milk, eggs, egg yolk, cream,
salt, pepper and nutmeg in a bowl.
Stir in the eggplant purée; blend well.
Pour into six buttered ¾-cup ramekins.

Place them in a deep roasting pan
lined with a double layer of newspaper.
This helps keep the heat even during cooking.
Add enough hot water to the pan
to come halfway up the sides of the ramekins.
Bake for 30 minutes,
or until the flans feel firm to the touch.

Let the flans rest in the water bath
for at least 30 minutes before unmolding.
Never unmold the flans when they just come out of the oven
or they will fall apart.

When ready to serve the flans, unmold them
on individual plates or on a serving platter.
The flans will contract slightly in the cooling
and should slide easily from the ramekins.

If the flans have cooled too much,
return to the oven for a few minutes to reheat
before unmolding.

Serves 6.

VITTORIO GASSMAN

Sautéed Sugar Snap Peas

Sugar snap peas are a very recent delicacy and if you have a garden, we urge you to plant the seeds so you will have an ample supply of your own if they are not in your market. These peas have edible pods as well as edible peas. Only the strings are not edible and must be removed. Not only are they delicious as a vegetable in themselves, but a handful added to a stew at the last moment brightens and crisps up the proceedings.

Kosher salt
1 pound sugar snap peas, strings removed
1 tablespoon lightly salted butter
Freshly ground black pepper
Lemon juice

Bring a large pot of salted water to a boil.
Add the peas and cook for 3 minutes
after the water returns to the boil.
Remove the peas and drop immediately into ice water.
Drain well.

Heat the butter in a skillet
and sauté the peas, shaking the pan.
Season with salt, pepper
and a few drops of lemon juice.

Serves 4.

Note:
This method of cooking vegetables can be used with beans.

Snow Peas in Shoyu

Chef Renggli gladly admits that he learns from other cuisines. However, he never takes a recipe intact; instead he understands the seasonings, ingredients and techniques and uses them, where they apply, in his own creations. In this recipe, he has taken a standard Chinese ingredient, snow peas, and a standard Chinese seasoning, soy sauce, and has used the Chinese stir-fry technique. However, the addition of clarified butter, lemon juice and black pepper, as well as the method of reducing the sauce, are distinctly his own.

1½ pounds fresh snow peas, strings removed
2 tablespoons clarified butter
2 tablespoons soy sauce
Juice of ½ lemon
Freshly ground black pepper

Cut each snow pea crosswise
on the diagonal into three pieces.
Heat the butter in a skillet until hot.
Add the snow peas and stir-fry 1 minute.
Make a well in the center of the snow peas
and add the soy sauce and the lemon juice.
Boil until the liquid is almost a glaze.
Cook, stirring,
until the snow peas are tender but still crisp.
Season with freshly ground pepper.
Serve hot.

Serves 6.

Crisp Sautéed Vegetables

Chef Renggli likes the freshness, texture and taste of good vegetables used in a recipe like this one. Other vegetables may be substituted depending on availability, always keeping in mind the balance of color, texture and taste.

Vegetables

1 small white turnip
1 kohlrabi
½ young parsnip
1 large carrot
1 small zucchini
1 small yellow squash
1 celery rib
1 bunch grass (wild) asparagus
½ cup snow peas, strings removed
1 bunch scallions, green part only
½ cup enoki mushrooms
6 cherry tomatoes (optional)

Peel the turnip, kohlrabi, parsnip and carrot.
Cut them,
as well as the zucchini and yellow squash, in half lengthwise.
Cut the halves on the diagonal into very thin slices.
Cut the celery on the diagonal into very thin slices.

Cut 2-inch tips of asparagus.
(Reserve remainder for another use.)
Cut the snow peas crosswise
on the diagonal into 1-inch pieces.
Cut the scallion greens into thin rings.
Trim the bottoms of the enoki mushrooms
and remove the stems from the tomatoes.

Sauce

⅔ cup sake
1 teaspoon soy sauce
½ pound lightly salted butter, cut into small pieces

Heat the sake in a small heavy saucepan.
Ignite.
When the flames subside,
cook the sake until it reduces to a glaze.
Beat in the soy sauce.
Beat in the butter, 1 or 2 tablespoons at a time,
until the sauce is thick and foamy.
It may be necessary to move the pan on and off the heat
to keep the sauce at the correct consistency.
Set aside and keep warm.

Assembly

2 tablespoons walnut oil
Kosher salt
Freshly ground black pepper

Heat a 10-inch skillet over moderate heat.
Add the walnut oil and spread to coat the bottom and sides.
Add the vegetables and sauté for 1 minute.
Season to taste with salt and pepper.
Stir in sauce.
Serve hot.

Serves 6.

Superb!

Harold Pinter

HAROLD PINTER

Dec. 8. 76

Steamed Vegetable Platter with Green Herb Sauce

This is a spectacular dish and certainly appropriate for a party. It also makes a great vegetarian dinner for two.

1 bunch broccoli, broken into stalks
1 small head cauliflower, broken into 2-inch flowerettes
2 large carrots, thinly sliced on the diagonal
⅓ pound fresh green beans, trimmed
¼ pound grass asparagus, trimmed
2 yellow squash, peeled and thinly sliced on the diagonal
2 zucchini, peeled and thinly sliced on the diagonal
6 mushroom caps
6 cherry tomatoes
1 avocado, peeled, pitted and cut into wedges
Sea salt
1 tablespoon imported green-herb Dijon mustard (see page 518)
½ cup Herb Sauce (recipe follows)
1 cup olive oil

Bring a large pot of salted water to a boil.
Add the broccoli, cauliflower, carrots and green beans and cook for 1 minute.
Drain and rinse under cold running water.
Drain again and pat dry.

Make a steamer as follows:
Use a cake rack which will fit into a roasting pan with a tight-fitting cover.
The pan must be deep enough so the rack can be raised about 1½ inches from the bottom.
Inverted custard cups are a good support for the rack.

Arrange all the vegetables, mushrooms, tomatoes
and avocado wedges attractively
in a heatproof serving dish
which will fit into your roasting pan.
Sprinkle the vegetables with sea salt.

Bring 1 inch of water to a boil
inside the large roasting pan.
When the water is boiling,
place the inverted custard cups in the pan.
Place the cake rack over the cups.
Make sure the rack is
above the level of the boiling water.
Place the serving dish on the rack,
cover the pan and steam for 15 minutes.

Meanwhile, prepare the sauce.
Beat the mustard into the prepared herb sauce.
Slowly beat in the olive oil.

Spoon the sauce over the vegetables.
Serve at once.

Serves 6.

Herb Sauce
2 tablespoons sea salt
2 teaspoons black peppercorns
½ whole nutmeg, cracked
2 tablespoons sherry wine vinegar
½ cup walnut oil
4 bunches parsley
1 pound spinach leaves, well washed
4 bunches scallion greens, trimmed
1 celery stalk, ribs separated
   and cut into 2-inch pieces
1 head garlic, peeled
1½ pounds onions, roughly cut up
10 fresh sage leaves

Heat the oven to 350°F.

In a spice or coffee grinder,
grind the salt, peppercorns and nutmeg to a powder.

In a large casserole,
cook the vinegar until it is reduced to a glaze.
Add the oil, then the parsley, spinach, scallions,
celery, garlic, onions and sage.
Stir in the spice powder.
Cover the casserole
and place in the preheated oven
to cook for 1 hour 45 minutes.

Purée the cooked mixture in a food processor.
Push the mixture through a fine strainer
into a clean bowl.

Makes 1 quart.

Note:
This sauce can be mixed with softened butter to make an
herb butter.

Lugar encantador, deliciosa comida

que más se puede pedir —

afectuoso recuerdo para Paul e Tom

Dolores Del Rio

DOLORES DEL RIO

Eggplant, Zucchini and Tomato Gratin

This is an attractive summer gratin and can be prepared ahead and baked just before serving.

Two 1-pound eggplants
½ cup olive oil
8 or 9 mixed crackers (Ritz, whole wheat, etc.)
2 tablespoons freshly grated Parmesan cheese
1 teaspoon fresh marjoram leaves
3 tablespoons lightly salted butter
2 (about 1 pound) ripe tomatoes, peeled, cored
    and cut crosswise into ¼-inch slices
2 pounds zucchini, cut into ¼-inch rounds
¼ teaspoon kosher salt
Freshly ground black pepper

Peel the eggplants.
Cut them crosswise into ½-inch slices.
Heat the olive oil in a 10- to 12-inch skillet
until very hot.
Sauté the eggplant in batches
until golden on both sides.
Remove from the skillet and drain on absorbent paper.

Heat the oven to 350°F.

Grind the crackers, cheese and marjoram until coarse in a food processor or a blender.

With about 1 tablespoon butter,
grease a 14- to 16-inch gratin pan.
Sprinkle 2 tablespoons of the crumb mixture
over the bottom.
Arrange alternate overlapping slices of tomato,
zucchini and eggplant down the length of the dish.
Season with salt and pepper.
Sprinkle with the remaining crumb mixture.
Dot with the remaining butter and bake for 20 minutes.

Heat the broiler.

Place the dish under the broiler to brown the top.

Serves 6.

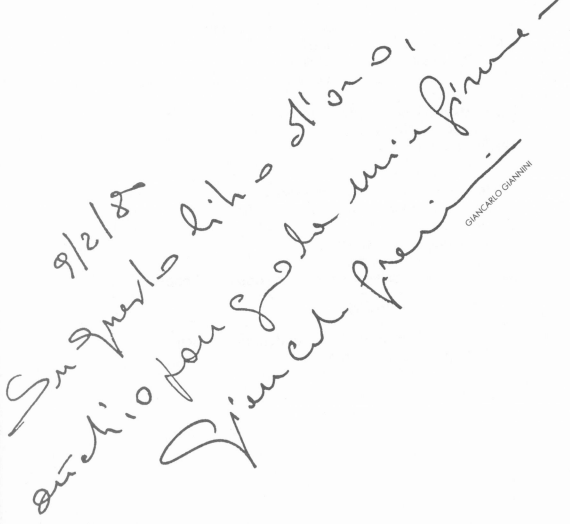

GIANCARLO GIANNINI

Asparagus

We love asparagus—the familiar thin green stalks; the seemingly wild reedlike variety; the thick, aggressive, mature stalks; and the positively obese, ivory-white stalks. We love them as a first course, as a vegetable, and as a salad. We love them hot, we love them cold, and particularly tepid. The only thing we have not yet discovered is how to use them for dessert. We have put together in the following pages a few asparagus recipes along with a basic procedure for cooking asparagus. We hope they give you as much pleasure as they give us.

Asparagus

24 to 36 fresh, firm asparagus spears,
  equal in size

Bring a large pot of well-salted water to a boil.
There should be enough water
to generously cover the asparagus.

Break off and discard
the tough stem ends of the asparagus.
Peel from tip to stem with a vegetable peeler.

Gently lower the asparagus spears
into the boiling water.
Bring the water back to a boil
and cook 6 to 12 minutes,
or until the tip of a knife can enter the stem
without resistance.
Cooking time varies with the thickness
of the asparagus.
They should be crisp, but tender, never limp.
Gently remove the asparagus with tongs.
Rinse them immediately under cold running water
to stop the cooking
and preserve the bright green color.
Drain well
before placing on a warmed serving dish.
Serve immediately.

Serves 6.

Note:
If you wish to cook the asparagus ahead, rinse them under
cold running water and then return them to boiling water for
a minute to reheat. If you want to keep them hot for a few
minutes, place them on a warm serving platter and cover
with a hot, damp kitchen towel.

Vinaigrette Sauce

2 red bell peppers,
  peeled and cut into ⅛-inch squares (see note, page 37)
1 small green bell pepper,
  peeled and cut into ⅛-inch squares (see note, page 37)
1 medium onion, finely chopped
½ cup cornichons, finely chopped
⅓ cup capers, coarsely chopped
¼ cup finely chopped fresh tarragon
1 teaspoon finely chopped fresh thyme
½ cup peeled, seeded and finely chopped cucumber
1 fennel bulb, finely diced (optional)
¼ cup peeled, finely diced sunchoke (optional)
1 tablespoon red wine vinegar
1 tablespoon imported Dijon mustard
¾ cup imported olive oil
Kosher salt
Freshly ground black pepper
24 to 36 cooked Asparagus spears,
  hot or at room temperature (see recipe, page 390)

Place the red and green peppers, onion, cornichons, capers, tarragon, thyme, cucumber, fennel and sunchoke in a bowl; mix thoroughly.

Mix the vinegar, mustard and olive oil.
Season well with salt and pepper.
Pour the mixture over the chopped vegetables and herbs.
Stir until blended.
Use immediately or cover and refrigerate overnight.

Arrange four to six asparagus spears on each of six individual serving dishes.
Spoon equal amounts of the sauce over the asparagus.

Serves 6.

Variation for Avocado Vinaigrette Sauce:

Force 1 ripe, peeled avocado through a fine mesh strainer. Immediately squeeze the juice of ½ lemon over the avocado to prevent it from turning dark. Beat the mixture into the vinaigrette sauce. This must be used immediately.

Sautéed Hazelnuts

16 to 24 hot, cooked Asparagus spears (see recipe, page 390)
4 tablespoons lightly salted butter
¾ cup skinned hazelnuts, coarsely chopped
Kosher salt
Freshly ground black pepper

Arrange the asparagus on a warm serving platter.

Heat the butter in a small skillet.
When the foaming subsides
and the butter begins to turn light brown,
add the hazelnuts.
Cook over medium heat
until the nuts are lightly toasted.

Season the asparagus with salt and pepper.
Pour the hazelnut mixture over the tips
and serve at once.

Serves 4.

Prosciutto
and Parmesan Cheese

16 to 24 hot, cooked Asparagus spears (see recipe, page 390)
Kosher salt
Freshly ground black pepper
2 tablespoons lightly salted butter
6 thin slices prosciutto, coarsely chopped
¾ cup freshly grated Parmesan cheese

Heat the broiler.

Arrange the asparagus on
an ovenproof serving platter.
Season with salt and pepper.

Heat the butter in a small skillet.
Add the prosciutto and cook for 2 minutes, stirring.
Pour the prosciutto and butter
over the asparagus tips.
Sprinkle with the cheese
and place under the heated broiler
until the cheese melts and is golden.
Serve at once.

Serves 4.

Eggs, Bread Crumbs and Herbs

16 to 24 hot, cooked Asparagus spears (see recipe, page 390)
¼ pound lightly salted butter
½ cup fresh bread crumbs
2 hard-boiled eggs, diced
¼ cup chopped parsley
1 tablespoon chopped fresh tarragon
2 teaspoons chopped fresh thyme
1 teaspoon chopped fresh basil
1 tablespoon chopped fresh chives
Kosher salt
Freshly ground black pepper

Arrange the asparagus on a warm serving platter.

Heat the butter in a skillet.
When the foaming subsides
and the butter begins to turn light brown,
add the bread crumbs and cook,
stirring, for 15 seconds.
Add the eggs and herbs, stirring.
Season with salt and pepper.

Spoon the mixture over the asparagus.
Serve immediately.

Serves 4.

Lemon Butter
and Fried Capers

16 to 24 hot, cooked Asparagus spears (see recipe, page 390)
Juice of 2 lemons
1 tablespoon heavy cream
¼ pound lightly salted butter,
   cut into 8 pieces
Pinch white or cayenne pepper
Kosher salt
Freshly ground black pepper
¾ cup Fried Capers (see recipe, page 82)

Arrange the asparagus on a warm serving platter.

Heat the lemon juice in a heavy, small saucepan
until it reduces to a glaze
just covering the bottom of the pan.
Do not let it burn.
Stir in the heavy cream.
Immediately whisk in the butter,
a piece at a time.
Add the pepper.

Season the asparagus with salt and black pepper.
Spoon the lemon butter sauce over the asparagus tips.
Sprinkle with the fried capers
and serve immediately.

Serves 4.

HALSTON

Salads

Salads are of course a wonderful way to herald
the changing seasons. We love to experiment
with them, seeking new ways to extoll the best
tomatoes, the freshest beets. Quick to do and
pretty to look at, these salads make a roast a
repast.

Dilled Cucumbers

Dilled cucumbers are a standard German and Austrian side dish, a sort of mild pickle to fight the rigors of their somewhat heavy food. Our food is infinitely lighter, and so are our dilled cucumbers. The combination of the julienned cucumbers and the thinly sliced red onions makes for a pretty dish as well.

2 tablespoons red wine vinegar
2 tablespoons olive oil
2 tablespoons imported Dijon mustard
¾ teaspoon sugar
1 teaspoon kosher salt
Freshly ground black pepper
¼ medium red onion, thinly sliced
2 tablespoons chopped dill
3 or 4 cucumbers, peeled, seeded
  and cut into very fine julienne strips

In a wooden salad bowl,
whisk together the vinegar, oil, mustard, sugar,
salt and pepper.
Blend well.
Add the onion and dill, then the cucumbers.
Toss to combine.
Serve as soon as possible.

Serves 6.

Bar Room Slaw

One of the most requested and most seasonal dishes of The Four Seasons and its Bar Room is Bar Room Slaw. The long list of vegetables has been given so that you too may be seasonal and creative. Certainly feel free to add to the list, keeping in mind the colors, textures and variations in taste. At The Four Seasons, this often comes with a paillard (see recipes, pages 253, 288, 306 and 320).

Vegetables

Carrot
Zucchini
Red bell pepper
Green bell pepper
Celery
Celery root
Summer squash
Chayote

Chinese cabbage
Daikon
Black radish
White cabbage
Red cabbage
Cucumber
Tomato

Dressing

2 egg yolks
½ teaspoon imported Dijon mustard
1 tablespoon lemon juice
Kosher salt
Freshly ground black pepper
1 to 1½ cups olive oil
1½ teaspoons red wine vinegar

Garnish

Romaine lettuce
Belgian endive
Danish watercress
Alfalfa sprouts

Choose the vegetables according to the season and your preference.
Cut them into fine julienne.
You will need about 4 cups julienned vegetables.

Make the dressing by combining
the egg yolks, mustard, lemon juice and salt and pepper
in a mixing bowl.
Stir briskly until well blended.
Slowly add olive oil, drop by drop,
beating without stopping.
When the mixture is thick,
add the remaining oil in a slow, steady stream.
Stir in the vinegar.

Pour the dressing over the julienned vegetables.
Line four serving plates with lettuce, endive and watercress.
Spoon the dressed vegetables over the greens and
sprinkle some alfalfa sprouts on top.

Serves 4.

Note:
To make the salad ahead, prepare all the vegetables,
wrap them in plastic and refrigerate
until you are ready to serve.
Make the dressing at the last minute.

Restaurants come + restaurants go
Summer, winter, spring + fall --
But one's the best --- forget the rest --
Because of Tom + Paul.

8/12/75 - 9/12/75

Cleveland Amory

CLEVELAND AMORY

Pickled Beets
and Endive Salad

Pickled beets are an English classic. Here they are a touch more interesting with the addition of red pepper and fresh ginger. While beets and endive are a classic combination, the beets alone would counterpoint a grilled or poached fish, hot or cold, with subtle harmony.

Pickled Beets

1½ pounds fresh beets, preferably 2 inches in diameter,
    washed well, leaves trimmed to about 1 inch
Kosher salt
1 cup red wine vinegar
4 cloves garlic
1 bay leaf
One 3-inch stick cinnamon
⅓ cup honey
¼ teaspoon crushed red pepper
2 slices fresh ginger

Place the beets in a pot and cover with water.
Add salt to taste.
Bring the water to a boil, then lower the heat to a simmer.
Cook until the beets are soft enough to be pierced
with a skewer.
Cooking time varies enormously
with the age and size of the beets.
It can take anywhere from 20 minutes to 1½ hours.

When the beets are cooked,
remove them from the pot with a slotted spoon.
Reserve the liquid.
As soon as the beets are cool enough to handle,
peel them (peels should come right off) and
slice them into ¼-inch slices.
Place in a bowl.

Meanwhile, add the remaining ingredients
to the beet cooking liquid and cook for 10 minutes.
Correct the seasoning.

Strain enough cooking liquid over the beets
just to cover.
As you pour, be careful not to get any of the sand
which settles to the bottom of the pot into the beets.
Cover the beets with an inverted saucer
and lightly weight it.
Refrigerate for 3 days before using.

Salad

1 small red onion, chopped
½ cup sour cream
¼ cup olive oil
1 tablespoon imported Dijon mustard
3 medium endives
Kosher salt
Freshly ground black pepper
Red wine vinegar

Soak the onion in ice water for 30 minutes.

Place the sour cream in a bowl.
Beat in the olive oil.
Drain the onion, wrap in a towel and squeeze dry.
Add the onion and mustard to the bowl.
Beat until smooth.

Slice the endives
lengthwise on a diagonal into ½-inch slices
and add to the sauce.
With a slotted spoon or tongs,
remove half the pickled beets with a little of the juice.
Combine well by tossing.
Season with salt and pepper and a little vinegar.

Serve in a crystal or earthenware bowl.

Serves 6.

Note:

The pickled beets will keep in the refrigerator for 1 to 2
weeks.
Serve extra beets with chopped onions and a little oil.

Beefsteak Tomato with Basil and Red Onions

This recipe has been popular at The Four Seasons since it opened. The beautiful, perfectly ripe tomatoes are brought to the table with a carving board and sliced there as if they are indeed the richest of steaks. It is a spectacular presentation, but you may prepare the salad ahead if you wish the flavors to mellow. There are some of us who prefer to add a little fresh crushed garlic to the dressing.

1 medium-large red onion, sliced ⅛ inch thick
2 large ripe but firm beefsteak tomatoes,
   stem ends cut off
12 large basil leaves
¼ teaspoon sugar
Freshly ground black pepper
Kosher salt
2 tablespoons red wine vinegar
⅓ cup olive oil

Soak the onion in ice water for 30 minutes.
Drain and pat dry.

Cut the tomato into ½-inch-thick slices,
or six slices per tomato.
Shake out any loose seeds.

Arrange the tomatoes, onion and basil leaves overlapping across a shallow serving dish.

Sprinkle with sugar, pepper, salt,
vinegar and olive oil.
Cover and leave at room temperature for 1 hour
if you wish to allow the flavors to develop.

Serves 4.

Red Peppers with Lemon and Oil

Red peppers seem, unfortunately, to have been relegated to the same role as parsley: color on the plate. They have a sweet, fresh flavor of their own which is taken full advantage of in this salad, full enough in flavor to be a first course.

4 large red bell peppers
Juice of 1 lemon
½ cup olive oil
Kosher salt
Freshly ground black pepper
8 Boston lettuce leaves
12 large fresh basil leaves
16 anchovy fillets
½ cup Fried Capers (see recipe, page 82)

Cut the stem ends off the peppers.
Quarter them, remove the seeds and de-rib.
Remove the peel with a vegetable peeler.
Peel difficult-to-reach surfaces with a small knife.

Place the peppers in a medium-sized bowl.
Pour the lemon juice
and ⅓ cup olive oil over the peppers.
Season with salt and pepper; toss and cover.
Let marinate at room temperature for 3 hours
to tenderize and flavor the peppers.

Line four individual salad plates
with two lettuce leaves each so the leaves curve down.
Arrange four pepper quarters over the lettuce
on each plate.
Garnish each with three basil leaves.
On each salad, crisscross four anchovies.

Spoon the remaining oil equally over the salads.
Sprinkle evenly with the fried capers.

Serves 4.

Potato Salad

Our version of this well-loved dish is far from the usual
picnic fare. It is served warm from salt-encrusted
potato shells.

Six 12-ounce baking potatoes
Kosher salt
½ cup finely chopped onion
2 large cloves garlic
⅓ cup white wine vinegar
¾ cup olive oil
Freshly ground black pepper
1 tablespoon imported Dijon mustard
2 tablespoons snipped fresh chives
10 strips bacon, cooked until crisp,
  drained and crumbled

Heat the oven to 400°F.

Wash the potatoes thoroughly.
While they are still wet, roll them in the salt,
completely covering the skin surfaces.
Place the potatoes on a baking sheet
and bake them in the preheated oven
for 45 minutes to 1 hour, or until tender.

While the potatoes are baking, prepare the dressing.

In a small, heavy saucepan,
place the onion, garlic, vinegar and oil.
Season to taste with salt and pepper.
Bring to a boil
and cook over medium-high heat for 5 minutes.
Discard the garlic.

Remove the pan from the heat, beat in the mustard,
and let rest for 30 minutes.

When the potatoes are cooked,
remove them from the oven
and let rest for 3 minutes.
Cut off ½ inch of potato from the top,
cutting lengthwise.
Very carefully,
scoop out rounded teaspoons of baked potato
from each shell,
leaving ¼ inch of potato lining the shells.
Place the scoops in a large bowl.
Add the chives and bacon to the potatoes.
Pour the dressing over the mixture and gently toss.
Taste and adjust the seasoning.

Spoon the potato salad into
the salted potato shells in mounds.
Serve warm.

Serves 6.

a most delicious,
elegant & wholesome
meal

Yehudi Menuhin

13 - April 1977

Zucchini with Basil Vinaigrette

Slightly related to Bar Room Slaw, this is a wonderful salad to know for the days of summer when one only wishes that the zucchini would stop growing.

6 small zucchini, ends trimmed
1 green bell pepper, peeled, seeded, de-ribbed and
    cut into julienne strips (see note, page 37)
1 red bell pepper, peeled, seeded, de-ribbed and
    cut into julienne strips (see note, page 37)
½ small red onion, cut into julienne strips
¼ cup finely chopped fresh basil
3 tablespoons olive oil
1 tablespoon red wine vinegar
Juice of ½ lemon
Kosher salt
Freshly ground black pepper
1½ tablespoons imported Dijon mustard

With a mandoline or long knife, make a few ⅛-inch-thick lengthwise slices of zucchini until you reach the seeds. Rotate a third and continue slicing until you reach the seeds again. Rotate and slice again. You should have a triangular length of seeds left. Discard the seeds. Repeat with the remaining zucchini.

Place the zucchini slices, peppers, onion and basil in a bowl.

Combine the rest of the ingredients in a small bowl for the dressing.

Before serving, toss dressing with vegetables until well coated.

Serves 4.

A Paul Kovi et Tom Margittai

les quatre saisons ?
c'est les trois étoiles de N.Y

cuisinement votre

Paul Bocuse

27 juin 1975

PAUL BOCUSE

Starches

Some of the dishes that follow are strictly made to accompany meat, poultry and fish. Others, like the Gorgonzola Polenta and the Spätzle, can make fine first courses. Likewise, some of our first courses, like the Risottos (pages 98, 100) and Gnocchi (page 96), make fine accompaniments. In any case, we do not think that a side dish is any less important than the main dish itself.

Gorgonzola Polenta

This dish was first created to go with Epigrammes of Wild Boar (page 351), although it also goes well with other game. The polenta combines the creamy mountain cheese of Italy with the Northern Italian staple of yellow cornmeal. We think the sharp edge of the cheese is a wonderful contrast to the creamy yellow cornmeal.

2 cups milk
4 tablespoons lightly salted butter
½ cup yellow cornmeal
Pinch freshly grated nutmeg
⅛ teaspoon freshly ground black pepper
3 ounces Gorgonzola cheese, 1 ounce chopped
   and the rest divided into 8 slices
¼ cup heavy cream
2 teaspoons kosher salt

In a saucepan, bring the milk and butter to a boil.
Add the cornmeal quickly,
stirring constantly with a wire whisk.
Cook over medium heat,
stirring constantly with a wooden spoon,
until the mixture becomes very thick.
Beat in the nutmeg, pepper
and the 1 ounce chopped cheese.
Beat to eliminate all lumps.
Off the heat,
beat in the cream and salt.
Readjust the seasoning to taste.

Heat the oven to 400°F.

Butter eight ⅓-cup muffin molds
and spoon in the cornmeal mixture.
Bang the molds against the work surface to settle the mixture.
Let stand 15 minutes to cool.

Butter a heavy ovenproof skillet
and turn the cornmeal molds into it.
Place a slice of Gorgonzola on top of each mold.
Heat slowly for a few minutes.
Do not let the cheese run down the sides.

Place the skillet in the preheated oven for 15 minutes,
or until the polenta molds begin to swell.
Glaze the cheese tops
under the broiler and serve at once.

Serves 8.

The Four Seasons est mon restaurant favori — new-york est favori /

FRANÇOIS TRUFFAUT

Spätzle

Spätzle is a dish that quite a number of countries claim, and each assures you that its name for the dish is the original and authentic one. In any case, in Chef Renggli's Switzerland it is spätzle and, therefore, calls for Swiss cheese. A spätzle machine looks like a food mill, only the holes are larger; the dough is alternately extruded through the holes and then cut off by the blade.

2 cups all-purpose flour
1 teaspoon kosher salt
Freshly ground black pepper
Freshly grated nutmeg
4 eggs
1¼ cups cold water
1 tablespoon vegetable oil
½ cup grated Swiss cheese
2 tablespoons lightly salted butter

Place the flour in a bowl
and make a well in the center.
Sprinkle in the salt, pepper and nutmeg.
Add 1 egg and ½ cup of water; mix well.
Add another egg and ¼ cup of water; mix well.
Continue in this way
until you have added all the eggs and water.
Beating vigorously, work the dough
for 5 minutes by hand until the mixture is batterlike.
Cover the dough and let rest 30 minutes.

Heat the oven to 375°F.

Bring 2½ quarts of salted water to a boil.
Add the vegetable oil.
Place a colander in the sink.
Pass the batter through a spätzle machine
into the boiling water.
If you don't have a spätzle machine,
use a spoon or rubber spatula to flick pieces of dough
off the side of the bowl into the water.
Cook the dough for 5 minutes.
Add some cold water to the pot to stop the cooking.
Pour the contents of the pot into the colander.
Toss to drain well.
Spread half the cooked spätzle
into a buttered shallow baking dish.
Sprinkle with half the Swiss cheese.
Top with the remaining spätzle in a layer.
Sprinkle with the remaining cheese
and dot with butter.

Bake in the preheated oven for 12 minutes,
or until the top is golden brown.

Serves 6.

Variation:
To make spinach spätzle, add ½ cup finely chopped cooked
spinach, well drained, to the batter.

the finest restaurant in N.Y.

Joe Levine

JOE LEVINE

Roesti Potatoes

This is another dish of Swiss origin that we have happily accepted into our repertoire. It goes well with any fairly zesty meat dish.

We present two versions of this crisp cake of cooked, then grated, potatoes—one plain and one layered with cheddar cheese—which would be very nice with a roast loin of pork or a roast chicken.

Kosher salt
4 large boiling potatoes
¼ cup bacon fat
¼ cup lard
Freshly ground black pepper
3 tablespoons lightly salted butter

Bring a large pot of salted water to a boil.
Add the potatoes and cook until they are almost done.
Drain and let cool,
then peel and coarsely grate them.

Heat the bacon fat and lard
in a heavy, shallow 10-inch skillet with sloping sides
until quite hot.
Spread half the potatoes over the bottom of the pan;
sprinkle with salt and pepper.
Cover with the remaining potatoes.
Cook over medium-high heat
until the bottom turns brown and crusty, about 10 minutes.
Turn the potatoes in one piece.
This is easiest to do
by placing a large plate over the pan
and turning both together.
Slip the turned-over potatoes off the plate
back into the pan, browned side up.
Cook until the bottom is browned, too.

Before serving,
smooth the edges of the potatoes with a spatula.
Sprinkle with salt to taste ·
and swish a pat of butter around the edge of the pan—
it will melt and run into the potatoes.
Cut into wedges to serve.

Serves 6.

Variation:

You can make Roesti Potatoes with cheddar cheese by making two thinner potato cakes. Top one with a layer of 7 ounces of sour cream, ½ cup cubed sharp cheddar cheese and 2 tablespoons chopped chives. Top with the second cake. Dot with 1 tablespoon of lightly salted butter and bake in a 400°F. oven for 5 minutes.

BERNARD HUGHES

Potato Galettes

Potato galettes are a French version of the potato pancake, and are made from a potato purée. We flavor ours with Champagne Cabbage (page 332), which makes them most unusual. These are so delicious we advise you to make many more than you think you'll need.

3 large (½-pound) baking potatoes
3 egg yolks
¼ recipe Champagne Cabbage
    or ½ pound sauerkraut, drained well
Kosher salt
Freshly ground black pepper
Freshly grated nutmeg
Cornstarch
Clarified butter

Heat the oven to 425°F.
Place the potatoes on a shelf
and bake until they are soft, about 1 hour.

While the potatoes are still hot, peel them
and put the pulp through the medium blade of a food mill.
Beat in the egg yolks until the mixture is smooth.
Beat in the Champagne Cabbage, salt, pepper
and nutmeg to taste.

When the mixture is well blended,
spread a layer of cornstarch on a tray.
Spoon the potato mixture on the tray
in a strip about 12 inches long.
Roll the strip back and forth with the palms of your hands
in the cornstarch until you have an even roll
2½ inches wide.
Cover lightly and chill for at least 1 hour.

When ready to serve,
cut the roll crosswise into 1-inch slices.
Lightly score both sides of each slice
with crisscrossing lines.

Over medium heat,
heat a layer of clarified butter on a griddle
or flat-bottomed skillet.
Add the slices of potato mixture in a layer
and cook until brown, about 8 minutes.
Turn and brown the second side, another 8 minutes.

Serve with the Beef Roulade (see recipe, page 327).

Serves 6.

CHRISTOPHER ISHERWOOD

Potatoes Paillasson

Julienne strips of potatoes are formed into a thin cake and cooked in butter until crisp for a perfect accompaniment for braised meats.

2 pounds boiling potatoes, peeled and cut into julienne
½ large carrot, peeled and cut into julienne
2 tablespoons snipped fresh chervil
4 tablespoons clarified butter
Kosher salt

Pat the potatoes dry and
mix with the carrots and chervil.
Heat the clarified butter
in a well-seasoned 10-inch skillet.
Add the potato mixture and pat into a cake-like form.
Cover and cook 6 minutes, shaking the pan often,
until the bottom of the potatoes is crisp and brown.

Place a plate over the skillet.
Turn the plate and skillet over together.
Slip the turned-over cake
back into the skillet, browned side up.
Continue cooking, uncovered, over low heat for 6 minutes.
Add salt to taste and turn out onto a serving platter.
Cut into wedges to serve.

Serves 6.

Wild Rice with Pine Nuts

The price of wild rice has put it in the category of truffles and other wild extravagances. Of course, it is not a true rice at all, but a grain of another family. There are dishes where its delicious nut-like flavor seems especially appropriate. In this recipe, we have amplified this flavor by adding pine nuts and think it is a perfect accompaniment to pigeon.

3 slices bacon, cut crosswise into ⅛-inch strips
½ cup minced onion
1 celery rib, cut into ¼-inch cubes
1 clove garlic
1 cup wild rice
Kosher salt
4 tablespoons lightly salted butter
½ cup pine nuts

Cook the bacon in a 10-inch skillet over medium heat.
When it has partially rendered,
add the onion, celery and garlic.
Cook for about 3 minutes, or until soft.
Add the rice and 3 cups of water.
Season with salt to taste.
Cover and simmer over medium heat for 45 minutes,
or until the rice has absorbed the water.
Set aside, uncovered, to cool and dry out.
Discard the garlic.

Just before serving, heat the butter in a skillet.
When it foams and begins to brown, add the pine nuts.
When they are brown, add the rice.
Cook and stir until heated through.

Serves 4 to 6.

WOODY ALLEN

Relishes

Relishes have a special place in our repertoire, adding their own color and grace to pâtés and game dishes. We've pulled together our favorites in the following pages, and we urge you to try them.

May & 1980—

Green Tomato Chutney

Chutney usually accompanies a curry. It can be used in an omelet, or in a tea sandwich, and with grilled seafood, poultry and meats.

½ dry red pepper
1 teaspoon coriander seeds,
  toasted in a dry skillet for 5 minutes
One 1-inch piece cinnamon stick
1 whole mace
1 cup cider vinegar
1 cup malt vinegar
1 pound dark brown sugar
½ teaspoon ground cumin seed
½ teaspoon ground turmeric
2 pounds cored, coarsely chopped green tomatoes
1 pound dried black currants
6 peaches, peeled, pitted and coarsely chopped
¼ cup grated fresh ginger
Rind of 1 lemon
1½ cups coarsely chopped shallots

Tie the red pepper, coriander seeds, cinnamon and mace into double-layered cheesecloth.

In a large heavy saucepan, pour in the vinegars. Add the brown sugar, cumin, turmeric and the spice bag. Bring to a boil.

Add remaining ingredients. Stir and bring back to the boil. Cover and simmer slowly for 2½ hours.

Remove the spice bag and lemon rind. Allow the mixture to cool to room temperature. Spoon into sterilized jars and cover tightly.

Let rest in the refrigerator for 3 to 4 weeks. Will keep for 1 month.

Cranberry Relish

While most people tend to think of cranberries only at Thanksgiving, we find that this relish is a refreshing accompaniment to have on hand. We often serve it tucked into the Pear Baskets (recipe follows). However, it is also delicious alone. We refrigerate it for at least a month before serving.

1 large navel orange
1 lime
1½ pounds sugar
1 tablespoon grated fresh ginger
1 cup black raisins
Two 3-inch cinnamon sticks
1 vanilla bean
3 pounds fresh cranberries, well picked over

Without peeling them,
cut the orange and lime into ¼-inch dice.

Place the sugar in a large heavy skillet
and cook carefully
until the sugar turns brown and caramelizes.
Do not let it burn.
Stir in the diced orange and lime, ginger, raisins,
cinnamon sticks and vanilla bean.
Cook over high heat, stirring constantly, for 5 minutes.

Fold the cranberries into the mixture,
coating each berry with the caramelized sugar.
Cook over medium heat for 10 minutes,
or until about half the cranberries break open.

Remove the pan from the heat and let the mixture cool.
Spoon it into sterilized jars.
Cover tightly and refrigerate for 1 month before using.
Will keep for about 3 months.

Makes about 1½ quarts.

Pear Baskets

While these pear baskets were specifically developed as a holder and accompaniment to the preceding Cranberry Relish, you can also fill them with a blanched almond or dried fruit mixture and use them as the accompaniment to a sorbet.

3 firm, ripe pears
½ cup dry white wine
¼ cup sugar
Juice of ½ lemon

Peel the pears and cut them in half lengthwise.
Remove the core with a melon baller or a small knife.
Cut a ¼-inch slice from the bottom of each half
so it will lie flat on the plate.

In a saucepan, heat the wine, sugar, lemon juice
and enough water to cover the pear halves.
When the sugar has dissolved, add the pears.
Bring the liquid to a boil,
lower the heat and simmer, covered, for 10 minutes,
or until the pears are tender
when pierced with a toothpick in their thickest parts.

Keep hot, or cool and reheat before serving.
Fill each with ¼ cup Cranberry Relish
(see recipe, page 421).

Serves 6.

It's always a delight to dine here!

ETHEL MERMAN

Pickled Onions

This is a relish to make when pearl onions are plentiful and then to keep and enjoy. A day's dedication to peeling onions will provide you with a fall's and winter's worth of this crisp accompaniment to pâtés.

2 cups small (¾-inch) pearl onions,
  all approximately the same size
2 tablespoons sea salt
Red wine vinegar

With very clean hands, peel the onions
and trim off both ends.
Place them in a 1-pint or 1½-pint sterilized jar.
Add the salt and enough red wine vinegar
to completely cover the onions.
Seal the jar tightly with its lid.

Refrigerate the onions for 3 weeks,
inverting the jar every week.

Remove the onions as needed
with a clean fork, tongs or spoon.
Never put your fingers in the jar
or the onions will lose their crispness.
They will keep for about 6 months.

Serve sliced with game pâtés.

Makes 2 cups.

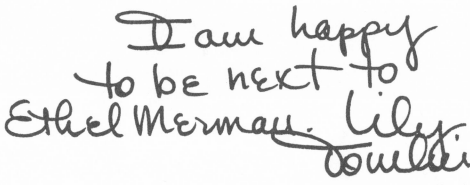

I am happy to be next to Ethel Merman. Lily Tomlin

LILY TOMLIN

With best musical and gastronomic wishes!

PLACIDO DOMINGO

1/31/79

Desserts

In a restaurant such as The Four Seasons, the desserts tend to be festive. We do, of course, have sorbets (pages 473 to 479) and ice creams (pages 481 to 486). Not all of our desserts can be made at home because some of them require special equipment. The chocolate Fancy Cake, for instance, which rides elegantly on top of our dessert cart and was invented by Albert Kumin when The Four Seasons opened, requires special chocolate rollers to create the great ribbons of chocolate which envelop the cake. We have chosen, therefore, some of our more popular desserts which can be made at home. Some of them may require more experience with pastry than others.

You always, of course, have the option of fruit and cheese for dessert, or you may wish to serve a hot soufflé (pages 487 to 493) for a different kind of gala finish to a meal. Certain special doughs are described on pages 519 to 529. We particularly call your attention to the Chocolate Puff Pastry (page 526). While this is used in the Bar Room Chocolate Cake (page 428), it is an unusual addition to your culinary repertoire and you can use it as a base for your own improvisations.

The question of which wine to serve with dessert is complex and one usually thinks of

Champagne or a sweet wine. The best of these wines are perhaps the Sauternes from France, the Spätlese of good years, as well as the Beerenausleses and Trockenbeerenausleses and Eisweins of the Moselle and Rhine valleys, but we cannot forget the great Tokays of our native Hungary or the fine late-harvest Rieslings now being produced in California. When desserts are extremely sweet, they may compete with and, indeed, kill the wines. Sweeter Champagnes are currently out of favor; for a change, try a demi-sec. With nut-based desserts, we often recommend a good, dry Madeira or a rich but not too sweet Port. Whatever your decision, do consider a wine with this course; it is too often neglected. At The Four Seasons, we always serve coffee separately after dessert.

Bar Room Chocolate Cake

This is like an intense chocolatey Napoleon or millefeuille without whipped cream. It is extremely popular in the Bar Room and its rectangular shape makes it easy to cut into even portions. Make your puff pastry dough at least a day in advance. The puff pastry may even be baked a day ahead if the weather is not humid. The puff pastry dough is pricked with a fork to prevent it from rising too much. The pastry should be layered and flaky but not puffed too high.

10 ounces Chocolate Puff Pastry (see recipe, page 526)
1 recipe Chocolate Buttercream (see recipe, page 533)
1 square semisweet chocolate
Confectioners' sugar

Roll the puff pastry into a 12 x 17-inch rectangle, $\frac{1}{16}$ inch thick.
Place it on a heavy, wet baking sheet.
Prick at $\frac{1}{4}$-inch intervals with the tines of a fork.
Chill for 1 hour.

Heat the oven to 450°F.

Bake the pastry in the preheated oven for 25 minutes.
Let cool to room temperature.
With a serrated knife,
cut the pastry crosswise into three equal pieces.
Put the best piece aside for the top.

Place one piece of the puff pastry on your work surface.
Spread with a $\frac{1}{2}$-inch layer of buttercream.
Top with another piece of pastry
and another layer of buttercream.
Place the last piece in place, flat side up.
Spread with a thin layer of buttercream.

Holding a square of chocolate over the cake,
make shavings with a vegetable peeler
so they fall directly onto the cake.
They should cover the whole top.
Chill.

When the buttercream is firm,
dip a long serrated knife into a glass of very hot water
and begin cutting.
First, trim the four edges so they are even.
Next, cut the cake in half lengthwise,
then crosswise in fifths
so you have ten equal pieces.
Sieve a light layer of confectioners' sugar
over the top.

Serves 10.

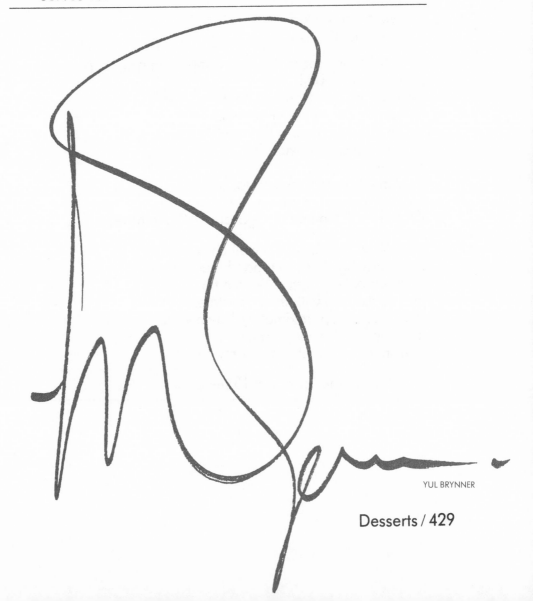

YUL BRYNNER

Chocolate Truffles

Chocolate truffles are actually a candy that normally follows the dessert and is served with coffee as a special extra surprise. However, many customers enjoy our truffles so much they would gladly make a dessert of them. These truffles will keep in the refrigerator for two weeks, providing no one in the family eats them, which is practically impossible. They seem to disappear as if by magic.

2 cups heavy cream
6 tablespoons sugar
¼ pound unsalted butter
31 ounces semisweet chocolate
6 tablespoons Grand Marnier
Unsweetened cocoa
Confectioners' sugar

Place the cream, sugar and butter in a saucepan
and bring to a boil.
Remove the pan from the heat
and stir in 21 ounces chocolate.
When the chocolate is thoroughly blended,
pour in the Grand Marnier.
Stir well.
Pour the mixture into a metal bowl
and refrigerate for about 1½ hours.
Every 10 to 15 minutes, vigorously stir the mixture.

When the mixture is well chilled and thick,
line a baking sheet with parchment paper.
Fit a pastry bag with a ⅝-inch tip
and fill the bag with the chocolate.
Pipe rounds, approximately 1 inch wide,
onto the parchment paper.
You should have about seventy rounds.

Refrigerate for about 15 minutes.

While the chocolate is chilling,
prepare the remaining 10 ounces chocolate for coating.
Melt the chocolate in the top of a double boiler
over simmering water.
The chocolate must be about 84°F. to coat properly.
If it is too warm, cool it by spreading it on a flat,
preferably marble, surface
and working it back and forth with a spatula
until it is cool enough.
Place the chocolate in a metal bowl
and warm it for a few seconds over simmering water
so the chocolate is about 87°F.
This is your tempered chocolate.
If, as you work, it gets too cold, reheat it gently again.

Mix equal parts of cocoa and confectioners' sugar,
about ¾ cup of each.
Remove the rounds from the refrigerator
and sift a light layer of the cocoa mixture over the top.
Coat your hands with the cocoa mixture
(this prevents sticking;
but only use a light layer since too much cocoa
will make the rounds difficult to coat).
Roll the rounds between your palms into smooth balls.
Return to the refrigerator for another 10 minutes.
The balls should be soft but firm.

Spread some of the tempered chocolate on your hands
and roll the balls between your hands to completely coat.
Return them to the parchment paper.
Add more chocolate to your hands as needed.
Return the coated balls to the refrigerator
for 2 minutes to harden the coating.

Place an inch of cocoa mixture in a bowl.
Again, coat your hands with the tempered chocolate
and coat the rounds completely with chocolate.
Drop them, still wet, into the cocoa and turn to coat.

Place the coated rounds in a flat sieve
and shake gently to remove the excess coating.
Refrigerate until ready to use.
The truffles will keep in the refrigerator for 2 weeks.

Makes about 6 dozen.

Frozen Chocolate Soufflé

Most frozen soufflés are based on a Bavarian cream type of mixture. Because chocolate has its own setting power when cold, it doesn't need the cooked custard base of the Bavarian. In fact, we get a lighter soufflé with our method.

¼ pound semisweet chocolate
2 ounces unsweetened chocolate
4 egg whites, at room temperature
⅔ cup sugar
2 tablespoons curaçao or orange liqueur
2 cups heavy cream

Fit a 1-quart soufflé mold with a collar (see directions for making a collar in the Basic Soufflé recipe, page 130).

Place the chocolates in a heavy saucepan and melt over low heat; set aside to cool.

In a clean bowl, beat the egg whites until frothy. Gradually pour in the sugar, and continue beating until you have slightly stiff peaks. Stir in the melted chocolate and curaçao.

In a separate bowl, whip the cream until stiff peaks form. Fold the cream into the egg white-chocolate mixture.

Spoon the mixture into the prepared mold. Cover and place in the freezer until solid, about 3 hours. About 15 minutes before serving, remove the soufflé to the refrigerator to defrost slightly.

Serves 8.

Almond Bavaroise

This creamy white dessert is the perfect end to a rich meal.

1 quart milk
¾ cup sugar
⅓ cup (3 ounces) almond paste
½ cup (2 ounces) finely ground almonds
½ cup cold water
Four ¼-ounce packages unflavored gelatin
2 cups heavy cream
2 tablespoons yellow chartreuse

Lightly oil a 12-cup mold.
Set aside.

Place the milk, sugar, almond paste and ground almonds in a saucepan.
Bring to a boil, stirring occasionally.
Remove from the heat and pour into a metal bowl; let cool.

Place the cold water in a bowl.
Sprinkle the gelatin over the top
and leave until it is dissolved,
then stir into the cooled almond mixture.

Fill a larger bowl with ice water
and set the metal bowl inside it.
Stir the mixture until it has thickened slightly.

In a separate bowl, whip the cream until stiff.
Fold it into the thickened mixture.
Fold in the chartreuse.

Pour the mixture into the oiled mold.
Tap to settle.
Chill in the refrigerator until completely set, about 4 hours.

When ready to serve, unmold onto a serving platter.

Serves 16 to 20.

Coconut Caramel Pudding

This is a very unusual version of a crème caramel, using cubes of sponge cake to add texture and definition. The custard itself is thickened and flavored by the coconut. You can prepare the sponge cake a day ahead. It is wonderful in taste, and we encourage you to use it as a base for other desserts.

1 ½ pounds (about 3 cups) sugar
4 cups milk
6 ounces sweetened shredded coconut (see note)
1 vanilla bean
9 eggs
Half 9-inch Sponge Cake (see recipe, page 531),
    cut into 1-inch cubes

Heat the oven to 375°F.

Place 1 pound sugar and 1 cup water in a skillet.
Cook over high heat, without stirring,
for about 10 minutes, or until the water evaporates
and the sugar caramelizes to a golden color.

Pour half the caramel into a 7½-inch soufflé dish.
Place in the refrigerator to chill.

Pour about ½ cup water
over the caramel remaining in the pan.
Stir until smooth, then set aside.

Place the milk, coconut and vanilla bean in a saucepan.
Slowly, bring to a boil and cook for 2 minutes.
Strain into a bowl; discard the coconut.
Split the vanilla bean and
scrape the seeds into the milk.

Place the eggs and the remaining ½ pound sugar
in a bowl and whisk until well blended.
Whisking the eggs, slowly pour some of the hot milk
into the eggs to raise their temperature.
When the eggs are hot, pour them into the milk,
whisking constantly.

Place the sponge cake over the caramel in the mold.
Pour in the hot custard.
It should fill the mold to the top.

Place the mold in a larger pan
and fill the pan with hot water
to come a third of the way up the sides of the mold.
Place in the preheated oven to bake for 45 to 50 minutes,
or until a knife inserted in the center comes out clean.

Remove the mold from the pan
and refrigerate for 1½ to 2 hours.

Unmold onto a platter.
Some of the caramel will remain in the mold.
Spoon the reserved caramel around the sides.

Serves 8.

Note:
Fresh coconut can, of course, be used. In that case, increase
the quantity of sugar to taste.

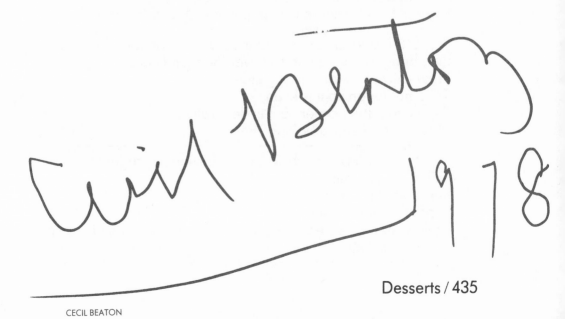

CECIL BEATON

Fig Strip

This dessert is like a spectacular giant-sized Fig Newton that combines figs, apricots, prunes and walnuts in a glazed sweet dough.

10 ounces dried figs, chopped
3 ounces dried apricots, chopped
3 ounces pitted prunes, chopped
¼ pound walnuts, chopped
¼ cup dry white wine
1 recipe Sweet Dough (see page 529)
Egg glaze (1 egg mixed with a pinch of salt
    and a pinch of sugar)
1 cup confectioners' sugar
1 egg white
½ teaspoon lemon juice
2 tablespoons apricot preserves, strained

Heat the oven to 375°F.

Place the figs, apricots, prunes and walnuts
in a food processor
and process until you have a smooth paste.
Remove the mixture to a bowl and stir in the wine.

On a floured work surface,
roll the dough out to a 12-inch square.
Starting about 1 inch in on three sides,
spread the fig mixture in a strip about 4½ inches wide.

Brush egg glaze around the side and bottom borders,
then bring the dough up to cover the fig mixture.
Press down to seal the long side.
Trim the dough so it is even,
them crimp the border so it is decorative.
Place on a greased baking sheet.

In a small bowl, whisk the confectioners' sugar
with the egg white
until very thick and white.
Stir in the lemon juice.
With a spatula, spread this glaze over the top of the fig strip.
Spread smooth.

Make a small cone
with a 3-inch square of parchment paper.
Fill the cone with the apricot preserves and cut off the tip.
Pipe lines of apricot lengthwise across the glaze.

Bake on the middle rack of the preheated oven
for 20 minutes, or until golden.
Turn off the oven and leave the strip for another 15 minutes.
If the oven retains the heat very well,
keep the door slightly ajar.

Let cool to room temperature.
Trim the sides so they are even
and cut crosswise into ¾-inch pieces.

Serves 14.

Feb. 8, 1977

A memorable day for me,

Louise Fletcher

LOUISE FLETCHER

Bourbon Pie

Every once in a while we serve a dessert, such as this one, which differs from our expected style. It is essentially a chiffon pie, and it's good enough to merit the change of pace. A very good bourbon served without ice in brandy snifters could be a dramatic accompaniment.

Crust
1½ cups all-purpose flour
½ teaspoon kosher salt
¼ pound unsalted butter, cut into 8 pieces
3 tablespoons vegetable shortening
2 to 3 tablespoons cold water

Place the flour and salt in a bowl.
Mix in the butter and shortening
with your fingers or two knives
until the mixture resembles coarse meal.
Slowly stir in the cold water,
adding only enough so the mixture holds together.
Knead briefly on a floured surface until smooth.
Wrap in waxed paper
and chill in the refrigerator for 1 hour.

Heat the oven to 425°F.

Roll the dough out on a floured surface
to a 10½-inch circle.
Fit into a 9½-inch pie pan.
With a fork, prick the bottom and sides of the crust
at ½-inch intervals.

Chill in the refrigerator for 10 to 15 minutes.
Line the chilled dough with a sheet of aluminum foil
and weight the dough with rice or beans.

Bake in the preheated oven for 10 minutes.
Remove the foil and weights
and continue baking until golden, 5 to 10 minutes longer.

Let the crust cool before filling.

Filling

4 egg yolks
½ cup sugar
2 tablespoons lemon juice
2 teaspoons grated lemon rind
2½ teaspoons unflavored gelatin
4 teaspoons cold water
2 tablespoons boiling water
5 tablespoons bourbon
1⅓ cups heavy cream
3 egg whites, at room temperature

Place the egg yolks in a mixing bowl.
Gradually whisk in 6 tablespoons sugar.
Stir in the lemon juice and rind.

Sprinkle the gelatin over the cold water
and set aside until the water absorbs the gelatin.
Add the hot water and stir to dissolve.
Stir into the egg yolk mixture, then add the bourbon.

Beat ⅔ cup cream until stiff,
then fold into the bourbon mixture.

In a clean bowl, beat the egg whites
until they hold soft peaks.
Add the remaining 2 tablespoons sugar
and beat until stiff.
Fold into the bourbon mixture.

Spread the filling into the baked pie shell,
letting it dome in the middle.
Chill in the refrigerator until firm.

Beat the remaining ⅔ cup cream until stiff,
then spread it over the top of the pie.

Serves 8 to 10.

JOHN V. LINDSAY

Pine Nut Galette

Raspberry preserves topped with crushed pine nuts, topped with a rich frangipane, topped with more pine nuts, and a dusting of sugar—all atop a rich, sweet cookie dough—clearly a most delectable dessert.

½ recipe *Sweet Dough* (see page 529)
3 tablespoons strained raspberry preserves
¼ pound (about 1⅓ cups) pine nuts
1 recipe *Frangipane* (recipe follows)
Confectioners' sugar

Heat the oven to 375°F.

Grease a 9-inch tart pan
with a removable bottom.

Roll out the dough
to a 9-inch circle about ¼ inch thick.
Fit it into the prepared pan.

Spread the bottom with a layer of the preserves.

Roughly crush 1 ounce of the pine nuts
with a rolling pin and sprinkle over the preserves.

Spread the frangipane over the nuts,
spreading it evenly.
Top with the remaining pine nuts.

Sieve a heavy layer of confectioners' sugar
over the top.
Place on a baking sheet
and bake in the preheated oven for 30 to 35 minutes.
Let cool to room temperature.

Serves 8.

Frangipane

7 ounces almond paste
¼ pound unsalted butter, at room temperature
2 eggs
3 egg yolks
1 lemon
¼ teaspoon almond extract
3 ounces (7 tablespoons) all-purpose flour

Place the almond paste and butter in a bowl
and beat until well blended, light and fluffy.
Slowly beat in the eggs and yolks,
beating well after each addition.
Grate in the lemon rind, then its juice.
Stir in the almond extract.
Mix well.
Whisk in the flour, beating until smooth.

Thank you so much for one of the Great lunches

Best Wishes,

Malcolm McDowell

MALCOLM McDOWELL

27 September 1979

Walnut Tart

This rather unusual tart has two crusts and a rich nut and caramel filling. It is probably something your guests have not seen before. We think it's especially good served with our Vanilla Ice Cream (page 482).

Filling

2¼ cups sugar
2 cups heavy cream
1 pound 2 ounces walnut halves or large pieces

Heat a 10-inch skillet.
Over low heat, add ½ cup sugar.
Stir with a wooden spoon until melted and light brown.
Then, stir in another ½ cup sugar
and stir until it melts.
Keep adding the sugar in this way.
Do not let it brown too fast.
Keep cooking until the sugar is dark brown
and no crystals remain.
The total cooking time for the sugar should be
about 10 to 15 minutes.

Slowly stir in the cream
and cook for about 2 minutes, stirring occasionally.
Stir in the walnuts and mix well.
Place the mixture in the refrigerator
to chill thoroughly, about 1 hour.

Assembly

1 recipe Sweet Dough (see page 529), chilled
Egg glaze (1 egg mixed with a pinch of salt and
  a pinch of sugar)
Confectioners' sugar

Heat the oven to 400°F.

Divide the dough into two pieces,
one almost twice the size of the other.
Place the larger piece of dough
between two sheets of waxed paper
and roll into a 13-inch circle.
Fit the dough into an 11-inch buttered tart pan
with a removable bottom.
Press the dough
so it fits completely and evenly into the pan;
trim off the excess.
Prick the bottom of the pastry all over with a fork.
Chill in the refrigerator for 15 minutes.

Line the pastry with aluminum foil
and fill it with beans or rice to weight it.
Place the pan on a baking sheet
and bake in the preheated oven for 15 minutes.
Remove the foil and weights;
return the crust to the oven
to bake for another 5 to 8 minutes,
or until lightly browned.

Place the crust on a rack
and let cool to room temperature.
While the crust cools, roll the remaining dough
between sheets of waxed paper to an 11½-inch round.
Place in the refrigerator to chill.

Fill the cooled crust with the walnut filling,
pressing it into all the corners
and making sure the top is fairly level.
Brush egg glaze around the edge of the cooled crust
and place the chilled round of dough over the filling.
Press the edges to seal.
Trim off the excess dough.

Brush egg glaze over the top,
place on a baking sheet and bake for 25 minutes.

Let cool to room temperature for at least 3 hours.
If desired, top with unsweetened whipped cream.

Serves 12.

WILLIAM SHIRER

William S. Shirer — Paris — 1929

Hazelnut Japonaise

This is a torte in the best Viennese sense of the word. It is built with layers of cake, meringue and buttercream, covered with buttercream and then finished with crushed hazelnuts. The sponge cake, meringue and buttercream can all be made ahead if the weather is not too humid, and then assembled before serving. The cake should be assembled at least an hour ahead for its flavors to blend, but if finished too far ahead, it will get soggy.

1 recipe Hazelnut Sponge Cake (recipe follows)
1 recipe Almond Meringue (recipe follows)
Praline Buttercream (see recipe, page 532)
Rum
Ground hazelnuts
Confectioners' sugar

Split the cake in half so you have two layers.

Place a meringue layer on your serving plate.
Spread with a thin layer of buttercream.
Then top with a sponge layer.
Sprinkle the sponge with some rum.
Spread a layer of buttercream about ⅛ inch thick.
Repeat the assembly.
Top with a meringue layer, flat side up.

Spread buttercream over the tops and sides, then press the ground nuts into the buttercream around the sides.

Cut strips of cardboard 1 inch wide and place them in parallel lines across the top of the cake, leaving a 1-inch space between them.
Sieve confectioners' sugar over the top, then carefully remove the strips.

Serves 8 to 10.

Hazelnut Sponge Cake

1 egg
2 egg yolks
3 ounces (1 cup) finely ground hazelnuts
½ cup sugar
1 teaspoon vanilla extract
3 egg whites, at room temperature
6 tablespoons all-purpose flour
1 teaspoon baking powder

Heat the oven to 375°F.
Grease and flour an 8-inch springform pan.

Place the egg and egg yolks in a bowl and
whisk to blend.
Stir in the hazelnuts and 6 tablespoons of sugar,
whisking until thick.
Blend in the vanilla.

In a separate bowl, beat the egg whites until thick.
Add the remaining 2 tablespoons sugar
and continue beating until stiff.

In a small bowl, mix the flour and baking powder.

Fold the egg whites into the nut mixture,
then fold in the flour mixture.
Pour into the prepared cake pan.

Place the pan on a baking sheet
and bake in the preheated oven for 35 minutes,
or until the top comes up when pressed in the center.

Makes one 8-inch layer.

Almond Meringue

2 ounces ground blanched almonds
2 tablespoons cornstarch
½ cup egg whites, at room temperature
¼ cup sugar

Take a piece of corrugated cardboard ⅛ inch thick.
Cut out a 9-inch circle with a handle.
Cut out an 8-inch circle inside the 9-inch circle
so you have a ring with a handle.
This is your mold.

Heat the oven to 350°F.
and line two baking sheets with parchment paper.

Mix the ground almonds and cornstarch together
to blend well.

Place the egg whites in a bowl and beat until foamy.
Slowly add the sugar
and continue beating until the egg whites are stiff.
Fold the almond mixture into the egg whites.

Place the cardboard mold on the parchment paper
and spread some of the mixture inside
so you have an 8-inch round, ⅛ inch thick.
Make the top flat with a spatula, removing excess batter.
Repeat until you have three circles, two on one sheet.

Place the baking sheets in the oven and
bake for 15 to 20 minutes,
or until the meringues are brown and dry.
Let cool, then peel off the paper.

Makes three 8-inch round meringues.

SEPT 23. 1975.
My best birthday to date
(seventy fifth!?)

Helen Hayes

HELEN HAYES

446 / Desserts

Hazelnut Cake with Chocolate Chunks

This loaf cake is the ultimate, elegant pound cake, although quite a bit lighter in texture. It is good enough to be a dessert at any dinner.

4 ounces semisweet chocolate
5½ ounces (about 1¾ cups) ground hazelnuts
4 ounces (about ¾ cup) all-purpose flour
1 ounce (about 3 tablespoons) cornstarch
11 tablespoons unsalted butter, at room temperature
2 ounces (about ¼ cup) almond paste
9½ ounces (about 1 cup plus 6 tablespoons) sugar
2 eggs
1 teaspoon vanilla extract
1½ to 2 tablespoons water
4 egg whites, at room temperature

Glaze
Apricot preserves, strained and heated
1 tablespoon lemon juice
¼ cup confectioners' sugar
1½ tablespoons water

Grease and flour a 4½ x 9½ x 2½-inch or two 4 x 5 x 2½-inch loaf pans.
Set aside.

Heat the oven to 350°F.

With a knife, roughly cut the chocolate into chunks no more than ¾ inch wide.
Place the chocolate in a bowl with the ground hazelnuts, flour and cornstarch.
Set aside.

Place the butter, almond paste and 6 ounces sugar
in the bowl of an electric mixer.
Beat until fluffy,
then beat in the eggs, one at a time,
beating well after each addition.
Beat in the vanilla.

Stir in the chocolate mixture and mix well.
Add 1½ tablespoons water and mix well.
If the mixture is very stiff,
add a little more water so it is creamy.

Beat the egg whites with a whisk.
When foamy, slowly add the remaining 3½ ounces sugar.
Beat until stiff but not dry.

Stir about one-fourth of the egg white mixture
into the flour mixture.
Fold in the remaining egg white mixture
until completely mixed.
Drop the batter into the prepared pan(s),
tapping lightly to settle.
When filled,
tap the pan gently on the work surface to settle.
Smooth the top.

Place the loaf pan(s) on a baking sheet
and bake in the preheated oven
for 55 to 60 minutes for the large pan
or 45 to 55 minutes for the small pans,
or until a knife in the center comes out clean.

Place on a rack and let cool in the pan(s) for 5 minutes.
Remove the cake from the pan(s) and place on a rack to
cool. While the cake is still hot,
spread a layer of apricot preserves over the top.
Let rest 10 minutes.

Mix the lemon juice, confectioners' sugar and water
to make a glaze.
Spread this over the top.
Let the cake cool to room temperature.
Do not refrigerate.
Cut in slices to serve.

Serves 20.

Crêpes Soufflés

Our version of this dessert has many components; the crêpes are filled with flavored pastry cream and poached beaten egg whites, then topped with a caramel sauce. However, all the elements can be prepared ahead. You will have to slip away from your guests just before you want to serve dessert, assemble the crêpes and pop them into a preheated oven. If you have ovenproof dessert plates, the crêpes soufflés can be prepared individually. The dessert is spectacular and worth the last-minute trouble. As with so many of Chef Renggli's recipes, the recipes for the components of this dish, such as the crêpe batter that uses carbonated water, are special and should be remembered for future use.

Filling

3 egg whites, at room temperature
9½ tablespoons sugar
1½ cups water
1½ cups milk

Beat the egg whites until frothy,
then slowly beat in the sugar.
Continue beating until the mixture is stiff.

Place the water and milk in a saucepan
and bring just to a simmer; do not let the liquid boil.

Drop about ¼ cup of the egg white mixture at a time
into the simmering liquid and poach 3 minutes.
Turn and poach 3 minutes longer.
Remove with a slotted spoon to a towel to drain.

Assembly

1 tablespoon Grand Marnier
1 cup Pastry Cream (see recipe, page 530), at room
   temperature
Confectioners' sugar

Heat the oven to 400°F.

Stir the Grand Marnier into the pastry cream.

Place about 2 tablespoons pastry cream
in the center of each of eight Crêpes (recipe follows).
Top each with a poached egg white.
Fold the sides in to cover.

Place the crêpes, open side down,
in a buttered 9 x 12-inch baking dish.

Bake in the preheated oven for 7 minutes.
Sieve confectioners' sugar over the top
and serve with Caramel Sauce (recipe follows) on the side.

Serves 8.

Crêpes

⅔ cup milk
2 eggs
1 cup minus 2 tablespoons all-purpose flour
⅔ teaspoon sugar
Pinch kosher salt
⅔ cup carbonated water
Clarified butter

Mix together the milk and eggs.
Stir in the flour, sugar and salt
to make a smooth pancake dough.
Let the dough rest 1 to 2 hours.

Just before cooking the pancakes,
stir in the carbonated water.

Heat a 7-inch crêpe pan.
When it is hot, add ¼ teaspoon clarified butter.
Let the butter melt and cover the bottom of the pan.

Pour a ladle of batter into the pan,
gently tipping and twisting the pan
so the batter covers the entire bottom.

Return the pan to the heat.
When the top of the batter bubbles,
turn the pancake over and cook for 4 or 5 seconds longer.
Remove from the pan.

Continue cooking until all the batter is used.
Add butter before each pancake is cooked.

Makes 8 to 10 crêpes.

Caramel Sauce

1 cup sugar
¾ cup water

Place the sugar and ¼ cup water in a skillet.
Cook, without stirring, until the water evaporates
and the sugar turns golden brown.

Pour in the remaining ½ cup water
and stir until smooth.

Makes about 1 cup sauce.

MARGAUX HEMINGWAY

Let's hope the next 3 seasons are as good as this one! my best.

Apple Pithiviers

Pithiviers is a sort of free-form, two-crusted pie, a giant turnover made with puff pastry and filled with almonds. Our apple and hazelnut version is even lighter than the classic. You might want to experiment with different fruits of your choice.

1 ½ pounds (5 or 6) McIntosh apples
2 lemons
2 ounces raisins
½ teaspoon ground cinnamon
¼ cup heavy cream
¾ cup sugar
1 egg
¼ pound unsalted butter
3 ounces (10 tablespoons) dry bread crumbs
3 ounces (1 cup) ground hazelnuts
1 pound Puff Pastry Dough (see recipe, page 523)
Egg glaze (1 egg mixed with a pinch of salt and
    a pinch of sugar)
Confectioners' sugar

Peel and core the apples.
Cut them in quarters,
then cut them crosswise into ½-inch slices.
Place in a bowl.
Grate in the rind from the lemons
and then squeeze in their juice.
Stir in the raisins and cinnamon.
Mix well.

In a separate bowl,
whisk the cream, sugar and egg until smooth.

Heat the butter in a 10-inch skillet until foamy.
Stir in the bread crumbs and hazelnuts
and cook until coated.
Add the apple mixture and stir to coat the apples.
Scrape in the cream mixture and stir to mix well.
Set aside to cool.

Line a baking sheet with parchment paper.

Roll the puff pastry out into a rectangle
12½ inches wide and ¼ inch thick.
Cut out two circles—one 9½ inches in diameter,
the other 12 inches in diameter.
Place the small circle on the parchment paper
and add the apple mixture,
leaving a ½-inch border all around.
Pack the mixture down so the sides are fairly straight
and the top fairly level.
It should be about 1½ inches high.

Brush egg glaze around the border.
Place the larger circle over the top
and press so it fits tightly around the apple mixture.
Press the border to seal well.
Trim the excess dough.
Then make a decorative edge by pinching the dough
with your fingers to make a scallop.

Starting about 1 inch from the center
and working until 1 inch from the edge,
cut curving lines through the pastry at
1-inch intervals around the dough.
Brush the top with egg glaze.
Chill for 30 minutes.

Heat the oven to 375°F.

Place in the preheated oven for 20 minutes,
or until the dough is crusty.
Sift a layer of confectioners' sugar over the top
and return to the oven.
After another 15 minutes,
sift another layer of confectioners' sugar on top
and turn the oven heat to broil.
Broil until the top is glazed.

Serve warm or at room temperature.

Serves 8 to 10.

Fresh Fruit Salad

The Four Seasons always offers some fruit compote (see next recipe) or fresh fruit for dessert. Our fruit salad is not so much a traditional salad as an artful arrangement of fresh fruit accompanied by a sauce.

Sauce

¼ cup raisins
1 tablespoon triple sec, kirsch, Grand Marnier, brandy or rum
¼ cup walnut pieces
1 cup crème fraîche
¼ cup thyme honey

Chop the raisins roughly.
Place them in a bowl and cover with the liquor.

Finely chop the walnuts and add to the bowl.
Stir in the crème fraîche and honey.
Stir to mix well.
Chill until ready to serve.

Fruit

1 grapefruit
6 oranges
12 strawberries
3 green apples
½ cantaloupe
⅛ honeydew melon

Prepare the fruit as follows:
With a knife, cut the rind completely from the grapefruit.
Cut it crosswise into ¼-inch slices.
Reserve six slices for the salad.

Cut pieces off the top and bottom of the oranges.
With a knife, cut off all the rind.
Then cut the oranges into quarters,
discarding the cores.

Wash the strawberries,
remove the stems and cut them in half lengthwise.

Cut the apples into quarters.
Then take each quarter
and cut across from one cut end to the other
so you have pieces flat on the bottom
and green on top.
Discard the core pieces.
Place the apple pieces flat on your work surface
and cut crosswise into even slices $\frac{1}{16}$ inch thick.

Peel the melons and remove all the seeds.
Slice the cantaloupe into twelve thin wedges
and the honeydew into six.

Assembly

Arrange the fruit on six 10-inch plates as follows:
Place two cantaloupe wedges
with a honeydew wedge between them
on the top of each plate, pointing toward the center.

Opposite the melon, place a grapefruit slice.
Arrange four strawberry halves around each grapefruit slice.

On either side of each plate,
place two orange pieces.
Between them, fan out a sliced apple section,
green side up.

Place a large dollop of sauce
on top of each grapefruit slice.

Serves 6.

Billy Carter

BILLY CARTER

Plains, Ga

8-29-77

Pineapple Compote

One of the various compotes we prepare daily at The Four Seasons, this is interesting enough to serve as a dessert after a special dinner.

1 pineapple
2 cups water
1 cup sugar
1 cup dry white wine
1 cinnamon stick
4 slices lemon
Sorbet
Strawberries soaked in cassis to cover

Place the pineapple on its side.
With a large sharp knife,
cut diagonally across the leaves
about 3 inches from their bottom.
Rotate the pineapple and cut again.
Rotate and cut two more times
so the leaves are neatly trimmed and come to a point.

With a large knife,
cut a thin slice off the bottom of the pineapple
so it can stand flat on your work surface.
Holding it that way,
cut off the peel by cutting from the leaves to the bottom
and rotating the pineapple until all the peel is removed.

Cut the pineapple, with its leaves,
into sixteen even wedges.
With a small knife,
cut out and discard the hard core from each wedge.

Divide the pineapple into two 10-inch skillets, and place
the wedges in a layer in each pan.
To each pan,
add 1 cup water, ½ cup sugar,
½ cup dry white wine,
½ cinnamon stick and 2 lemon slices.
Place over medium heat
and cook until the sugar dissolves.
Cover the pans and cook 5 minutes longer.
Turn off the heat and let the pineapple cool in the syrup.

Place two pineapple wedges,
leaves pointing in the same direction
and curves facing each other, on each of eight plates.
Place two or three scoops of sorbet
in the middle of the plate.

Garnish with some macerated strawberries.

Serves 8.

*A memorable day
when Mrs. Citizin Kane
met Mrs. Orson Welles
and her beautiful daughter,
who might have been mine!
Salud!
Ruth Warrick*

RUTH WARRICK

Figs with Whipped Cream

Really ripe figs have a short season; but when they are available, they are a splendid dessert topped as they are here with whipped cream lightly seasoned with a touch of Grand Marnier.

16 very ripe figs, preferably purple
1 cup heavy cream
2 tablespoons sugar
1 teaspoon Grand Marnier

With a small knife, peel the figs.
Cut off and discard the very tips.
Cut each fig into even quarters,
stopping about ¼ inch from the bottom.

Arrange four figs on each of four plates,
spreading them open so they resemble stars.

In a chilled bowl,
whip the cream until thick.
Beat in the sugar
and continue beating until soft peaks form.
Beat in the Grand Marnier.

Spoon dollops of whipped cream into the open figs.

Serves 4.

Pear Mousse with Poached Pears

Although there is an actual pear mousse in this recipe, the finished dessert has the assembled look of a torte. The sponge cake layer, the mousse, and the poached pears can all be prepared ahead.

Mousse

1½ packages (¼ ounce each) unflavored gelatin
¼ cup cold water
2 cups pear purée (see note)
2 to 3 tablespoons pear brandy
Juice of 1 lemon
4 egg whites, at room temperature
¾ cup sugar
½ cup heavy cream

Sprinkle the gelatin over the cold water.
Set aside until the water absorbs the gelatin,
then heat gently until the gelatin dissolves.
Set aside to cool.

Stir the gelatin into the purée.
Then stir in the pear brandy and lemon juice.

In a clean bowl, beat the egg whites until foamy.
Gradually beat in the sugar
and continue beating until stiff peaks form.
Fold into the pear purée.

In a separate bowl, whip the cream until stiff.
Then, fold into the purée.

Pour the mixture into an 8-inch round mold
and chill for several hours, or until set.

Assembly
⅓-inch layer Sponge Cake (see recipe, page 531)
1 recipe Pears Poached in Red Wine (recipe follows)
Sweetened whipped cream

To unmold the mousse, dip the pan briefly in hot water.
Place the sponge layer over the mousse
and turn them over together onto a serving platter.

Garnish with the poached pears and whipped cream.

Serves 8.

Note:
To make pear purée, cook pears as for Pear Baskets (see
recipe, page 422), not bothering to trim them to lie flat.
When cooked through, purée them in a food processor or
through a food mill. You will need 4 or 5 pears for 2 cups of
purée.

Pears Poached in Red Wine

This simple dessert is extremely pretty, since the red wine tints the pears a deep red bordering on maroon.

2 cups sugar
1 bottle (about 3 cups) dry red wine
One 5-inch cinnamon stick
4 whole cloves
4 ripe pears, peeled, halved and cored

Place the sugar, wine, cinnamon and cloves in a 10-inch frying pan.
Bring to a boil and stir to dissolve the sugar.

Add the pear halves, lower the heat to simmer and cook for 10 minutes,
or until the pears are just barely cooked through.

Remove the pears to a side dish.
Discard the cinnamon and cloves.

Cook the liquid slowly until it reduces to a thick syrup, about 15 minutes.
Return the pear halves, cut side down, to the pan.
Cook for another 5 minutes,
continually spooning syrup over the pears.

Serve hot or cold.

3/23/77

ORSON WELLES

Feuilleté with Fresh Fruit

These are individual puff pastry shells filled with pastry cream and fresh fruit. If you slice the fruit ahead, put a little bit of lemon juice on it so that it does not discolor. The feuilleté should be prepared ahead but not baked until just before dinner. The fruits can be varied according to the season, in which case you may want to vary the white alcohol as well so that the fruit flavors mingle harmoniously.

6 unbaked *feuilleté boats* (see *Puff Pastry recipe, page 523*)
Sugar
½ cup plus 9 strawberries, hulled
1½ cups *Pastry Cream* (see *recipe, page 530*)
1½ teaspoons framboise
½ cup heavy cream
1 small cantaloupe, peeled, seeded and sliced
3 kiwis, peeled and sliced
Apricot preserves, strained and heated

Heat the oven to 425°F.

Place the cut puff pastry dough on a wet baking sheet and freeze for 10 minutes.
Sprinkle the tops with a layer of sugar.

Place in the preheated oven, lower the heat to 400°F. and bake for 25 minutes.

Meanwhile, purée the ½ cup strawberries in a food mill or food processor.
Stir the purée into the pastry cream and add the framboise.

Whip the cream until stiff and fold into the strawberry mixture.

Cut the tops off the baked feuilleté boats and set aside.
Pull out the center of the bottoms and fill with the prepared cream mixture.

Cut the remaining strawberries in half lengthwise.
Place a row of each fruit over the pastry cream
on each feuilleté.

Brush a layer of apricot preserves over all the fruit.
Top with the feuilleté tops set over the fruit at an angle.

Serves 6.

Note:
Vary the fruit according to the season.
In making your selection, try to contrast colors and textures.

Four Seasons
are not enough
when the food
is as superlative
as it is at
The Four Seasons!

Garson Kanin

GARSON KANIN

20. X. 75

Fruit Tart

This is more elaborate than the usual fruit tart as it is built up into a dome with layers of sponge cake in graduated sizes and the pastry cream spread in between. This keeps the fruit from sinking into the pastry cream and gives a better texture to the finished tart. As with our other fruit desserts, choose the fruits according to your taste and the season.

Melted semisweet chocolate
One 9-inch baked Linzer Dough tart shell
  (see recipe, page 528)
One 9-inch Sponge Cake (see recipe, page 531)
1 cup green grapes
1 cup black grapes
2 bananas
1 cup heavy cream
1 cup Pastry Cream (see recipe, page 530)
Apricot preserves, strained and heated

Spread a thin layer of melted chocolate along the bottom and sides of the tart shell. Let dry.

Slice the sponge cake into three equal layers. Trim one layer into an even 8-inch circle and one into a 5-inch circle. Set one whole layer and the trimmings aside for another use (see note).

If the grapes have seeds, cut them in half lengthwise and discard the seeds. If they do not have seeds, you may leave them whole.

Peel the bananas and cut them crosswise into ¼-inch-thick slices.

Whip the heavy cream until stiff, then fold into the pastry cream.

Spread a layer of the cream mixture about ½ inch thick
in the tart shell.
Top with the 8-inch sponge layer.
Add more pastry cream so it slopes in from the sides.
Top with the 5-inch sponge layer.
Top with more cream.
Using a long metal spatula, spread some more cream
over everything except the tart shell
and smooth it so it comes to a gentle dome.

Arrange alternating rows of concentric circles
of banana slices, black grapes and green grapes
over the cream until it is completely covered.

Brush a layer of preserves over all the fruit.

Serves 8.

Note:
The extra sponge cake may be used for the Coconut
Caramel Pudding (see recipe, page 434).
If wrapped well, the cake will keep in the freezer for several
months.

— With fond recollections of
many delightful evenings
at the Four Seasons —

Lillian Ross

LILLIAN ROSS

7/31/75

Fruit Flan

A version of this fruit flan, made with crisp, flaky puff pastry, is almost always on our dessert cart. Sometimes we replace the pastry cream with a thin layer of liqueur-soaked sponge cake; other times we omit both and let the natural freshness of a fruit such as raspberries stand alone. In any case, the fruits vary with the market and our whim. The apricot preserves we use here not only add flavor but help to seal the pastry and keep it from getting soggy after the pastry cream and fruit have been placed on it. The extra apricot preserves are used to glaze the fruit.

1 pound Puff Pastry (see recipe, page 523)
Egg glaze (1 egg mixed with a pinch of sugar and
 a pinch of salt)
Confectioners' sugar
2 very ripe peaches
½ honeydew melon
Apricot preserves, strained and heated
1 cup Pastry Cream (see recipe, page 530)
¾ cup blueberries

On a lightly floured surface,
roll the puff pastry into a 10 x 15-inch rectangle, ⅟₁₆ inch thick.
From this, cut an even 9 x 14-inch rectangle.
From that, cut off two strips, each 1 x 14 inches long.
Brush egg glaze over the large rectangle.
Place one 1-inch strip on top of the rectangle along one side,
lining up the edges so they are even.
Repeat with the second strip on the other side.

Place the dough on a wet baking sheet.
If desired, take a 1-inch round pastry cutter and
cut a decorative pattern along the long sides
by cutting away half circles of dough.
Freeze the dough for 30 minutes.

Heat the oven to 400°F.

Place a weight down the center of the strip
so the bottom will not rise as high as the sides.
Bake for 15 minutes,
then sift a layer of confectioners' sugar over the sides.

Bake 10 minutes longer, then remove the weight and
bake until cooked through and golden,
about another 10 minutes.
Let cool before filling.

While the shell bakes, peel and pit the peaches
and cut each into ¼-inch wedges.
Peel and seed the melon and
cut it into ¾-inch balls with a melon baller.

When the shell is cool,
brush a layer of apricot preserves along the bottom.
Spread an even layer of pastry cream over the preserves.
Arrange the fruit in rows down the pastry cream.
Place the peaches in two rows against the edges.
Place a row of melon next to each row of peaches.
Fill the center with blueberries.

Spread apricot preserves over the fruit.
To serve, cut crosswise into eight slices.

Serves 8.

We came back to celebrate our first big date—
10 years, here—before I went to Vietnam.
So much has changed—but the main—
the best restaurant for lovers!
Thanks for the champagne for our anniversary!
Dan & Pat

DAN & PAT ELLSBERG

Chestnut Couronne

Chestnuts, with their firm brown shells, are quite a bit of work to split, heat and then peel. Fortunately, this exceptional and impressive confection thoroughly rewards your efforts. When chestnuts are out of season, canned purée makes a satisfactory substitute.

2 egg whites, at room temperature
½ cup sugar
Confectioners' sugar
1 recipe Purée of Chestnuts (see page 344)
1 cup heavy cream

Draw an 8-inch circle on a sheet of parchment paper. Place on a baking sheet.

Heat the oven to 200°F.

Beat the egg whites until fluffy.
Gradually beat in the sugar and continue beating until the mixture is stiff and shiny.

Fit a pastry bag with a ½-inch tip.
Fill with the meringue mixture
and pipe a spiral inside the circle
beginning at the outside and working in.
Fill in any holes with extra mixture.

Bake in the oven until completely dry
but not brown, about 1½ hours.
The meringue should not stick at all to the paper.

Sprinkle an 8-inch tube pan
with a layer of confectioners' sugar.
Fit a pastry bag with an ⅛-inch round tip.
Fill the bag with the chestnut purée
and pipe the purée randomly into the mold to fill.
The result should look something like tangled string.

Center the meringue over the mold
and turn the meringue and mold over together
onto a serving plate.

Whip the cream until soft peaks form.

Fit a pastry bag with a ⅜-inch tip
and fill it with the cream.
Pipe the cream into the center of the chestnut purée
and make dots around the top and outer rim.
If desired, garnish with chestnuts packed in syrup,
drained.

Serve with Chocolate Rum Sauce (recipe follows).

Serves 12.

Chocolate Rum Sauce

9 ounces semisweet chocolate
6 tablespoons hot water
3 tablespoons dark rum
¼ cup heavy cream

Melt the chocolate in the top of a double boiler.
Whisk in the water and rum,
then the heavy cream.
Set aside to cool to room temperature and thicken.

Makes 1½ cups.

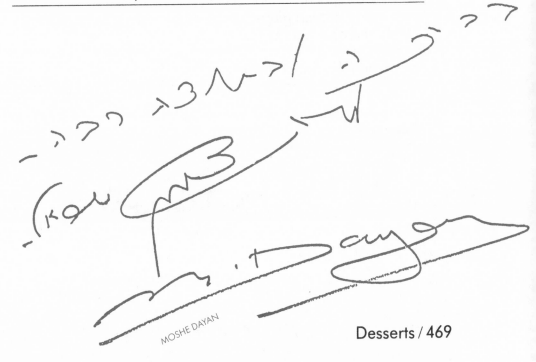

MOSHE DAYAN

The Four Seasons Christmas Fruitcake

Every Christmas, we send gift baskets to our cherished customers and in it we include our fruitcake. After being asked for the recipe for many years, we have finally agreed to share it. We think it is very special—light in color and kept moist by a marzipan wrapping rather than by soaking it, as is usual, in brandy.

1 pound 10 ounces unsalted butter
1 pound 10 ounces (about 3½ cups) sugar
20 eggs
2 pounds 12 ounces (about 11 cups) bread flour
3 pounds candied fruit
   (oranges, lemons, angelica, red and green cherries),
   chopped
1 vanilla bean
½ cup rum
½ teaspoon ground cinnamon
½ teaspoon ground ginger
Grated rind of 2 lemons
Juice of 1 lemon
2 cups roughly chopped walnuts

21 Dec. 76
There is _no_ better place
to celebrate winter

William Goldman

WILLIAM GOLDMAN

Topping
Confectioners' sugar
3 pounds marzipan
Simple Syrup (see recipe, page 474)
Granulated sugar
Melted semisweet chocolate (optional)

Grease and flour five 8 x 4 x 2½-inch loaf pans.
Set aside.

Heat the oven to 400°F.

Place the butter in a mixing bowl
and beat until smooth.
Slowly add the sugar and keep beating
until the mixture is very light and fluffy.

Begin adding the eggs, three at a time,
beating well after each addition.
When half the eggs have been added,
beat in about ½ pound flour.
Add the rest of the eggs, three at a time.

Add about 1 cup flour to the candied fruit and
toss to coat.
Add the remaining flour to the mixing bowl.
Split the vanilla bean lengthwise and
scrape the seeds into the batter.
Stir in the remaining ingredients
except the fruit and nuts.
Blend well.

Add the fruit and nuts and
stir just to mix.
Divide the batter among the prepared pans,
tapping them against the work surface
to settle the mixture.
Smooth the top with a spatula.

Place the pans on a baking sheet
and bake in the preheated oven for 1 hour 15 minutes.
Let cool completely.
If the top is rounded, trim it so it is flat.

PETER MAAS

Sprinkle your work surface with confectioners' sugar.
Divide the marzipan into five parts.
Roll each into a ¼-inch-thick rectangle.
Add more confectioners' sugar as needed
to prevent sticking.
Trim the marzipan to an even 8 x 14-inch rectangle.

Brush the marzipan with simple syrup.
Place a cooled fruitcake over the marzipan
and roll up to completely coat (except for the short ends)
in the marzipan.

Place granulated sugar on a sheet of waxed paper.
Brush the top and sides of the marzipan coating
with sugar syrup
and then dip the marzipan in the sugar to coat.

With a knife, make a crosshatch design on top.
If desired, melt some semisweet chocolate
and decorate the sides with a row of chocolate
and the top with chocolate leaves or other designs.
Repeat with the remaining fruitcakes and marzipan.

Makes 5 fruitcakes.

JIMMY BRESLIN

It is almost as nice as Maas fayr

Sorbets

Often a complex and rich meal is best completed by what appears to be a simple sorbet but which is, in fact, a very special course.

Most of the sorbets which follow balance a fruit, an alcohol and a simple syrup—a bland mixture of sugar and water which controls the crystallizing quality of the sorbet. What follows then is a simple syrup recipe and the ingredients for the various sorbets as well as general procedural instructions. There are also a few sorbets which use a slightly different technique.

At The Four Seasons, we serve a combination of four different scoops of sorbet in a pastry shell.

Fruit Sorbets

General Procedure

Have the simple syrup at room temperature
or colder.
Mix the fruit purée or juice with the flavorings,
then stir in the simple syrup.

Place in an ice cream freezer and
freeze according to the manufacturer's directions.
If not serving immediately, keep in the freezer.
Just before serving,
beat the sorbet in a blender or food processor.

Makes a generous 4 cups.

Simple Syrup

1 cup sugar
2 cups water

Place the sugar and water in a saucepan.
Stir to dissolve the sugar.
Bring the water to a boil and cook for 5 minutes.
Let cool before using to make sorbets.

This will keep practically indefinitely
in a covered jar in the refrigerator.

Makes about 2 cups.

Grapefruit and Tequila Sorbet

2 cups fresh grapefruit juice, preferably pink
Juice of 1 lemon
2 tablespoons tequila
1 recipe Simple Syrup

Melon and Port Sorbet

1 pint puréed melon
1 cup port wine
Juice of 2 lemons
1 recipe Simple Syrup

Cassis Sorbet

2 cups puréed black currants packed in syrup, drained
Juice of 2 lemons
2 tablespoons cassis
1 recipe Simple Syrup

Cantaloupe Sorbet

2 cups puréed cantaloupe
Juice of 2 lemons
1 recipe Simple Syrup

Kiwi and
Champagne Sorbet

2 cups puréed kiwi
1 cup Champagne
1 recipe Simple Syrup (see page 474)

Papaya and Lime Sorbet

2 cups puréed papaya
Juice of 2 limes
1 recipe Simple Syrup (see page 474)

Mango and Lemon Sorbet

2 cups puréed mango
Juice of 2 lemons
1 lightly beaten egg white
1 recipe Simple Syrup (see page 474)

Raisin and Grappa Sorbet

3 cups seedless green grapes
1 recipe Simple Syrup (see page 474)
½ cup raisins soaked overnight in grappa to cover

Place the grapes in a blender or food processor
and blend until liquid.
Strain through a fine sieve.
You should have 2 cups of juice.
If not, purée more grapes.

Mix the grape juice with the simple syrup and raisins.
Place in an ice cream freezer
and freeze according to the manufacturer's directions.

Makes a generous 4 cups.

For the Four Seasons
Divine Love & Peace

BILLY DEE WILLIAMS

Tea Sorbet

½ cup English Breakfast tea leaves
2 cups cold water
2 strips orange rind
1 recipe Simple Syrup (see page 474)
¼ cup crème de menthe
Fresh mint leaves
Lemon juice
Sugar

Place the tea leaves and the orange rind into a bowl with
1 cup cold water.
Press down with a saucer
so the tea leaves stay under water.
Leave overnight, then strain; discard the leaves.

Stir in the remaining 1 cup water,
the simple syrup and the crème de menthe.

Pour the mixture into an ice cream freezer
and freeze according to the manufacturer's directions.

Garnish with sugared mint leaves.
Dip fresh mint leaves in lemon juice,
dust with sugar and let dry.

Makes about 4 cups.

SANDY DENNIS

Chocolate Rum Sorbet

6 ounces unsweetened chocolate
2 cups water
1 cup sugar
3 tablespoons rum
½ teaspoon vanilla extract

Chop the chocolate into very small pieces,
either in a food processor or with a knife.
Place the chocolate, water and sugar in a saucepan.
Place over medium heat
and bring to a boil, stirring constantly.
Reduce the heat
and let cook for about 8 minutes,
stirring all the while,
or until the mixture is completely smooth.
Let cool to room temperature.
Stir in the rum and vanilla.

Place in an ice cream freezer
and freeze according to the manufacturer's directions.

Makes about 2½ cups.

I remember my birthday cake thank you

Lovely to see you again!

Joan Sutherland Bonynge

1st March 1976.

How nice to be on the same page with a woman
of such talent + courage –
Thank you, Rod Steiger

Ice Creams

Though ice cream is thought a characteristically summer dessert—and we are certainly grateful for its refreshing coolness on those sweltering summer days—it is equally refreshing in winter, and therefore we serve it year round.

Vanilla Ice Cream

2 cups heavy cream
3 cups milk
2 vanilla beans, halved lengthwise
10 egg yolks
9½ ounces (1 rounded cup) sugar

Place the cream, milk and vanilla
in a heavy saucepan.
Bring to a boil.

In a separate bowl,
beat the egg yolks and sugar together
until well blended.
Whisking the egg yolks,
slowly pour some of the hot milk
into the egg yolks to raise their temperature.
When the egg yolks are hot,
pour them into the cream mixture,
whisking constantly.

Cook the mixture over low heat, stirring constantly,
until the mixture thickens; do not let it boil.
Strain the mixture into a mixing bowl.
Scrape the vanilla beans with a knife
so the seeds go into the cream; discard the beans.

Let the mixture cool to room temperature,
stirring every few minutes.
When cool,
place in the refrigerator to chill thoroughly.

Pour the mixture into an ice cream freezer
and freeze according to the manufacturer's directions.

Makes 6 cups.

Variation:

For Rich Vanilla Ice Cream, substitute cream for the milk
and use four vanilla beans instead of two.

For Wild Honey Ice Cream,
substitute wild honey for the sugar.

Caramel Ice Cream

The tricky part in this recipe is the caramel. Watch the sugar carefully, and when it reaches the color you are looking for, remove it immediately from the heat. Otherwise, your caramel will continue to cook from the heat retained in the pan and will be too dark.

9½ ounces (1 rounded cup) sugar
2 cups heavy cream
3 cups milk
10 egg yolks

Place the sugar in a heavy saucepan
and cook, stirring constantly,
until the sugar melts and turns brown (caramelizes).

Place the cream and milk in a saucepan.
Bring to a boil.

Off the heat,
slowly pour the boiling cream and milk into the caramel,
whisking constantly.
Make sure the caramel is completely dissolved
and the mixture is smooth.

In a separate bowl, beat the egg yolks.
Whisking the yolks, slowly pour some of the hot cream
into the egg yolks to raise their temperature.
When the egg yolks are hot,
pour them into the cream mixture, whisking constantly.

Cook the mixture over low heat, stirring constantly,
until the mixture thickens slightly.
Do not let it boil.
Strain the mixture into a mixing bowl.

Proceed with the cooling and freezing procedure
as explained in the recipe for Vanilla Ice Cream (page 482).

Makes 6 cups.

Praline Ice Cream

This ice cream, a variation of the vanilla, is enhanced by the flavor of the praline powder. Since the powder keeps indefinitely and takes longer to make than the ice cream itself, you might want to make a larger quantity to keep on hand. You'll find it's lovely to flavor buttercreams or to sprinkle over ice cream.

9½ ounces (1 rounded cup) sugar
1 cup blanched hazelnuts
2 cups heavy cream
3 cups milk
10 egg yolks

Place the sugar in a heavy pan and cook,
stirring constantly,
until the sugar melts and turns brown (caramelizes).
Stir in the nuts
and continue cooking until brown.

Pour the caramel into an oiled pan
and let cool completely.
When cold, break into pieces
and place in a food processor or blender
and blend until very fine.
This is praline powder.
(It will keep indefinitely in a jar in the refrigerator.)

Proceed with the recipe for Vanilla Ice Cream
(page 482),
omitting the vanilla beans and sugar
but stirring the praline powder
into the thickened cream mixture
before it cools.

Proceed with the cooling and freezing procedure
as explained in the basic recipe.

Let rest in freezer for several hours before serving.

Makes 6 cups.

Where to Eat In America?

Espresso and Sambuca Ice Cream

Since sambuca, a clear liqueur, is often served with floating coffee beans, the combination of sambuca and coffee to make a rich ice cream seems a natural. You may want, in turn, to garnish the ice cream with coffee beans or powdered espresso.

2 cups double-strength espresso
2 cups heavy cream
10 egg yolks
7 ounces (scant cup) sugar
¼ cup sambuca

Follow the recipe for Vanilla Ice Cream (page 482), omitting the vanilla beans and milk and boiling the double-strength espresso with the cream.

When the mixture is cool, stir in the sambuca.

Pour the mixture into an ice cream freezer and freeze according to the manufacturer's directions.

Makes about 5 cups.

A question answered !! with affection and admiration

william Rice

WILLIAM RICE

Coconut Banana Ice Cream

This ice cream combines two of our favorite flavors, blending the chewy texture of shredded coconut with the rich fragrant sweetness of ripe bananas.

2 very ripe bananas, approximately
2 cups heavy cream
3 cups milk
½ cup shredded unsweetened coconut
10 egg yolks
9½ ounces (1 rounded cup) sugar
¼ cup coconut liqueur

Push the bananas through a sieve to make a fine purée. You should have 1 cup purée. Set aside.

Proceed with the recipe for Vanilla Ice Cream (see page 482), cooking the coconut instead of the vanilla beans with the cream and milk. Do not strain the mixture.

When the mixture cools to room temperature, stir in the banana and coconut liqueur.

Proceed with the cooling and freezing procedure as explained in the basic recipe.

Makes about 7 cups.

Dessert Soufflés

For some reason, we still view a soufflé as a special treat, a kind of culinary magic. Not only do The Four Seasons' dessert soufflés taste marvelous, they also are created to hold in proud perfection for a longer time than the normal soufflé. These soufflés will be creamy on the inside, which creates a nice contrast with the crisp crust.

When The Seasons opened, some of its soufflés were served individually in coffee or demitasse cups. It is an attractive way to give each person their own special soufflé and special crust. Instructions for making individual soufflés can be found in the serving note at the end of the Cappuccino Soufflé (page 492).

Basic Dessert Soufflé

This is our basic procedure for making soufflés, and it is at the heart of the soufflé recipes that follow it. Once you master the basic soufflé, you can make a limitless variety of elegant desserts. For example, replace part of the milk with orange juice, grate in a little orange rind, add a tablespoon or so of an orange-flavored brandy such as Triple Sec, and you'll arrive at an orange soufflé. The possible variations are endless. It is only the proportions that have to be preserved.

4 tablespoons unsalted butter
4 tablespoons all-purpose flour
1½ cups milk, scalded
½ cup sugar
6 egg yolks
6 egg whites, at room temperature

Follow the procedure for making the Basic Soufflé (see recipe, page 130),
with the following changes:
prepare the mold with butter and sugar
instead of butter and flour.

When heating the milk,
add the ½ cup sugar to it to dissolve.

Cream Cheese and Riesling Soufflé

An extremely unusual soufflé, the mold could be served surrounded by seedless grapes dipped in lightly beaten egg white and then rolled in sugar.

1 recipe Basic Dessert Soufflé
½ pound cream cheese
⅓ cup Riesling
Confectioners' sugar

Heat the oven to 400°F.

Prepare an 8-cup soufflé mold as described in the basic recipe.

Whip the cream cheese until fluffy.
Add the wine and continue beating until smooth.
Stir into the base mixture before adding the egg whites.

Spoon into the prepared mold.

Bake in the preheated oven for 35 minutes.
As soon as the soufflé is done,
sieve some confectioners' sugar over the top.
Serve immediately.

Serves 6.

Macaroon and Maraschino Liqueur Soufflé

The macaroon in this variation on the basic soufflé adds a hint of texture along with its flavor.

1 recipe Basic Dessert Soufflé (see page 488)
⅓ cup maraschino liqueur
1 cup finely crushed macaroons

Heat the oven to 400°F.

Prepare an 8-cup soufflé mold as described in the basic recipe.

Stir the liqueur and macaroons into the base mixture before adding the egg whites.

Spoon into the prepared mold.

Bake in the preheated oven for 35 minutes. Serve immediately.

Serves 6.

Thanks for everything all these years!

MORT GOTTLIEB

Cappuccino Soufflé

You can, of course, serve coffee instead, but this is perhaps the most glorious version we know of a coffee end to a meal.

4 ½ tablespoons unsalted butter
4 ½ tablespoons all-purpose flour
1 tablespoon instant coffee, preferably instant espresso
1 ½ cups milk, scalded
6 egg yolks
⅓ cup coffee liqueur
Ground cinnamon
8 egg whites, at room temperature
Pinch salt
⅓ cup sugar
Confectioners' sugar

Heat the oven to 400°F.

Butter and sugar an 8-cup soufflé mold
and fit it with a collar
(see directions for making a collar in the
Basic Soufflé recipe, page 130).
Set aside.

Melt the butter in a saucepan.
Stir in the flour and cook,
stirring constantly, for 2 minutes
without letting the mixture brown.
Stir the coffee into the milk
and stir to dissolve.
Stir the milk into the butter-flour mixture
and whisk until smooth and thickened.

Remove the pan from the heat
and stir in the egg yolks, two at a time,
beating well after each addition.
Stir in the coffee liqueur and
½ teaspoon ground cinnamon.

In a separate bowl,
beat the egg whites with a pinch of salt
until frothy.
Gradually add the sugar
and continue beating until stiff peaks form.

Stir about one-fourth of the beaten egg whites
into the base mixture to lighten it.
Fold in the remaining whites.

Spoon the mixture into the prepared mold
and bake in the preheated oven for 35 to 40 minutes.
As soon as the soufflé is done,
sieve some confectioners' sugar and cinnamon over the top.

Serve immediately with Cappuccino Sauce (recipe
follows).

Serves 6.

Please stay just as you are.

Yours sincerely

DANA ANDREWS

Cappuccino Sauce

1 cup milk
2 teaspoons instant coffee, preferably instant espresso
¼ cup sugar
2 egg yolks, lightly beaten
¼ cup coffee liqueur

Place the milk, coffee and sugar
in a small saucepan.
Place over medium heat and stir until dissolved.

Remove the pan from the heat
and gradually stir some of the milk mixture
into the egg yolks
to raise the temperature of the eggs.
Pour the egg yolks into the milk and cook,
stirring constantly,
until the mixture thickens slightly.
Do not let the mixture boil.

Remove the pan from the heat
and stir in the coffee liqueur.
Let cool.

Makes about 1¼ cups.

Note:
If you prefer, make smaller soufflés as follows: Fill six 1½-cup soufflé molds each with 1¼ cups of the mixture and bake for 15 minutes; fill fourteen ¾-cup soufflé molds each with a generous ½-cup mixture and bake for 10 to 12 minutes; fill twenty-four ⅓-cup demitasse cups each with ⅓ cup of the mixture and bake for 10 minutes.
In all cases, butter and sugar your molds but eliminate the collar. Place the molds on a baking sheet and bake in a preheated 400°F. oven.
If you do not want so many small soufflés, make half the recipe.

Thank you not only for the excellent cuisine but also for the wonderful service !

Zubin Mehta

Basic Preparations

We have created a polyglot category which, for want of a better name, we call "Basic Preparations." In some cases, they are in fact basic; in others, such as mayonnaise and croissants, they are finished dishes. But they are, in some particular way, capable of combination or they are basic in that, at our restaurant, they are used daily, such as the croissants which go on our table at lunch and dinner in the Pool Dining Room. Many of these basic preparations can be made ahead, even in quantity, and frozen or refrigerated for future use. If you do this where applicable, you will find that you can prepare many of our recipes rather rapidly.

Chicken Stock

½ carrot, halved lengthwise
1 small leek, well washed and trimmed
1 sprig fresh rosemary
1 small celery rib with leaves
½ parsnip, halved lengthwise
3 pounds chicken wings, legs, backs and necks
1 large onion, stuck with 4 whole cloves
1 bay leaf
½ whole nutmeg
4 cloves garlic
1 celery root, peeled and cut into 2-inch chunks
1 tablespoon white peppercorns, coarsely crushed
1 tablespoon kosher salt

Tie the carrot, leek, rosemary, celery
and parsnip together with kitchen string.

Place the chicken pieces in a large stockpot.
Add the remaining ingredients and vegetables.
Add cold water just to cover everything.
Slowly, bring the liquid to a boil.
Skim off the scum which rises to the top.
Reduce the heat and simmer for 2½ hours,
skimming every 30 minutes.

Line a colander with a dampened kitchen towel
or several layers of dampened cheesecloth.
Place the colander over a bowl
and pour the stock through,
pressing on the solids to extract all the liquid.
Discard the solids.

Let the stock cool to room temperature, uncovered;
then refrigerate.
When the stock is cold, remove fat surface.
Refrigerate or freeze until ready to use.
If refrigerating for more than 2 days,
bring the liquid back to the boil every few days
to keep it from souring.

Makes about 2 quarts.

Brown Veal Stock

1 tablespoon vegetable oil
3 pounds veal bones and knuckles
1 celery rib, quartered
1 carrot, quartered
½ celery root, quartered
1 parsnip, quartered
1 medium onion, peel on, quartered
3 cloves garlic
4 whole cloves
½ teaspoon dried marjoram
1 tablespoon kosher salt
1 teaspoon freshly ground black pepper
1 bay leaf, crumbled
2 cups dry white wine

Heat the oven to 450°F.

Heat the oil in a 5-quart ovenproof saucepan.
Add the veal bones and knuckles.
Stir and brown over high heat for a few minutes.
Place the pan in the preheated oven for 35 minutes.
Drain off as much fat as possible,
then add the vegetables, herbs and spices.
Mix well and return the pot to the oven
for another 30 minutes.

Remove the pan from the oven.
Place the bones and vegetables in a clean stockpot.
Pour the fat out of the saucepan
and pour in the wine.
Stir, scraping the bottom of the pan,
to release the browned particles.
Simmer until the wine is reduced to 1 cup.

Pour the reduced wine
over the bones and vegetables
and add cold water to cover, about 7 cups.
Bring to a boil,
reduce the heat and simmer for 3 hours.
Skim the surface and spoon off fat occasionally.

Line a colander
with a dampened kitchen towel
or several layers of dampened cheesecloth.
Place the colander over a bowl
and pour the stock through,
pressing on the solids to extract all the liquid.
Discard solids.

Let the stock cool to room temperature, uncovered;
then refrigerate.
When the stock is cold,
remove the fat that has risen to the surface.
Refrigerate or freeze until ready to use.
If refrigerating for more than 2 days,
bring the liquid back to the boil every few days
to keep it from souring.

Makes about 1 quart.

My soul is happier for my sole

Thank You,

Donald Pleasence

DONALD PLEASENCE

Demi-Glace

6 pounds veal bones
3 large cloves garlic
2 medium onions, roughly chopped
2 small celery ribs, roughly chopped
1 carrot, roughly chopped
3 bay leaves
1 whole nutmeg, crushed
10 whole cloves
1 tablespoon freshly crushed black peppercorns
½ teaspoon dried thyme leaves
½ cup mushroom stems and peelings
1½ cups tomato paste
1½ cups all-purpose flour
2 quarts Brown Veal Stock (see recipe, page 498)
2 cups dry red wine

Heat the oven to 400°F.

Place the veal bones in a large, deep casserole
and let them brown in the oven for 1 hour,
turning them over after 30 minutes.
Add the chopped vegetables, herbs and spices.
Return to the oven to brown for 15 minutes,
stirring often.

Stir in the tomato paste
and return to the oven for an additional 15 minutes.
Stir in the flour
and let brown in the oven for an additional 5 minutes.

Transfer the casserole to the top of the stove.
Add the stock, about 1 gallon water and the wine.
Bring the mixture to a boil.
Skim the scum that rises to the surface.
Lower the heat and simmer for 5 hours,
skimming as needed.

Place a chinois over a bowl
and pour the stock through,
pressing on the solids to extract all the liquid.
Discard the solids.

Let the demi-glace cool to room temperature, uncovered;
then refrigerate.
When the demi-glace is cold,
remove the fat that has risen to the surface.

Makes 3 quarts.

The Four Seasons
is a most handsome restaurant
and the food is so delicious (with or without calories)
Blessings to Tom and Paul!
Thank you for a "super" meal —

GINGER ROGERS

Glace de Viande (Meat Glaze)

Glace de viande is a very useful thing to keep in your refrigerator. It will keep practically indefinitely, and used by the spoonful, lasts a long time. Many home cooks we know devote a day to making stock so as to prepare glace in quantity; they keep one jar available in the refrigerator and the rest tightly sealed and frozen.

1 quart Brown Veal Stock (see recipe, page 498)

Place the stock in a saucepan and let simmer until it has reduced by two-thirds. Strain it through a fine sieve into a clean, small saucepan. Cook very slowly, being careful not to let the stock burn as you reduce it to a thick syrup. This is your glaze.

Let the glaze cool; then bottle and refrigerate.

Makes about ½ cup.

Thank you — there is nothing better in life than having a drink with friends!

Chris Evert

CHRIS EVERT

Beef Bouillon

6 pounds beef bones
1 celery rib
1 carrot, sliced
4 cloves garlic, lightly crushed
1 onion, halved and browned under a broiler
2 leeks, well washed and halved
1 whole nutmeg, crushed
1 small bunch parsley
1 potato, quartered
1 sprig Italian parsley
1 sprig fresh marjoram
2 tomatoes, halved
3 bay leaves
8 whole cloves
1½ teaspoons freshly crushed black peppercorns

Fill a stockpot with enough cold water
to cover the bones.
Bring the water to a boil.
Add the bones and boil for 10 minutes.
This will draw out much of the scum in the bones.
Drain the bones and rinse them briefly.

Rinse out the pot;
return the bones to it with the remaining ingredients.
Add cold water just to cover everything.
Bring the liquid to a boil; lower the heat so the stock simmers.

Let the stock simmer for 4 to 5 hours,
or until the liquid has reduced to 1 gallon.

Line a colander with a dampened kitchen towel
or several layers of dampened cheesecloth.
Place the colander over a bowl
and pour the stock through,
pressing on the solids to extract all the liquid.
Discard the bones and vegetables.

Let the bouillon cool to room temperature, uncovered;
then refrigerate.
When the stock is cold,
remove the fat that has risen to the surface.
Refrigerate or freeze until ready to use.
If refrigerating for more than 2 days,
bring the liquid back to the boil every few days
to keep it from souring.

Makes about 1 gallon.

Spring, Summer
Winter, Fall
Milton and I
Have EATEN them all!

Much thanks

Meryl Streep

MERYL STREEP

and Milton Goldman

MILTON GOLDMAN

27 April / 1979

Fish Stock

4 pounds fish bones and heads
   (do not use salmon or other oily fish)
2 leeks, well washed and split
1 medium onion
2 cloves garlic, unpeeled and lightly smashed
1 celery rib
1 parsnip, peeled and sliced
3 to 4 sprigs parsley
½ teaspoon freshly crushed black peppercorns

   Wash the fish bones and heads well
under cold running water to remove all traces of blood.
Remove the gills.

   Place the bones and heads in a stockpot
and add cold water to cover.
Bring the liquid to a boil and skim carefully
to remove the scum that rises to the surface.
Add the remaining ingredients.
Add more water to generously cover everything.
Bring the liquid to a boil.
Lower the heat and simmer for 45 minutes,
skimming as necessary.

   Line a colander with a dampened kitchen towel
or several layers of dampened cheesecloth.
Place the colander over a bowl
and pour the stock through,
pressing on the solids to extract all the liquid.
Discard solids.

   Let the stock cool to room temperature, uncovered;
then refrigerate.
When the stock is cold,
remove the fat that has risen to the surface.
Refrigerate or freeze until ready to use.
If refrigerating for more than 2 days,
bring the liquid back to the boil every few days
to keep it from souring.

   Makes 2 quarts.

Glace de Poisson (Fish Glaze)

This is a reduction of fish stock just as the glace de viande is a reduction of veal stock. It can be used, similarly, to enrich sauces. It is somewhat more unusual, but we find it equally useful.

2 quarts Fish Stock (see recipe, page 505)

Place the stock in a saucepan and let it simmer until it has reduced by two-thirds.

Strain it through a fine sieve into a clean 2-quart saucepan. Let it cook until it has reduced to about 2 cups. Strain again into a clean, small pan. Cook very slowly at this point, being careful not to let the stock burn as you reduce it to a thick syrup. This is your glaze.

Let the glaze cool; then bottle and refrigerate.

Makes about 1 cup.

STEVE McQUEEN

FishVelouté

4 tablespoons lightly salted butter
¼ cup all-purpose flour
2⅔ cups Fish Stock (see recipe, page 505), heated

Melt the butter in a saucepan and stir in the flour.
Stir and cook for 2 minutes without letting the flour brown.

Gradually whisk in the fish stock and
stir until the sauce is smooth.
Bring the mixture to a boil.
Lower the heat and
let the sauce simmer for 20 minutes, whisking often.

Makes 2 cups.

Thankyou for dinner –
Peace.
— Ali MacGraw .

ALI MACGRAW

Civet Marinade

Much game or other meat that you wish to flavor like game is marinated in a pungent liquid which is then used to make the appropriate sauce. The reason it is called a civet marinade is that it is often used as one of the ingredients of the civet sauce. Civet sauces are usually thickened with blood. Sometimes, in the place of the blood, or in addition, dark, bitter chocolate is used.

10 juniper berries,
  toasted in a dry skillet for 5 minutes
½ cup red wine vinegar
1 bottle (about 3 cups) dry red wine
1 bunch parsley stems
1 medium onion, quartered
½ leek, well washed and chopped
1 celery root, roughly chopped
1 clove garlic
1 carrot, roughly chopped
5 bay leaves
10 whole cloves
1½ teaspoons freshly crushed black peppercorns

Combine all the marinade ingredients
in a non-aluminum bowl
and add the meat.
This is enough for 4 to 5 pounds of wild hare, wild boar,
venison or sauerbraten, or 3 mallard ducks.

Let the meat marinate for 2 weeks in the refrigerator.

Game Sauce

2 tablespoons vegetable oil
2 pounds venison bones,
    preferably soaked in Civet Marinade (see preceding recipe)
    for up to 2 weeks, drained
1 parsnip, roughly cut up
1 carrot, roughly cut up
½ leek, well washed and roughly cut up
1 medium onion, roughly cut up
6 garlic cloves, unpeeled
1 tablespoon plus 1 teaspoon juniper berries,
    toasted in a dry skillet for 5 minutes
1 teaspoon whole cloves
1 teaspoon black peppercorns
3 bay leaves
4 tablespoons tomato purée
¼ cup all-purpose flour
¼ cup gin
1 cup Civet Marinade (if used for the bones) or dry red wine
1 quart Brown Veal Stock (see recipe, page 498)
2 tablespoons grappa
1 tablespoon freshly crushed black pepper
1 teaspoon unsweetened chocolate
1 tablespoon red currant jelly
Kosher salt
2 tablespoons beef blood (optional)
4 tablespoons lightly salted butter

Heat the oven to 400°F.

Heat the oil in a roasting pan.
Add the bones and stir to coat.
Place them in the preheated oven to brown for 30 minutes.
Add the parsnip, carrot, leek, onion, garlic, 1 tablespoon
juniper berries, cloves, peppercorns and bay leaves.
Return to the oven for another 15 minutes.

Pour off all the fat.
Place the pan over medium heat.
Make a well in the center of the bones
and pour in the tomato purée.
Stir well, then stir in the flour.

Next, stir in the gin and civet marinade,
scraping the bottom of the pan to loosen any stuck bits.

Pour in the veal stock and bring to a boil.
Lower heat to simmer; cover pan; cook 2 hours,
or until the liquid is reduced to 2 cups.

Strain the liquid into a clean saucepan.
Skim all the fat and bring to a boil, skimming again.

Place the grappa, crushed pepper, chocolate
and remaining 1 teaspoon juniper berries in a saucepan.
When hot, stir in the currant jelly.
When it dissolves, pour in the boiling sauce.
Cook until the sauce is thick enough to coat a spoon,
about 10 minutes.
Add salt to taste,
then stir in the blood, followed by the butter.
Strain into a sauceboat if ready to serve
or a clean saucepan for gentle reheating.

Makes about 3 cups.

To the Four Seasons
What a lonely Place —!
Thank You, All Best Wishes
Madeline Kahn

MADELINE KAHN

Aspic

2 calf's feet, each weighing about 2 pounds, split
1 pound very lean ground beef
1 leek, white part only, well washed and sliced
1 carrot, sliced
1 celery root, peeled and sliced
1 medium onion, unpeeled, sliced
1 celery rib, sliced
1 small bunch parsley
1 branch fresh sage or ¼ teaspoon dried sage
2 cloves garlic
3 lightly beaten egg whites
½ whole nutmeg, crushed
6 whole cloves
1 bay leaf, crumbled
1 tablespoon black peppercorns, crushed
1 cup dry white wine
2 cups crushed ice
Kosher salt
1 teaspoon unflavored gelatin

Place the calf's feet in a pot with water to cover.
Bring the liquid to a boil.
Drain the feet and rinse them; rinse out the pot.

Return the feet to the pot.
Add 3 quarts cold water, or enough to cover the calf's feet
with about 1 inch to spare.
Slowly bring the water to a boil;
reduce heat to a simmer and let cook for 3 to 5 hours.
Skim as needed.
Add water if necessary to keep the calf's feet covered.

Strain the liquid through a colander
lined with a dampened kitchen towel.
Let cool and remove any fat.

Meanwhile, grind the beef, leek, carrot, celery root,
onion, celery, parsley, sage and garlic
through the coarse blade of a meat grinder.
Mix with the remaining ingredients, except the salt and
gelatin.
Pack into a container with the crushed ice.

Place the iced ground meat mixture and
the calf's feet stock in a heavy stockpot over low heat.
When the stock is hot, check to be sure
the meat mixture is not sticking
to the bottom of the pan.
If it is, stir gently to prevent it from burning.
If not, leave it alone.
Bring the liquid just to the boil,
then lower the heat and let the mixture simmer
without stirring for 2 hours.

Line a colander
with a dampened kitchen towel
or several layers of dampened cheesecloth.
Place the colander over a clean pan
and carefully ladle the mixture in,
being careful not to stir.
Let strain slowly.

Taste the clarified stock
and season with salt if necessary.
Bring back to the boil.
Skim the surface with strips of absorbent paper
to remove any remaining fat.
Continue cooking until reduced to 3 cups.
Gradually stir in the gelatin.

Cool and refrigerate until set.

Makes 3 cups.

With all good wishes,
Antonia Fraser

ANTONIA FRASER

Quick Aspic

Ideally, of course, aspics should be lovingly made from scratch as in the previous recipe. However, in today's world, when we are in need of a quick aspic, this one is of a good and satisfactory kind.

4 cups Chicken Stock (see recipe, page 497)
2 ripe tomatoes, quartered
3 tablespoons unflavored gelatin
¼ cup dry Madeira wine or Cognac
3 egg whites, lightly beaten
1½ teaspoons kosher salt
½ teaspoon freshly cracked black peppercorns

In a saucepan,
combine the stock with the remaining ingredients.
Slowly bring the liquid to a boil, stirring constantly.
Lower the heat to a simmer and
cook, without disturbing the pot, for 15 minutes.
Do not cook longer.

Line a colander
with a dampened kitchen towel
or several layers of dampened cheesecloth.
Place the colander over a bowl
and slowly ladle the liquid in.
Do not stir.
Let the stock drain slowly.
The liquid should be clear.
If not, repeat the straining.

Let cool to room temperature, then chill.

Makes 1 quart.

Lemon Butter Sauce

This is a simple, light sauce. The secret in keeping it frothy and light, and yet held together, is to have a heavy pan, cold butter and a fire at moderate heat. Whisk constantly. The addition of a little glace de viande or glace de poisson enhances the flavor of the sauce. In fact, any compound butter, such as the Crayfish Butter that follows, can also be used to flavor the sauce.

⅓ cup heavy cream
Juice of 2 lemons
1 tablespoon Glace de Viande (meat glaze)
   (see recipe, page 502)
½ pound lightly salted butter, cut into pieces

Place the cream in a small saucepan.
Cook until thickened and reduced to about half.

Place the lemon juice in a skillet.
Cook until reduced to a glaze.

Pour the reduced cream into the lemon glaze.
Whisk in the glace de viande and
stir over heat until smooth.
Whisk in the butter, a few pieces at a time,
until the sauce is smooth and thick.

Keep warm until serving.

Serves 4.

Note:
If using this sauce for fish, substitute Glace de Poisson (see recipe, page 506) for glace de viande.

Crayfish Butter

In some way, crayfish butter tastes more strongly of crayfish than the meat of the crayfish itself. This is equally true of the lobster or shrimp butters made in the same way. They are all valuable and freeze well.

1 ½ cups dry white wine
½ cup Cognac
Kosher salt
1 tablespoon freshly crushed black peppercorns
2 pounds lightly salted butter
4 ½ pounds chopped crayfish heads

Place the wine, Cognac, salt, peppercorns and butter in a large saucepan.
Heat slowly.
When the butter melts, add the crayfish.
Simmer, uncovered, for 1 ½ hours.

Strain the mixture through a fine sieve, pushing down on the crayfish to extract all the juices.
Chill in the refrigerator.
When the mixture is cold, lift off the butter.
Wrap it securely in plastic and keep in the refrigerator or freeze.

Crayfish butter will last several months in the refrigerator and longer in the freezer.

Makes about 1 pound.

Variation:

For Lobster or Shrimp Butter, follow the recipe for Crayfish Butter, substituting lobster or shrimp shells for the crayfish heads.

Béchamel Sauce

Béchamel is a basic white sauce whose reputation suffered in the period when it was indiscriminately used on top of everything. However, in our times it is useful not only on its own but as a base for other sauces.

3 tablespoons lightly salted butter
3 tablespoons all-purpose flour
1½ cups milk
Kosher salt
Freshly ground white pepper
Freshly grated nutmeg

Heat the butter in a saucepan.
Add the flour and stir to mix.
Cook for 2 minutes without letting the mixture brown.
Add the milk and stir until smooth.
Bring to a boil.
Season with salt, pepper and nutmeg to taste.

Makes 1½ cups sauce.

HERMIONE GINGOLD

MAUREEN STAPLETON

SIDNEY POITIER

Mayonnaise

Mayonnaise is a good sauce in its own right and also as a base. We sometimes use lighter oils in place of the olive oil, if, in a given recipe, we wish a less prominent olive taste. This is particularly true when we intend to use the mayonnaise in combination with other sauces, such as tomato.

2 egg yolks
1½ teaspoons imported Dijon mustard
1 tablespoon lemon juice
Kosher salt
Freshly ground black pepper
1½ cups olive oil
1½ teaspoons white wine vinegar

Combine the egg yolks, mustard, lemon juice, salt and pepper in a mixing bowl.
Whisk briskly until well blended and the egg yolks are thick.

Slowly pour in the oil, drop by drop, beating vigorously without stopping.
When the mixture is thick, add the remaining oil in a slow, steady stream.
Stir in the vinegar.

Makes about 1¾ cups.

I came I saw — I over ate —

"   "   "

"   "   "

Green Herb Mustard

You will note that many of the recipes in this book call for imported green-herb mustard. It is currently unavailable in this country, but we have managed to make a very satisfactory equivalent. The mustard should be used within twenty-four hours.

3 bunches watercress, leaves only
1 bunch parsley, leaves only
1 cup tarragon wine vinegar
2 tablespoons imported Dijon mustard
1 teaspoon imported tarragon Dijon mustard
¾ teaspoon sugar

    Bring two pots of salted water to a boil.
Cook the watercress in one pot for 6 minutes
and the parsley in the other for 1 minute.
Drain well and purée in a food processor; squeeze dry.

    Place the vinegar in a small pan
and cook until reduced to 3 tablespoons; cool.

    Mix together the purées, vinegar, mustards and sugar.
Press the mixture through a drum sieve into a bowl.
Use within a day,
or the mustard will lose its bright green color.

    Makes about 5½ tablespoons mustard.

Sweet Dough, Puff Pastry and Dessert Bases

Of all the basic preparations, these are perhaps the most satisfying in that the ingredients vary relatively little and you can be quite sure of the results once you have the techniques under control.

Croissants

Since The Four Seasons opened, tight crisp brown croissants
have been a signature item in the shining silver bowl that sits
on an elevated silver tripod holding the breads. The
following recipe is scaled to make twelve breakfast
croissants. If you wish to make the miniatures that we serve,
instead of cutting your 12 x 18-inch rectangle into 6-inch
squares, cut it into 3-inch squares. These should only be
baked for 12 minutes.

1 tablespoon sugar
2½ teaspoons kosher salt
1 cup milk
11 ounces unsalted butter
2 packages (¼ ounce each) active dry yeast
3¾ cups all-purpose flour
1 egg
1 tablespoon water

Place the sugar, salt and milk in a saucepan.
Cook over low heat
until the sugar and salt dissolve.
Add 2 tablespoons butter
and continue cooking until beads form around
the edge of the pan and the butter melts.
Remove the pan from the heat
and let cool for a few minutes.
Sprinkle the yeast into the pan and stir to dissolve.
Set aside for a few minutes,
or until the mixture is foamy.

Spread 3¼ cups flour on your work surface
into a ring about 15 inches across.
Gradually pour in the milk mixture
and gently stir the flour and milk together with your hand.
When all the liquid has been absorbed,
knead the dough thoroughly,
stretching it out and folding it back on itself
until the dough is smooth.

Place the dough in a warm greased bowl.
Turn the dough to grease the top,
then cover with a cloth and set in a cool place
until tripled in bulk, about 3 hours.
If you want to stretch the time,
let the dough rise in the refrigerator.

Punch the dough down with your fist.
Place it on your work surface and knead briefly.
Return the dough to the bowl,
cover and return to the cool place to rise
until doubled in bulk, about 1½ hours.
Place the dough in the refrigerator to chill
for 30 minutes.

While the dough chills,
mix the remaining 10 ounces butter
with the remaining ½ cup flour.
Using the palm of your hand or a scraper,
spread the butter and work it
until it is about the same consistency as the dough.

Place the dough on a lightly floured board
and roll it out into a 21 x 7-inch rectangle.
Spread the butter as evenly as possible
over two-thirds of the dough,
leaving about a ½-inch unbuttered border all around.

Fold the dough as you would a business letter,
folding the unbuttered third in first.
Brush off any excess flour.
Then fold in the remaining third.
This is your first turn.
Turn the dough so the short edge faces you.
Roll out and fold in three again.
Wrap the dough in plastic wrap
and refrigerate until firm, about 30 minutes.

Give the dough two more turns,
for a total of four turns.
Wrap the dough in a clean cloth
and refrigerate for 1½ hours.

On a lightly floured board,
roll the dough to a 12 x 18-inch rectangle.
Cut it in half lengthwise
and then across at 6-inch intervals
so you have six 6-inch squares.
Cut each square on the diagonal into two triangles.
Refrigerate half the dough.

Take the triangles one at a time
and place them on a lightly floured board.
Gently pull each corner of the dough
to slightly elongate the sides.

Place one hand on each corner
of the long side of the triangle.
Roll the dough tightly toward the extending point.
Continue until all the dough is rolled in.
Bring the ends of the roll toward each other
to form a crescent shape.

Continue forming the rest of the dough.
When it is all shaped,
remove the dough from the refrigerator and shape that.

Place the crescents (croissants)
on a buttered baking sheet,
leaving enough room around each for them to rise.
Cover with a clean towel
and let rise for about 1½ hours at room temperature,
or until tripled in bulk.

Heat the oven to 475°F.

Mix the egg and water
and brush this glaze on the croissants.

Place the croissants in the oven and bake for 5 minutes.
Lower the oven temperature to 450°F.
and bake 15 minutes longer.
Serve warm.

Makes 12.

Puff Pastry

In our introduction to Puff Pastry in Hot Appetizers (page 114), we describe this dough in some detail. The only thing we feel we should add to this recipe is an indication that puff pastry freezes well. When making it, you may wish to take more time to make several batches, cut out various finished shapes, wrap them tightly and freeze them. They can then be baked, still frozen, on a preheated baking sheet.

Use for:
Feuilleté with Fresh Fruit
Apple Pithiviers
Fruit Flan
Feuilletés
Millefeuilles

1 tablespoon kosher salt
1¾ pounds plus ¼ cup (7¼ cups total) all-purpose flour
3 cups heavy cream
2 pounds unsalted butter, cold

Place the salt and 1¾ pounds flour in a mixing bowl.
Stir to mix.
Pour in the cream and
blend together to form a soft ball of dough.
Turn onto a floured work surface
and knead until the dough is smooth and elastic.
Wrap the dough in waxed paper and refrigerate 30 minutes.

If you wish to mix the dough in a food processor,
proceed as follows:
Place 3½ cups flour and 1½ teaspoons salt in the work bowl.
With the machine running, pour in 1½ cups cream.
Let run for 1½ minutes.
If the machine overheats and stalls,
turn it off and wait 1 minute before continuing.
Repeat.
Knead the two portions of dough together until smooth.
Wrap the dough in waxed paper and refrigerate 30 minutes.

Place the butter on a heavily floured work surface
and beat with a rolling pin until somewhat softened.
Sprinkle the remaining ¼ cup flour over the butter and
knead together until the butter is smooth and pliable.
Shape the butter into a 7 x 12-inch rectangle.
Keep in a cool place until needed.
The butter and dough should be equally supple.

Place the dough on a floured surface
and roll it into a 14 x 18-inch rectangle.
Brush any excess flour off the surface of the dough.
Place the butter over half the dough,
leaving about a 1-inch border on three sides.
Brush the edges of the dough with water and
then fold the dough in half to enclose the butter,
pressing the edges to seal together.

Gently beat the dough with a rolling pin
to soften and distribute the butter.
Roll the dough into a 12 x 30-inch rectangle.
Lightly flour the dough as needed;
brush excess flour from surface before folding.
Fold the ends in to meet in the middle,
leaving a 1-inch space between them.
Fold the two halves together like a book.
This is one turn.
Wrap the dough and refrigerate for 20 to 30 minutes.

Repeat the rolling and folding process four more times,
for a total of five turns.
Each time you begin rolling,
place the dough in front of you so it is like a closed book.
Always let the dough rest in the refrigerator
for 20 minutes between turns.
If you let it rest longer, the butter may get very hard.
In that case,
let it rest at room temperature for a few minutes
before rolling.

You may wrap the dough securely in plastic at this point
and freeze until needed
or shape for a specific recipe and freeze that way.
See the directions which follow.

Makes about 5 pounds puff pastry.

To make feuilleté boats:

Heat the oven to 425°F.

Cut off 1½ pounds dough
and roll it into a 10 x 12-inch rectangle.
Cut the rectangle into six 4 x 5-inch rectangles.
Trim the rectangles into diamonds which are 4½ inches
on each side.

Place the diamonds on a wet baking sheet
and freeze for 10 minutes.

Mix 1 egg yolk with 1 teaspoon water for a glaze
and brush it on the chilled dough,
not letting the glaze drip on the sides of the dough
or on the baking sheet.

Place in the preheated oven,
lower the temperature to 400°F.
and bake for 25 minutes.

Makes 6 feuilleté boats.

To make baked millefeuilles:

Because the dough shrinks after it is baked,
roll it out so it is at least 3 inches wider and 3 inches longer
than you will need for the finished product.
The dough should be no more than 1/16 inch thick.
Place the rolled-out dough on a wet baking sheet
and prick all over with a fork.
Freeze for 1 hour.

Bake in the middle of a preheated 450°F. oven
for 16 minutes,
or until cooked through and golden brown.

You will need about 1½ pounds dough
to make a 9 x 12-inch or 8 x 14-inch baked millefeuille.
For a 10 x 15-inch rectangle or 12-inch square,
use 2 pounds dough.

Chocolate Puff Pastry

The problems and the potential rewards of a chocolate puff pastry have always tempted pastry chefs. Our chefs have worked out a solution which is the base of our Bar Room Chocolate Cake. It is unusual in that it does not work with cocoa powder added to the dough, but rather with chocolate added to the butter. This in turn is used as the butter between the layers. Use this recipe as a base for your own creations.

Use for:
Bar Room Chocolate Cake

½ pound semisweet chocolate
1 pound unsalted butter, cold
1 pound bread flour
⅔ to 1 cup cold water

Place the chocolate
in the top of a double boiler over simmering water
and heat until melted.
Let cool to 90°F.

Place the butter in an electric mixer
and beat until smooth.
Stir in the chocolate and
beat until well blended and fairly smooth.
Wrap in plastic and chill until firm.

Place the flour
in the work bowl of a food processor or an electric mixer.
Take one-fourth of the chocolate mixture,
cut it into small pieces and add to the flour.
Process until the mixture resembles coarse meal.
With the machine running, add just enough water
to bring the dough together to form a ball.
Knead briefly on a floured board until smooth.
Wrap in waxed paper
and chill in the refrigerator for 2 hours.

Shape the remaining chocolate-butter mixture
into an 8-inch square.
Keep in a cool place.

Place the dough on a floured surface
and roll it into a 10 x 18-inch rectangle.
Brush any excess flour off the surface of the dough.
Place the chocolate-butter square over half the dough,
leaving about a 1-inch border on three sides.
Brush the edges of the dough with water
and then fold the dough in half to enclose the butter.

Roll out the dough and make four turns
as explained in the recipe for Puff Pastry (see page 523).
The rectangles will be smaller
because the quantity of dough is less.

See recipe for Bar Room Chocolate Cake (page 428)
for baking directions.

Makes about 3 pounds of dough.

I only write for money!

Judith Krantz

JUDITH KRANTZ

Linzer Dough

This very rich tart dough is named after the linzer torte and also the cookies of the same name. Once you get used to working with it, we think you will find that it adapts to many delicious fruit tarts.

Use for:
Fruit Tart

½ cup sugar
1 egg
7½ tablespoons unsalted butter
1 rounded cup ground hazelnuts
1 cup all-purpose flour
Pinch ground cinnamon
Pinch kosher salt

Mix the sugar and egg until creamy and well blended.
Beat in the butter.
When smooth, beat in the nuts,
then the flour, cinnamon and salt.
Wrap in waxed paper and chill until firm.

Heat the oven to 400°F.

Roll the dough out on a heavily floured board
or between sheets of waxed paper to a 10-inch circle.
Place in a 9-inch tart pan with a removable bottom.
Line the pan with aluminum foil
and weight the dough with rice or beans.

Bake in the preheated oven for 10 minutes.
Remove the foil and weights
and continue baking until golden, 5 minutes longer.

Let cool before filling.

Makes one 9-inch tart shell.

Note:
If you have some extra dough, roll it into 2-inch rounds to make cookies. Bake in a 400°F. oven for 8 to 10 minutes. Serve spread with jam.

Sweet Dough

Sweet dough is a simple, basic, multi-use dough.

Use for:
Walnut Tart
Fig Strip
Pine Nut Galette

12 tablespoons unsalted butter, at room temperature
½ cup sugar
2 cups cake flour, sifted
1 egg, lightly beaten
Pinch salt

    Beat the butter until soft, then beat in the sugar.
When well blended, beat in the flour,
then the egg and salt.
Wrap the dough in waxed paper and chill until firm.

April 5, 1978

Frank Langella

FRANK LANGELLA

A wonderful way to begin spring!

Thank you!

Pastry Cream

The addition of cornstarch to this custard makes it a
particularly stable mixture and one that is not liable to curdle.

Use for:
Fruit Flan
Fruit Tart
Crêpes Soufflés

2 cups milk
5 egg yolks
6 tablespoons sugar
2½ tablespoons cornstarch
2 tablespoons Grand Marnier, kirsch or other liqueur

Place the milk in a saucepan and heat.

In a separate bowl,
beat the egg yolks, sugar and cornstarch until blended.
Slowly beat in the hot milk.

Return the mixture to the saucepan
and cook over medium heat, stirring constantly,
until the mixture comes to a boil.
Let boil for 1 minute, stirring constantly.
Stir in the liqueur.

Makes 2 cups.

Thank you again Joseph Losey

JOSEPH LOSEY

Sponge Cake

Do not let the name of this recipe mislead you. It is the European idea of a sponge cake, which is truly a génoise and not the light American sponge cake at all.

Use for:
Pear Mousse
Coconut Caramel Pudding

4 eggs
⅔ cup sugar
Grated rind of 1 lemon
Scant ¾ cup flour
¼ cup cornstarch
4 tablespoons unsalted butter, melted

Butter and flour a 9-inch round springform pan.
Heat the oven to 375°F.

Place the eggs, sugar and lemon rind
in the top of a double boiler over simmering water.
Whisk the mixture until tripled in volume and warm.

Carefully transfer the egg mixture to a bowl
and whisk until it is back to room temperature.

Sift the flour and cornstarch directly over the egg mixture.
Gently fold in.
Then fold in the melted butter.

Pour the mixture into the prepared pan
and bake in the preheated oven for 25 to 30 minutes,
or until done.

Basic Buttercream

The basic buttercream can be variously flavored to decorate simple cake layers and make practically an infinite variety of desserts. Here, we give you the chocolate and praline variations, but different liqueurs and different extracts can, of course, be used.

Use for:
Bar Room Chocolate Cake
Hazelnut Japonaise

4 egg whites
1 ½ cups confectioners' sugar
½ pound unsalted butter, softened
½ teaspoon vanilla extract (or to taste)

Place the egg whites and confectioners' sugar
in the top of a double boiler
and whisk until the mixture is heated through
and thick.
The sugar will completely melt.

Transfer the mixture to the bowl of an electric mixer
and beat at high speed
until the mixture cools completely to room temperature.

In a separate bowl, beat the butter
until it is fluffy and very smooth.
Beat the egg whites into the butter until smooth.
Beat in the vanilla.

Makes 3 cups.

Variation:
To make Praline Buttercream,
add ⅓ cup praline powder
(see directions in recipe for Praline Ice Cream, page 484)
to the Basic Buttercream.

Chocolate Buttercream

4 egg whites
1 ½ cups confectioners' sugar
½ pound unsalted butter, softened
2 teaspoons instant coffee,
    dissolved in 2 teaspoons hot water
4 ounces semisweet chocolate,
    melted and cooled to room temperature
2 tablespoons dark rum

Follow the recipe for the Basic Buttercream
(see preceding recipe),
adding the chocolate, coffee and rum to the softened butter
before adding the beaten egg whites.

Makes about 3 cups.

This is my second
and equally enjoyable visit—
I will return!

Richard Burton

RICHARD BURTON

Notes on Ingredients

Almond Paste

A smooth paste of ground almonds and sugar available commercially in delicacy stores, usually in cans or bars. We use it primarily in baked desserts.

Anchovies

We use Portuguese flat fillets packed in olive oil. They should be firm, not mushy or furry, but not too stiff or bristly. Drain well before use.

Arugula

A green known by many different names, the most common being "rocket." It belongs to the mustard family and has a pungent, slightly bitter flavor.

Asparagus, grass

Straw-thin wild asparagus which can be eaten raw.

Belly Bacon

Pork from the belly that has been salt-cured, not smoked. It is sometimes called streak of lean.

Black (Russian) Radish

A large radish with a dull black skin, white meat and a sharp flavor. We usually use it raw in salads.

Brockflower

A cross between broccoli and cauliflower in appearance and taste; the buds are purplish.

Butter

Clarified—Butter is clarified by gently heating it so it melts and the butter fat separates from the liquid and any solids. This clear yellow fat is the clarified butter. It does not burn as quickly as normal butter and will keep for a long time.

Lightly Salted—Good lightly salted butter is made from sweet cream to which a small amount of salt has been added. We like it because it makes sauces lighter and less fatty-tasting.

Unsalted—This is sweet butter made without any salt. We always use it in the bake shop. The label should read "unsalted" as well as "sweet" since most salted butter is also sweet butter.

Cabbage, Chinese

We use the variety that is similar in color to ordinary cabbage but elongated, resembling celery in shape.

Calabaza

A member of the squash family with a yellowish-green rind and vivid orange-yellow flesh. Can be found in Latin American markets.

Calf's Brains

The brains should be creamy white in color and the tiny blood veins on the surface should be red and look fresh.

Calvados

Apple brandy distilled from cider in the Calvados department of France. The best Calvados is from Vallée d'Auge. Applejack is our domestic version of Calvados.

Candied Fruits

Fruits preserved by slow cooking in a sugar syrup. Rather than purchasing small packages, buy from stores that carry the fruits in bulk and do a large business.
If you cannot find a good assortment in your area, write to:
>   Maison Glass
>   52 East 58th Street
>   New York, NY 10022

Capers

Capers are a gray-green, slightly salted vinegar pickle made from the unopened flower buds from a Mediterranean shrub. We prefer the large, soft kind.

Caviar

Though the roe or eggs of any fish may be called caviar, when we speak of caviar we mean specifically the roe of fish in the sturgeon family. The three main types are beluga, with the largest eggs, followed by sevruga and osetra with progressively smaller eggs. The hallmarks of good caviar are freshness, intactness of the individual eggs, lack of gumminess and absence of a great deal of salt. Excellent caviar is being produced in Oregon and California, although the traditional sources have been Russia and Iran.

Celery Root

A globular-shaped root with rough, brownish skin and an intense celery taste.
It is also called celeriac and knob celery.

Chayotes

Tropical, pear-shaped squash, ranging in color from white to dark green. Found in Latin American markets.

Chicken Fat

Unless otherwise specified, recipes call for unrendered fat from a chicken. If there should be any blood on the fat, wash it off or, if necessary, cut it off. To render chicken fat, put it in a very heavy pan and cook over very low heat until all the liquid fat separates from the small nut-brown cracklings. The cracklings can be eaten as is or sprinkled over a green salad. The fat should be put through a cloth or filter paper. It will keep in the refrigerator for a long time.

Chicory
Although many different greens are called chicory, we mean the flat open heads with curly, rather spiky thin leaves. They have a pungent, sharp, bitter taste.

Chinois
A cone-shaped metal sieve, used with a wooden pestle or wooden spoon to purée foods. See *Equipment* for source.

Chipolatas
Chipolatas are small, coarse, spicy fresh pork sausages, available from Spanish butchers.

Cider
Hard cider is fermented apple juice. There are both bubbly and still varieties. For cooking, we use the still. Sweet cider is made from fresh apple juice and at its best when it's made without sugar or preservatives. There is also sweet pasteurized cider but it's not as fresh-tasting and fruity. Hard cider is alcoholic, sweet cider is not. Austrians, Northern French, Swiss and English drink cider in great quantities, and some of the best ciders available are made in those countries.

Coriander
Also known as cilantro or Chinese parsley, this is an earthy-flavored, aromatic herb.

Cornichons
Cornichons are baby pickles that are picked when the flower is still attached. They are usually packed in white wine vinegar with onions and tarragon and are a classic accompaniment to pâtés. You can order them from:

Maison Glass
52 East 58th Street
New York, NY 10022

Crayfish
Small fresh-water lobsterlike crustaceans. Purchase them live or frozen, whole or peeled tails. You can order them in season (February to June) from:

Bayouland Seafood
Route 3, Box 478
Breaux Bridge, LA 70517

Cream, Heavy
Also called sweet whipping cream, this is cream which has approximately 33 percent butterfat. We do not use the ultra-pasteurized or stabilized types.

Crème Fraîche

Crème fraîche is sweet heavy cream that has picked up free-floating yeast either through exposure to the air or exposure to a culture. The yeast causes the cream to thicken and gives a very special taste. We use a commercial brand, available in some areas, called Santé. However, you can make your own either by using buttermilk as a culture agent or by simply leaving the cream in a shallow container at room temperature, exposed to the air, lightly covered with cheesecloth. After 24 hours, spoon the thickened cream off the top. It will keep in the refrigerator for a week or more. The watery residue can be used in place of water in pastry-making.

Currants

Red or black, round berries. The red are pleasantly sour, the black are sweetish. Black currants packed in sweet syrup are available from:

Bremen House
200 East 86th Street
New York, NY 10028

Daikon

A large, oriental radish that we frequently use raw in salads.

Dandelion

The young leaves of this common weed have a bitter but pleasant flavor. Best when small, before the flower appears.

Drum Sieve

A round, fine mesh wire sieve set into a wooden frame resembling a drum. It gives a very fine purée. See *Equipment* for source.

Duck Livers

These are larger and paler in color than chicken livers and have a more delicate taste. They are difficult to find in quantity, so save them from your ducks.

Ducks

There are several breeds of this bird but the white Pekin or Long Island, 4 to 5 pounds, are the ones we use. All domestic ducks are descended from the small mallard, which is leaner and more intensely flavored than the Long Island duck and weighs 1½ pounds. See *Game* for source for mallard ducks.

Eggs

All recipes in this book call for fresh USDA large eggs.

Equipment

Specialty equipment needed for some of our recipes can be obtained from:

Williams-Sonoma
P.O. Box 3792
San Francisco, CA 94119

Bridge Kitchenware Corporation
214 East 52nd Street
New York, NY 10022

Escarole

This is a broad-leafed green, sometimes referred to as endive. The heads are compact with a yellowish base from which white-ribbed curly green leaves fan out.

Fatback

This is firm clear fat from the back, covering the loin, of an overfed pig. It is unsalted and sometimes called "pork fat." When cured in salt, it is "salt pork."

Fennel

A firm pale-green crisp bulb with stalks at the end, this winter vegetable has a licorice-like flavor.

Fennel Sticks (Fenouille)

The dried stems of the fennel bulb; often used in an open fire to flavor grilled fish, or directly in the dish itself. You can order them from:

Embassy Grocery Corporation
57-10 49th Street
Maspeth, NY 11378

Fiddlehead Ferns

These are the heads of young wild ferns. They are shaped like fiddleheads and are somewhere between asparagus and mushrooms in flavor. They are abundant in woodlands in spring.

Field Cress

A small, peppery-flavored variety of cress.

Flour

It is always more accurate to weigh flour for baking than to use volume measure.

All-Purpose Flour—Also called plain or white flour; bleached or unbleached.

Bread Flour—This flour is higher than all-purpose flour in gluten, the natural protein component of flour, and tends to give greater strength to certain kinds of dough and improve the texture of bread. It is typically made from a combination of high-protein wheat flour along with other specialty flour. Several mills now make bread flour for the general public.

Cake Flour—Cake flour is a highly refined, bleached flour used in delicate preparations. In purchasing it, make sure it does not have any baking powder mixed in.

Gado-Gado

An Indonesian condiment based on peanuts and hot peppers ground together. Mixed with water, it develops into a paste. You may order from:

H. Roth & Son
1577 First Avenue
New York, NY 10028

Game

Although availability depends on the season, you can order pheasant, quail, partridge, venison, squab, boar and the like from:

Czimer Foods
R.R. 1
Box 285
Lockport, IL 60441

Geese

We find the best birds are 4 to 6 months old, weighing 6 to 14 pounds.

Ginger

The rhizome of a plant indigenous to South Asia. We use the root fresh, ground or preserved. It is available in oriental markets.

Grappa

An Italian brandy distilled from pressed grape skins, similar to French marc.

Grenadine

A sweet red syrup with the flavor of pomegranates.

Jícama

Large, brown tuber with white flesh that looks somewhat like a sweet potato; eaten raw, it has a crisp, delicate taste. Found in Latin American markets.

Juniper Berries

The dried fruit of an evergreen shrub often used to season game dishes. Always toast before using.

Kidney Fat

The kidney fat is the purest of all fats, white and flaky.
It is also called leaf lard or suet.

Kiwi

This tropical fruit has become available and popular in the last few years. Rough and greenish-gray on the outside, it has a bright green pulp with small black seeds. The peel is inedible but the pulp is refreshing and tart. Pick fruits that are ripe and not hard.

Kohlrabi

This member of the cabbage family has an oblong base from which sprout leaves. Look for small kohlrabi with thin rinds.

Larding Needle

A heavy, pointed needle into which strips of fat are fitted in order to thread them through meat to add both flavor and tenderness. See *Equipment* for source.

Leeks

These cylindrical-shaped members of the onion family have a wide base and dark green leaves, resembling an overgrown scallion.

Mandoline

A device for cutting vegetables into uniform shapes. The better mandolines have adjustable blades that can slice to different thicknesses, julienne or ripple. The blade is stationary and you move the foods through it. See *Equipment* for source.

Mango

This originally Malaysian fruit has a taste somewhere between an apricot and a pineapple but is infinitely richer than both. The fruit is kidney-shaped and either a golden yellow or a yellow-greenish red, and should only be purchased ripe. The pit is very large.

Marrow Bones

The shinbone, usually of beef, more rarely of veal, prized for its flavorful soft interior. Generally cut into 2-inch lengths.

Marzipan

Sweetened almond paste.

Mortadella

This is a large round pink sausage made with finely ground pork and strips of fat. Available in Italian specialty stores.

Mushrooms

Chanterelles are orange-yellow mushrooms that grow in a funnel or crater shape. They appear across most of our country in summer or fall. They can be purchased fresh or dried. Dried they are available from:

>Amazon-Dechoix
>35-17 31st Street
>Long Island City, NY 11106

Royal Trompette is an unusual purplish-black cousin of the chanterelle.

The very expensive dried Italian mushrooms can be found in Italian stores such as:

>Manganaro Foods
>488 Ninth Avenue
>New York, NY 10018

Enoki mushrooms, a slender white Japanese variety with a tiny cap and long stem, are now available fairly extensively in this country.

Shiitake, the mushrooms most commonly used in Chinese and Japanese cooking, are available dried in oriental shops. Available fresh in some markets.

Nasturtium

Beautiful mid-summer vine with flowers ranging from yellow to orange. Leaves, stems and flowers can be used in salads.

Olive Oil

Extra virgin cold-pressed, where the pits have not been broken and the oil is a clear, light green, is the most aromatic and best. You can order from:

Williams-Sonoma
P.O. Box 3792
San Francisco, CA 94119

Olives

Kalamata olives are shiny, almond-shaped olives from Greece. They are purple-black to mahogany, cured in olive oil, vinegar and salt, or in brine alone.

Niçoise olives are those tiny black Provençal olives, deep amethyst to jet-black, either cured in brine or packed with oil and Provençal herbs.

Both are available by mail from:

Fantis Foods
179 Franklin Street
New York, NY 10013

Pancetta

Lightly cured bacon used in Italian cooking. Available from Italian specialty stores.

Papaya

A tropical South American or Caribbean fruit. The rind is yellow; the meat, a bright, startling orange. The seeds that go down the center look like black caviar.

Paprika, Hungarian Sweet

Made from the pods of certain sweet peppers, this brilliant red spice is available ground or creamed in tubes from:

Paprikas Weiss
1546 Second Avenue
New York, NY 10028

Peas

In addition to the usual sweet peas we use two delicious varieties: snow peas, the flat, green edible pod, and sugar snap peas, a cross between snow peas and sweet peas, also with an edible pod.

Pepita Seeds

Hulled, unsalted pumpkin seeds; best are long, thin and dark green. Buy from:

Casa Moneo Spanish Imports
210 West 14th Street
New York, NY 10014

Pepper

We use many different kinds of pepper, among them: Black peppercorns from Tellicherry or Malabar, India; white peppercorns, which are used in light-colored sauces; green peppercorns, available packed in salt water or freeze-dried; and red peppercorns, also called poivre rose, available freeze-dried.

We also use cayenne, which is ground red pepper; dried red pepper pods, both whole and crushed into flakes; grains of paradise, also known as guinea pepper, from Liberia; and Szechuan peppercorns.

For maximum flavor, grind whole peppercorns just before use. All these peppers except for the red (poivre rose) are available by mail from:

Aphrodisia
28 Carmine Street
New York, NY 10014

The red pepper is available from:

H. Roth & Son
1577 First Avenue
New York, NY 10028

Periwinkles

Tiny black sea snails, available from fish stores year round but most abundant in July and August.

Phyllo Dough

Thin sheets of Greek pastry similar to strudel dough which can be purchased fresh or frozen. Available from Greek specialty stores.

Pine Nuts (Pignoli)

The edible seeds from the cones of pine trees are pale and somewhat soft, usually sold shelled and blanched. Available from Italian and other specialty stores.

Prosciutto

Salted, air-cured ham. Though Italian prosciutto cannot be legally imported, good American varieties are available in Italian specialty stores. The meat should be soft, reddish-pink, not dark red.

Quail and Quail Eggs

Our quail usually weigh between 3 and 4 ounces. Their eggs, which are very small, with brown-speckled hard shells, are difficult to crack neatly. Use a small knife and work carefully.

Ramp

A wild leek which grows naturally in Appalachia in late spring; there are also hothouse varieties. It is known for its very strong taste.

Red-leaf Lettuce

A loose, open-headed green lettuce with red-topped leaves; it is soft and pleasant.

Rice

Arborio—Italian round rice which absorbs more liquid than ordinary rice. Available in Italian specialty stores or by mail from:

Manganaro Foods
488 Ninth Avenue
New York, NY 10018

Long Grain—This is the usual American rice. The grains are longer than short- or medium-grain. Do not purchase precooked.

Wild Rice—This is not related to regular rice, but is an undomesticated cereal grass. The varieties we use are usually from the Great Lakes area and can be ordered by mail from:

Consolidated Wild Rice
Industrial Park
Bemidji, MN 56601

Rutabaga

Also called "swede," this is a root vegetable related to the turnip.

Saffron

The most expensive of spices, saffron comes from the stigma of the crocus. Its delicate flavor and rich yellow color make it the essential ingredient in many dishes.

Sake

Slightly sweet Japanese fortified rice wine.

Salsify

Also known as "oyster plant," this root plant tastes somewhat like oysters.

Salt

We always use coarse salt, most often kosher, but sometimes the larger sea-salt crystals, which impart a different flavor to the dish. Rock salt has even larger crystals which haven't been purified; it is used to heat oysters.

Scallions

Also called green onions, these shoots from white onions have white bulbs and green tops.

Shallots

These small cousins of the onion are purplish to gray in color and more delicate in taste. Look for firm bulbs.

Soft-Shell Crabs

Crabs caught just after they have shed their shells and before new ones have grown; usually available live in the spring.

Sorrel

Related to sour grass, this is a spring and early summer perennial. The leaves are used in soups, sauces, and occasionally in uncooked salads; acidic and refreshing. Jarred sorrel is available from:

Amazon-Dechoix
35-17 31st Street
Long Island City, NY 11106

Spätzle Maker

A metal machine that looks like a food mill with larger holes; used to make spätzle. It can be ordered from:

H. Roth & Son
1577 First Avenue
New York, NY 10028

Sprouts

Alfalfa sprouts are threadlike and white; mung bean sprouts are greener and more robust. Buy fresh, not canned.

Squash Blossoms

Blossoms from a summer squash plant, usually dipped in a light batter and fried.

Squid

Also called inkfish or cuttlefish, this is a close relative of the octopus. Small squid (approximately 6 inches) are usually served whole; larger squid are cut into rings and pieces.

Sunchokes

Sunchokes are a California version of Jerusalem artichokes. They bear no resemblance to artichokes and, in fact, the name is a misnomer because they grow underground and have no chokes. They have a nutty flavor and can be used in salads or cooked as a vegetable.

Sweetbreads (Veal)

The large pair of thymus or smaller pair of thyroid glands of a calf.

Swiss Chard

Leafy green vegetable, similar to spinach but more delicate in flavor.

Truffles

A fungus with a rough skin and pungent aroma. Most black ones come from France, white from Italy. Fresh are difficult to come by but there are good, though expensive, canned varieties. You can order fresh from:

Paul A. Urbani
P.O. Box 2054
Trenton, NJ 08607

Venison

Venison is the meat of deer. The prime cut for roasting is the saddle, available from select butchers. See *Game* for source.

Vesiga

The spinal marrow of the great sturgeon may, in some places, be bought from fish stores, more usually dried than fresh. If dried, it needs to be soaked before using.

Vinegar

Almost every fruit, alcohol and liquid can be fermented by yeast to make vinegar. Vinegars vary from brand to brand in quality, color, acidity and taste. If you can't find a good selection in your neighborhood, write:

Williams-Sonoma
P.O. Box 3792
San Francisco, CA 94119

Walnut Oil

This is not only an oil from nuts but an oil with an elegant nutty flavor. The imported variety is better than the cold-pressed and is available from:

Williams-Sonoma
P.O. Box 3792
San Francisco, CA 94119

Wasabi Powder

Dried green horseradish powder available from Japanese stores.

Watermelon Rind

Watermelon rind is inedible in its natural state, but is very good when pickled or preserved. See *Candied Fruits* for source.

White Alcohol

Clear brandies distilled from different fruits, the most popular of which are kirsch (from cherries), poire (pear) and framboise (raspberries).

Index

TOM MARGITTAI